The Multiculturalism Backlash

Over a relatively short period, many European governments have been purposefully dropping the notion 'multicultural' from their policy vocabularies. More and more politicians and public intellectuals have criticized a perceived shift towards 'too much diversity'. This volume goes beyond the conventional approaches to the topic by offering a careful examination of not only the social conditions and political questions surrounding multiculturalism but also the recent emergence of a 'backlash' against multicultural initiatives, programmes and infrastructures.

Featuring case-study based contributions from leading experts throughout Europe and North America, this multidisciplinary work seeks to assess key questions with reference to recent and current trends concerning multiculturalism, cultural diversity and integration in their respective countries, evaluating questions such as:

- Is there is a common 'sceptical turn' against cultural diversity or a 'backlash against difference' sweeping Europe?
- How have public discourses impacted upon national and local diversity management and migration policies?
- Are the discourses and policy shifts actually reflected in everyday practices within culturally, linguistically and religiously diverse settings?

The Multiculturalism Backlash provides new insights, informed reflections and comparative analyses concerning these significant processes surrounding politics, policy, public debates, and the place of migrants and ethnic minorities within European societies today. Focusing on the practice and policy of multiculturalism from a comparative perspective this work will be of interest to scholars from a wide range of disciplines including political science, anthropology and sociology.

Steven Vertovec is Director of the Max-Planck Institute for the Study of Religious and Ethnic Diversity, Göttingen and Honorary Joint Professor of Sociology and Ethnology, University of Göttingen, Germany.

Susanne Wessendorf is a Postdoctoral Research Fellow at Max-Planck Institute for the Study of Religious and Ethnic Diversity, Göttingen, Germany.

The Multiculturalism Backlash

European discourses, policies and practices

Edited by
Steven Vertovec and Susanne Wessendorf

Routledge
Taylor & Francis Group

LONDON AND NEW YORK

First published 2010
by Routledge
2 Park Square, Milton Park, Abingdon, Oxon, OX14 4RN

Simultaneously published in the USA and Canada
by Routledge
270 Madison Avenue, New York, NY 10016

Routledge is an imprint of the Taylor & Francis Group, an informa business

Typeset in Times New Roman by
Taylor & Francis Books Ltd

British Library Cataloguing in Publication Data
A catalogue record for this book is available from the British Library

Library of Congress Cataloging in Publication Data
The multiculturalism backlash : European discourses, policies, and
practices/ edited by Steven Vertovec and Susanne Wessendorf.
    p. cm.
Multiculturalism–Europe. 2. Minorities–Government policy–Europe. 3.
Immigrants–Cultural assimilation–Europe. 4. Europe–Ethnic relations. 5.
Europe–Race relations. I. Vertovec, Steven. II. Wessendorf, Susanne, 1973-
    D1056.M86 2009
    306.094–dc22
                          2009018032

ISBN 10: 0-415-55648-1 (hbk)
ISBN 10: 0-415-55649-X (pbk)
ISBN 10: 0-203-86754-8 (ebk)

ISBN 13: 978-0-415-55648-4 (hbk)
ISBN 13: 978-0-415-55649-1 (pbk)
ISBN 13: 978-0-203-86754-9 (ebk)

Contents

Notes on contributors

Gianni D'Amato is Professor at the University of Neuchâtel and Director of the Swiss Forum of Migration and Population Studies (SFM). His research interests are focused on citizenship, transnationalism, populism and the history of migration. He is author of *Vom Ausländer zum Bürger. Der Streit um die politische Integration von Einwanderern in Deutschland, Frankreich und der Schweiz* (Lit Verlag 3rd edition, 2005) and has co-authored and co-edited, among others, *Herausforderung Stadt. Städtische Migrationspolitik in der Schweiz und in Europa* (Seismo Verlag, 2005) and *Mit dem Fremden politisieren. Rechtspopulismus und Migrationspolitik in der Schweiz seit den 1960er Jahren* (Zurich, Chronos Verlag, 2008).

Ralph Grillo is Emeritus Professor of Social Anthropology, University of Sussex. He is author of *Ideologies and Institutions in Urban France: The Representation of Immigrants* (Cambridge University Press, 1985) and *Pluralism and the Politics of Difference: State, Culture, and Ethnicity in Comparative Perspective* (Clarendon Press, 1998); editor of *The Family in Question: Immigrant and Ethnic Minorities in Multicultural Europe* (Amsterdam University Press, 2008); and co-editor of *Legal Practice and Cultural Diversity* (Ashgate, 2009).

Ulf Hedetoft is Professor of International Studies and Director of the SAXO Institute at the University of Copenhagen. He is also Chairman of the Nordic Association for Migration Research. His research interests include European nationalism, international migration and political cultures in Europe and North America. He is currently working on the politics of migration control and shifting integration regimes in small European states. His recent publications include contributions to the *Handbook of Socio-Cultural Psychology* (Cambridge University Press, 2007), *Russia and Globalization* (Woodrow Wilson Center Press/Johns Hopkins University Press, 2008), *Nations and Nationalism – a Global Historical Overview* (ABC-CLIO, 2008) and *Global Ordering* (University of British Columbia Press, 2008).

Will Kymlicka holds the Canada Research Chair in Political Philosophy at Queen's University, and is a Visiting Professor in the Nationalism Studies programme at the Central European University in Budapest. He is the author of six books published by Oxford University Press, including *Multicultural Citizenship* (1995) and most recently *Multicultural Odysseys: Navigating the New International Politics of Diversity* (2007), and co-editor with Keith Banting of *Multiculturalism and the Welfare State: Recognition and Redistribution in Contemporary Democracies* (Oxford Uniersity Press, 2006).

David Ley is Canada Research Chair of Geography at the University of British Columbia in Vancouver. His research examines the social geography of large cities, particularly immigration and urbanization, and gentrification and housing markets. Books include *The New Middle Class and the Re-making of the Central City* (Oxford University Press, 1996) and *Millionaire Migrants: Trans-Pacific Life Lines* (Blackwell, forthcoming), a study of wealthy East Asian trans-migrants to Canada.

Baukje Prins is Lecturer in Social and Political Philosophy at the University of Groningen, the Netherlands. She is currently working on a book about the history and dynamics of inter-ethnic relationships through the life-stories of her former Dutch and Moluccan classmates at a primary school in the 1960s. Publications include *Voorbij de onschuld* (Van Gennep, 2004), a study of the Dutch debate on immigrant integration, and articles in the *European Journal of Women's Studies*, *Ethnicities* and *Social Theory and Practice*.

Sawitri Saharso is Professor of Intercultural Governance at the Faculty of Management and Administration of the University of Twente and Associate Professor at the Department of Sociology of the VU University Amsterdam. Her research interests include migration and gender with a special focus on value conflicts within a European comparative perspective. Her recent publications include *The Rights of Women and the Crisis of Multiculturalism*, special issue of *Ethnicities* 8(3) (co-edited with A. Phillips, 2008) and *The Veil: Debating Citizenship, Gender and Religious Diversity*, special issue of *Social Politics: International Studies in Gender, State and Society* 16(4) (co-edited with S. Kilic and B. Sauer, 2008).

Valérie Sala Pala is Lecturer in Political Science at the University of Saint-Etienne, France. She has primary research interests in the sociology of inter-ethnic relations, ethnic discriminations, racism, and anti-racism, as well as urban and social policies in an international comparative perspective. Her most recent publications include: 'Differentialist and universalist anti-discrimination policies on the ground: how far they succeed, why they fail: a comparison between Britain and France', *American Behavioral Scientist*, 2009 (forthcoming), 'The construction of Islam as a public issue in western European countries through the prism of the Muhammad cartoon controversy: a comparison between France and Germany' (with Frauke Miera), *Ethnicities*, 2009 (forthcoming). She is also the co-editor (with

Lionel Arnaud, Sylvie Ollitrault and Sophie Rétif) of *Mobilisations, dominations, identités* (L'Harmattan, 2009, forthcoming).

Karen Schönwälder is a Research Group Leader at the Max-Planck Institute for the Study of Religious and Ethnic Diversity in Göttingen, Germany. She previously worked at the Social Science Research Center (WZB) in Berlin. Her current projects investigate issues of diversity and cohesion in European cities and the political incorporation of immigrants. Her publications focus on migration and integration policies and processes, with a focus on Germany and Britain, e.g. 'Immigrant settlement structures in Germany: general patterns and urban levels of concentration of major groups', *Urban Studies*, 46(7), 2009 (with Janina Söhn), 'Reformprojekt Integration', in Jürgen Kocka (ed.), *Zukunftsfähigkeit Deutschlands. Sozialwissenschaftliche Essays* (Bonn, 2008, pp. 315–34).

Patrick Simon is Director of Research at INED (Institut National d'Etudes Demographiques – National Demographic Institute), Paris, where he heads the research unit 'International Migration and Minorities' and is fellow researcher at CEVIPOF, Sciences Po. He is doing research on anti-discrimination policies, ethnic classification and the integration of ethnic minorities in European countries. He is involved in several European projects, such as EMILIE (A European Approach to Multicultural Citizenship: Legal Political and Educational Challenges). He chairs the scientific panel 'Integration of immigrants' at the IUSSP (International Union for the Scientific Studies of Population). He has recently co-edited (with C. Bonifazi, M. Okolski and J. Schoorl) *International Migrations in Europe: New Trends, New Methods of Analysis* (University of Amsterdam Press, 2008) and a report for the Council of Europe (2007) *Ethnic Statistics and Data Protection*.

Steven Vertovec is Director of the Max-Planck Institute for the Study of Religious and Ethnic Diversity, Göttingen and Honorary Joint Professor of Sociology and Ethnology, University of Göttingen. Previously he was Professor of Transnational Anthropology at the Institute of Social and Cultural Anthropology, University of Oxford and Director of the British Economic and Social Research Council's Centre on Migration, Policy and Society (COMPAS). His research interests surround globalization and transnational social formations, international migration, ethnic diasporas and multiculturalism. He is author of *Hindu Trinidad* (Macmillan, 1992), *The Hindu Diaspora* (Routledge, 2000) and *Transnationalism* (Routledge, 2008), and editor or co-editor of twenty-seven volumes including *Islam in Europe* (Macmillan, 1997), *Migration, Diasporas and Transnationalism* (Edward Elgar, 1999), *Migration and Social Cohesion* (Edward Elgar, 1999), *Conceiving Cosmopolitanism* (Oxford University Press, 2003), *Civil Enculturation* (Berghahn, 2004) and *Migration: Major Works* (Routledge, forthcoming).

Susanne Wessendorf is a Postdoctoral Research Fellow at the Max-Planck Institute for the Study of Religious and Ethnic Diversity, Göttingen. She is currently working on patterns of 'super diversity' in a London neighbourhood. Her recent publications include 'Culturalist discourses on inclusion and exclusion: the Swiss citizenship debate', *Social Anthropology/ Anthropologie Sociale* (2008, 16). 'Roots-migrants: transnationalism and "return" among second-generation Italians in Switzerland', *Journal of Ethnic and Migration Studies* (2007, 33(7)) and 'Migration and cultural, religious and linguistic diversity in Europe: an overview of issues and trends' (with Steven Vertovec) in Rinus Penninx, Maria Berger and Karen Kraal (eds) *The Dynamics of International Migration and Settlement in Europe: A State of the Art* (Amsterdam University Press, 2006, 171–200).

Ricard Zapata-Barrero is Associate Professor of Political Theory at the Department of Social and Political Science, Universitat Pompeu Fabra (Barcelona). He is director of the interdisciplinary research group on immigration (GRITIM: http://www.upf.edu/gritim/) and of the Master's degree in Immigration Management at UPF. He is currently working on issues such as the link between different types of cultural pluralisms, an ethics of migration politics, the political theory of borders, the regional Euro-Mediterranean politics of immigration and diversity accommodation policies. His publications include *Multiculturalism, Muslims and Citizenship: A European Approach* (co-edited with T. Modood and A. Triandafyllidou, Routledge, 2006), *Fundamentos de los discursos políticos en torno a la inmigración* (Trotta, 2008), *Conceptos Políticos en el contexto español* (edited, Síntesis, 2007) and *Immigration and self-government: normative questions and institutional prospects* (edited, Peter Lang, 2009).

1   Introduction

Assessing the backlash against multiculturalism in Europe

Steven Vertovec and Susanne Wessendorf

'Multiculturalism is dead.' This was a headline in Britain's *Daily Mail* on 7 July 2006 – the first anniversary of the London bombings. Such a pronouncement followed a long course of public criticism – indeed, over several preceding years – suggesting that a particular liberal ideology had dominated politics since the 1970s, had failed miserably, and moreover had produced a dangerous social condition in which Islamic terrorism could flourish. This growing scepticism, culminating in a verbal backlash against multiculturalism, had reached such a point that *The Economist*'s (2007) columnist Bagehot commented:

> Once it connoted curry and the Notting Hill carnival; these days, when applied to British politicians or their policies, 'multiculturalism' is almost as derogatory a term as 'socialist' or 'neocon'. Even more than they agree about most other things, the main political parties are united in their convictions that multiculturalism is a perniciously naïve idea whose time has gone, or ought never to have come at all.

The backlash, moreover, was certainly not confined to Britain. Since the early 2000s across Europe, the rise, ubiquity, simultaneity and convergence of arguments condemning multiculturalism have been striking. How and why have such seemingly similar public debates unfolded across such varied social and political situations?

This volume addresses this question through studies examining public policies and debates concerning multiculturalism (inherently combined with issues of immigration and immigrant integration) in seven European contexts. It also benefits from broader reflections on these issues by two prominent Canadian observers. Together the chapters provide a comparative look at public and political processes concerning multiculturalism – or more accurately, what multiculturalism is often purported to be. While a number of shared processes are identifiable across nation-states (part of the task of this Introduction), the contributing chapters underscore the importance of examining specific, or nationally contextualized, debates and local developments surrounding the seemingly widespread turn against multiculturalism.

Multiple modes of multiculturalism

Despite the '-ism' suggesting a distinctive ideological canon, multiculturalism is actually rather hard to pin down. Numerous philosophies, institutional frameworks and political interventions have been referred to under a collective rubric of multiculturalism. Yet social scientists have identified a wide variety of types of multiculturalism. (Here we are focusing on multiculturalism by way of specific policies and public institutions; that is, in this volume we are less concerned with debates over multiculturalism in political philosophy, as represented for instance by Charles Taylor (1992), Will Kymlicka (1995), Bhikhu Parekh (2000), Brian Barry (2001), Tariq Modood (2007) and Anne Phillips (2007).) A divergent set of civic programmes might be labelled as 'radical multiculturalism' or 'polycentric multiculturalism' (Shohat and Stam 1994), 'insurgent multiculturalism' (Giroux 1994), 'public space multiculturalism' (Vertovec 1996), 'difference multiculturalism' (Turner 1993), 'critical multiculturalism' (Chicago Cultural Studies Group 1994), 'weak' or 'strong' multiculturalism (Grillo 2005). Indeed, Steven Vertovec (1998) has pointed to at least eight different kinds of multiculturalism while Garard Delanty (2003) suggests another list with nine types of multiculturalism.

When attempting to bracket together an array of public measures as 'multiculturalism', the task is further complicated if undertaken comparatively across countries most known for the implementation of policies deemed, officially or not, multicultural: Australia, Canada, the United States, Great Britain, Sweden and the Netherlands. These countries – and different cities within them – have not undertaken the same approach, introduced the same measures nor set up the same institutions (cf. Martiniello 1998, Bennett 1998, Rogers and Tillie 2001). Even within a single country, policies relevant to an overall multicultural agenda have not taken the same perspectives, aims and course of development. Hence, as Stuart Hall (2001: 3) observes, 'Over the years the term 'multiculturalism' has come to reference a diffuse, indeed maddeningly spongy and imprecise, discursive field: a train of false trails and misleading universals. Its references are a wild variety of political strategies.' That it is difficult to formulate a specific corpus of tenets or practices around multiculturalism should come as no surprise. Gary Freeman importantly points out that practically everywhere governments have dealt with immigrant and ethnic minority incorporation through a rather disordered closet full of measures. 'No state possesses a truly coherent incorporation regime', Freeman ((2004): 946) notes. 'Instead, one finds ramshackle, multifaceted, loosely connected sets of regulatory rules, institutions and practices in various domains of society that together make up the frameworks within which migrants and natives work out their differences.' Such a patchwork of policies indeed characterizes numerous domains of public governance. Rather than a singular set of well-integrated policies and institutions, most often we find 'subsystem frameworks that are weakly, if at all, coordinated' (ibid.).

Moreover, Freeman observes, 'immigrants are mostly managed via institutions created for other purposes' (ibid.: 948). That is, immigrants and ethnic minorities engage, and are incorporated through, a range of public institutions including: various levels of administration from neighbourhood associations and municipal councils to regional and national government departments; schools and universities; libraries; hospitals and health clinics; law courts and the police; social services; youth clubs; employment agencies; sports and leisure facilities; and various forms of print, radio, television and internet media.

Within and cutting across such varied institutions, the rubric multiculturalism has entailed diverse measures such as:

- Public 'recognition': support for ethnic minority organizations, facilities and activities; public consultative bodies incorporating such organizations.
- Education: consideration for dress codes, gender-specific practices and other issues sensitive to the values of specific ethnic and religious minorities; creation of curricula reflecting the backgrounds of ethnic minority pupils (intended to teach non-ethnic minority children about the background of their peers, and to bolster the self-images of ethnic minority pupils); mother tongue teaching and language support; the establishment of minority groups' own schools (usually religious, publically financed or not).
- Social Services: information, restructuring and retraining for delivering culturally sensitive practices among public employees, social workers, healthcare providers, police and courts.
- Public materials: state-sponsored information (such as health promotion campaigns) provided in multiple languages.
- Law: cultural exceptions to laws (such as Sikhs being allowed to wear turbans instead of motorcycle helmets); oaths on sacred books other than the Bible (e.g. Qur'an, Bhagavad Gita); recognition of other marriage, divorce and inheritance traditions; protection from discrimination or incitement to hatred.
- Religious accommodation: permission and support for the establishment of places of worship, cemeteries and funerary rites; allowance of time off work for worship.
- Food: allowance of ritual slaughter; provision of proscribed foods (halal, kosher, vegetarian) in public institutions.
- Broadcasting and media: monitoring of group images to ensure non-discrimination or to avoid stereotypes; provision of own media facilities for minority groups.

A singular principle does not equally infuse all these domains. That is not to say, however, that within and across these domains, and within a number of countries since the 1960s, a range of institutional initiatives have not had some broad, complementary objectives. Foremost among these we can

identify tenets aiming to: reduce discrimination; promote equality of opportunity and overcome barriers to full participation in society; allow unconstrained access to public services; recognize cultural identities (as opposed to
assimilation) and open up public spaces for their representation; and foster
acceptance of ethnic pluralism and cultural understanding across all groups.
These are dissimilar objectives requiring different public measures, but
obviously they sit well together. In this way, multiculturalism can at best be
described as a broad set of mutually reinforcing approaches or methodologies
concerning the incorporation and participation of immigrants and ethnic
minorities and their modes of cultural/religious difference.

The slow death of multiculturalism?

Since the 1970s when multicultural policies were increasingly operationalized
in various nation-states, criticism has never been lacking. For instance in
Britain, the Swann Report, Honeyford affair and Rushdie (*Satanic Verses*)
affair represented a few of the issues that prompted considerable public debate
about multicultural initiatives and frameworks throughout the 1980s (see
respectively Verma 1989, Halstead 1988, Lewis 2002). From the beginning of
the 1990s in the Netherlands, there have also been political attacks on dominant Dutch policies meant to assist ethnic minorities (see Prins and Saharso,
this volume). In Canada during the 1990s, some representatives of ethnic
minorities themselves increasingly expressed criticism against multiculturalism, emphasizing concerns of marginalization and the reproduction of
cultural difference (see Ley, this volume). Indeed, several chapters in this
volume point to longstanding and diverse national controversies surrounding
multiculturalism.

Yet beginning around the turn of the millennium, sporadic critical voices
seemingly became harmonized into a chorus. (To push the metaphor, however, as described below it is questionable as to whether the critics have been
singing from the same hymn sheet.) Perhaps the main reasons for this – as
with most political processes – are events. Since 2000 one occurrence or prominent public statement after another sparked a flurry of debates in government
assemblies, newspapers and journals, TV talk shows and radio phone-in programs. Immigrants, Muslims and multiculturalism were at the heart of these.
By no means exhaustive and mostly drawing on cases in Britain (the context
known best to the authors of this Introduction), some key incidents are listed
below. These and further examples are also described in chapters throughout
this volume.

January 2000. In the Netherlands, journalist Paul Scheffer (2000) publishes
an article entitled 'The multicultural drama', in which he points out that
ethnic minorities are overrepresented in statistics concerning unemployment,
poverty, criminal activity and school drop-outs. In what purports to be the
first outspoken criticism from the Left, Scheffer claims multicultural policy
has made politicians blind to these facts.

May 2001. Riots, largely pitting British Bangladeshi and Pakistani youths against White youths, break out in three northern British cities. An official report into the disturbances (known as the Cantle Report) suggests that:

> Separate educational arrangements, community and voluntary bodies, employment, places of worship, language, social and cultural networks, means that many communities operate on the basis of a series of parallel lives. These lives often do not seem to touch at any point, let alone overlap and promote any meaningful interchanges.
>
> (Home Office 2001: 9)

September 2001. 9/11 and the terrorist attacks in the USA make the threat of Islamic terrorism in the West an uppermost public concern.

2001 to May 2002. Rise (and death) of Pim Fortyn, outspoken Dutch politician who openly castigated Muslim immigration and Muslims' inherent unassimilability.

February 2003. Results of 2001 UK Census published, showing extremely poor socio-economic conditions among some groups (especially Bangladeshis and Pakistanis). Public debates ask whether multicultural policies are to blame, or migrants (and their Muslim cultures) themselves.

February 2004. Prospect magazine editor David Goodhart (2004) publishes 'Too Diverse?' It is an article, again from left-of-centre, which controversially suggests that collective attitudes toward welfare are threatened by ethnic diversity. Also in this month, the French parliament votes in favour of a new law to ban the wearing of Islamic headscarves in schools. Throughout Europe commentators weigh up the issue in their own societies.

March 2004. Madrid train bombing prompts further fears of Muslim terrorists-among-us in Europe.

April 2004. In yet another critique from the Left, the chair of the Commission for Racial Equality, Trevor Phillips, proclaims that 'multiculturalism' should be ditched, as it suggests separatism when there is an increased need for common British identity.

November 2004. The murder of filmmaker Theo van Gogh by a Muslim extremist sparks more public discussion about tolerance, free speech and intolerant Muslim minorities.

July 2005. London terrorist bombings. Especially because the perpetrators were British-born and bred Muslims, there is much public comment on how such a condition could have arisen, and what should be done about it.

September 2005. In Denmark the *Jyllands-Posten* publishes notorious Muhammad cartoons, causing considerable controversy that in many places across Europe pits Western/'host' country open-mindedness vs. Islamic/migrant intolerance. In the UK, this month Trevor Phillips makes another contentious speech, this time suggesting the country is 'sleepwalking into segregation' by way of increasingly separate communities.

October–November 2005. Riots in Paris suburbs and other localities throughout France are depicted as troubles wrought by migrant youths (despite considerable activity among White French youths too); some reports even portray the disturbances as caused by Muslim youth.

October 2006. Cabinet Minister Jack Straw says he would prefer Muslim women not to wear veils which cover the face. The ensuing debate entails questions as to how much conformity a society should demand of minorities vs. to what extent they should be allowed to practice values no matter how disagreeable to the majority.

Although most of these cases specifically involved issues around Muslims and Islam, they each represent events flagged by critics in order to condemn, for various intents and purposes, policies of migrant/minority cultural accommodation. These events seemed to provide for critics, who had long been seeking to pronounce – and to ensure – the death of multiculturalism, nails with which to seal its coffin.

Backlash against multiculturalism: core idioms

Prompted by the public debates around these and other (usually nationally specific) events, the backlash against multiculturalism has involved specific idioms or tactics of condemnation. Sometimes these are used in conjunction, or argued through one line of reasoning that depends on another. In each case the discursive strategy is posited upon portrayals of multiculturalism that are set up to be readily and plainly impugned. The portrayals themselves, it will be shown below, are demonstrably partial, erroneous or false. Nevertheless in these ways across Europe, we witness remarkably common claims by way of critical assessments of multiculturalism (in the process of discursive convergence, though, one is unsure how much of a particular national commentator's argument has been adopted directly from another country's: e.g., a Brit drawing upon Paul Scheffer, a Dane or German inspired by David Goodhart). Drawing upon a few exemplary statements again mostly from Britain, but resonating in backlash discourse elsewhere, we outline the core critiques found since the turn of the millennium in the backlash against multiculturalism – we should say, what critics claim to be multiculturalism.

Multiculturalism is a single 'doctrine'

A basic device common to most such critiques is to describe and emphasize multiculturalism as a singular, fixed ideology or dogma. In this way 'it' can be more readily condemned. Proponents of backlash discourse either don't know about, overlook or purposefully ignore the diffuse and myriad patchwork of policies, practices and institutional adjustments through which immigrant and ethnic minority accommodation and incorporation are actually undertaken. Instead, critics find it important to paint an undemanding picture of an integrated and dominating 'multicultural industry' comprised of White liberals and ethnic minority activists. In this way columnist Melanie Phillips (2006a) suggests that 'Multiculturalism became the driving force of British life, ruthlessly policed by an army of bureaucrats enforcing a doctrine of state-mandated virtue to promote racial, ethnic and cultural balkanization'; *Sunday Times* writer Jasper Gerard (2006) describes how 'many immigrants, encouraged by multicultural orthodoxy, retreat into their differentness'; Patience Wheatcroft (2006) writes in the *Daily Telegraph* how 'The doctrine of multiculturalism dictated that all beliefs should be allowed to flourish'; while the *Daily Mail*'s James Slack (2006) describes 'the dogma of multiculturalism' and 'the Left-wing doctrine' which 'dictates that different communities should not be forced to integrate. Instead, they are allowed to maintain their own cultures and identities.' With such a consolidated enemy to fight, politicians can mount campaigns. Hence in 2007 Conservative Party leader David Cameron criticized 'the creed of multiculturalism' for contributing to a 'deliberately weakening of our collective identity' (in *The Economist*, 2007); Cameron has therefore picked a fight with, as he calls it, the 'disastrous' and 'discredited doctrine of state multiculturalism' (*Daily Mail*, 26 February 2008).

Multiculturalism stifles debate

Drawing on the idea that multiculturalism comprises a single, prevailing ideology that has been foisted on the country, critics contend that this has created an atmosphere in which thought and speech is controlled. In this way many backlash critics claim to speak out daringly against a 'tyranny of political correctness' (Wheatcroft 2006) that has stifled any attempt to discuss race and immigration in, as they see it, real terms. For instance David Cameron has attacked multiculturalism and its concomitant 'fear of causing offence or being branded a racist' (*Daily Mail*, 26 February 2008). With another way of positing this, a senior politician of the German CDU party, Volker Kauder, said that certain subjects had become 'taboo' in public and that 'the time of looking away and blindness resulting from a false multi-culti ideology is over' (*Bild*, 1 April 2006). Another example comes from Britain's *Daily Express* (2007a), which asserted that Muslims and Islamist terrorists have been 'allowed to live an existence entirely separate from the non-Muslim neighbours'; consequently, 'The era of politically correct cultural surrender must be brought to an end.'

Multiculturalism has fostered separateness

With multiculturalism presumably identified so concretely, probably the most common complaint is that 'it' has led directly to social breakdown. This is particularly claimed in terms of multiculturalism promoting ethnic separatism, an explicit rejection of common national values, and a lack of interest in social integration. For instance, David Davis, the then Conservative shadow

Home Secretary, in saying that Muslims must start integrating into mainstream British society (*Daily Telegraph*, 4 August 2005), 'signaled a shift away from the policy of multi-culturalism, which allows people of different faith and cultures to settle without expecting them to integrate'. He suggests that 'often, the authorities have seemed more concerned with encouraging distinctive identities rather than promoting the common values of nationhood'. John O'Sullivan (2007) wrote in the *Daily Telegraph* that ' "multiculturalism" encourages minorities to retain their culture and identity. Thus, our rulers set out, eager and well-intentioned, to maximize the differences and therefore the tensions inherent in diversity'. The tide of backlash discourse (again, seemingly underpinned by events) eventually led members of the ruling New Labour party to adopt the argument. Thus in 2006 the then Secretary of State for Communities and Local Government, Ruth Kelly MP, said that 'we have moved from a period of uniform consensus on the value of multiculturalism, to one where we can encourage that debate by questioning whether it is encouraging separateness' (*Daily Mail*, 24 August 2006). The Conservatives happily continued this theme, with David Cameron warning that 'multiculturalism – the idea that different cultures should be respected to the point of encouraging them to live separately – had dangerously undermined Britain's sense of identity and brought about "cultural apartheid" ' (*Daily Mail*, 26 February 2008).

Much of this kind of discourse stems from the 2001 Cantle Report and its image of 'parallel lives' (see Grillo, this volume). In Germany, where the notion of *Parallelgesellschaften* ('parallel societies') has existed since a prominent report of the 1990s (see Heitmeyer 1996), the backlash against multiculturalism has been argued directly in terms of self-separating, 'parallel societies' (*Focus*, 24 October 2004; *Tagesspeigel*, 17 January 2008). Similarly in France, this image of increasing separateness of some parts of the population has been expressed by way of the fear of a 'balkanization' of French society and concerns about 'communitarianism' (Simon and Sala Pala, this volume).

Multiculturalism refuses common values

Another aspect of the argument that multiculturalism promotes separatism is that it is thereby not interested in any form of commonality. This was even the view of one New Labour Home Secretary in Britain, David Blunkett, who was weary of an 'unbridled multiculturalism which privileges difference over community cohesion' (Blunkett 2002: 6). Since, some suggested, 'a blend of multiculturalism and Europeanism [has] drained all pride and meaning out of Britishness' (O'Sullivan 2007), the solution must be to drop multiculturalism and promote national identity. This was exactly Trevor Phillips' 2004 argument, mentioned above, which was depicted as the Left 'waking up' to the damage multiculturalism had done. For the Right, this has been clear all along. For example, in 2007 a report by the right-wing think tank Policy

Exchange castigated 'multi-cultural policies implemented since the 1980s which have emphasized difference at the expense of shared national identity and divided people along ethnic, religious and cultural lines' (*Daily Mail*, 29 January 2007). In Germany, too, such discourse is present (despite the clear lack of multicultural policies; see Schönwälder, this volume); there, Stefan Lust has argued in that multiculturalism's insistence on recognizing identities-of-origin, instead of a common host-culture, 'must lead to disaster' (*Tagesspeigel*, 17 January 2008; also reiterated in his 2008 book *Abschied von Multikulti* – 'Farewell to Multiculti'). Multiculturalism has, he claims, inherently led to separation and ethnic conflict in places like the UK and the Netherlands.

Multiculturalism denies problems

The idea that a single ideology has controlled the ability to see things clearly, to speak about them truthfully, and to promote commonality have been conjoined in an argument that multiculturalism refuses to acknowledge social problems connected with immigrants and ethnic minorities. This was a key feature of Paul Scheffer's (2000) original critique: that is, that a new divide has emerged within Dutch society, particularly represented by a new class of the economically and socially unsuccessful – a group made up of non-Western migrants and their second and third generation offspring. The government turns a blind eye towards this new division, Scheffer said, since it seeks only to praise the multicultural society from an illusory cosmopolitan viewpoint. A similar claim has been made by the Mayor of Berlin's borough of Neukölln, Heinz Buschkowsky: he castigated a 'multi-culti-romanticism' that closed the eyes of politicians to a 'ticking time-bomb' situation of ethnic separatism and disaffected youth (*Focus*, 24 October 2004). A further example came in 2006 when *Bild* newspaper interviewed historian Arnulf Baring, who represented the view that *Ausländer* ('foreigners') in Germany don't accept German culture and that this is simply overlooked by many. 'It's not the Germans who are the fools', Baring said, 'but the politicians and do-gooders who have given us decades of a multicultural dream' (*Bild*, 5 April).

Multiculturalism supports reprehensible practices

Cultural relativism – itself portrayed as all-aspects-of-all-cultures are good – is depicted as the underpinning the blindness of the doctrine of multiculturalism. For this reason multiculturalism, critics say, supports backward minority cultures' unequal treatment of women, forced marriages, honour killings and female genital mutilation. Critics draw on such examples to profess moral outrage, again boldly and candidly against an overbearing climate of political correctness. Paul Cliteur (2001), writing in *NRC Handelsblad*, condemned politicians and the intellectual elite for upholding their view that all cultures are equal. Cultural relativism, he said, serves only to suppress an open debate about common values. According to Cliteur, it is nonsensical to state that all cultures are equal since some cultures are evil, some cultures suppress women and some cultures excessively punish misdemeanours. As discussed by Ulf Hedetoft (this volume), in Denmark such arguments have made their way into government documents, where 'culture' – described in terms of fixed 'core values' – is used as a yardstick by which immigrants' integration is to be measured. This fixed notion of 'culture' and 'cultural differences' is thereby directly related to notions of a 'cultural battle' (*kulturkamp*) which must be fought against both new immigrants and the enemy within (including left-wing liberals).

Such views have been long present in Britain too (especially around the Rushdie affair and its depiction of Muslim intolerance), but the tragedy of the 7/7 terrorist attacks particularly sparked this backlash idiom. Immediately after the event, *Daily Mail* columnist Melanie Phillips (2005) wasted no time in blaming multiculturalism. She contested that in the wake of the London bombings, 'Muslims have been presented not as the community which must take responsibility for this horror, but as it principal victims.' Combining several of the backlash tropes outlined above, Phillips continued:

> This moral inversion is the result of the cultural brainwashing that has been going on in Britain for years in the pursuit of the disastrous doctrine of multiculturalism. This has refused to teach Muslims – along with other minorities – the core of British culture and values. Instead, it has promoted a lethally divisive culture of separateness, in which minority cultures are held to be equal if not superior to the values and traditions of the indigenous majority.
>
> Even worse, multiculturalism causes the moral paralysis of 'victim culture', whereby to say an ethnic minority is at fault is to invite immediate accusations of racism.
>
> We have already paid a terrible price for multiculturalism and this cancer of moral inversion and irresponsibility.

This argument is expanded in her book *Londonistan: How Britain is Creating a Terror State Within* (Phillips 2006a). Elsewhere, she also carries on this combined line of argument, based on the core assumption that 'At the heart of multiculturalism lies a radical egalitarianism by which everyone's culture and lifestyle has equal validity and moral stature. The consequence is that people are increasingly unable to make moral distinctions based on behaviour' (Phillips 2006b). Phillips' reasoning has been persuasive, or at least rehashed. On the anniversary of 7/7 and with the flagrant headline 'Multiculturalism has let terror flourish in Britain', Britain's *Daily Express* (2007b) wrote about Muslims:

> Many will not understand our culture, our attitude to women, our liberal values. Many will not even want to try. At best they will be out of touch,

at worst they will be inclined to radicalize the young and spread the word that leads to death and terror. The pernicious doctrine of multiculturalism has allowed this situation to develop. The Government must not allow it to continue.

Indeed, as part of his growing backlash campaign, Tory leader David Cameron warned that the ultimate outcome of multiculturalism, if unchecked, could be the recognition of Sharia law in Britain. Managing to combine three key idioms (multiculturalism as single doctrine, the fear of concession to Islam, the fostering of separatism) in one sentence, Cameron said:

The reality is that the introduction of Sharia law for Muslims is actually the logical endpoint of the now discredited doctrine of state multiculturalism – instituting, quite literally, a legal apartheid to entrench what is the cultural apartheid in too many parts of our country.

(*Daily Mail*, 26 February 2008)

Multiculturalism provides a haven for terrorists

As already indicated by Melanie Phillips' interventions, among others, public discourses comprising strands of a backlash against multiculturalism have combined with fears surrounding terrorism (or, some would say, a manipulation of such fears). Following the arrest of 17 Muslims charged with terrorism in Canada, Phillips (2006c) herself wrote:

In particular, both Canada and Britain need to face the fact that multiculturalism, which for both countries is an article of faith, has brought havoc in its wake. This doctrine holds that all minority cultures must enjoy equal status with the majority, and that any attempt to impose the majority culture over those of minorities is by definition racist. It has helped create a cultural vacuum into which has roared militant Islamism – the interpretation of Islam that preached holy war. Multiculturalism not only creates the environment in which this clerical fascism can flourish but – crucially – also undermines our ability to defend ourselves against it.

… Multiculturalism has exacerbated the alienation that has left so many British Muslims vulnerable to the siren song of jihad.

In a more condensed form, Phillips (2006b) states, 'Multiculturalism plus radical Islam is an explosive cocktail.' To be sure, others have taken this cue. In its coverage of a report by the defence and security think tank Royal United Services Institute, the *Daily Mail* (15 February 2008) proclaimed 'Multiculturalism is making Britain "a soft touch for terrorists".' Moreover, said the then Tory shadow Home Secretary Dominic Grieve (*Guardian*, 27 September 2008), multiculturalism in the UK has left a 'terrible' legacy, creating a vacuum that has been filled by extremists from across the political spectrum. He said 'long-term inhabitants have been left fearful'.

Backlash against multiculturalism: themes and stratagems

As the current phase of multiculturalism debates were getting under way, Baukje Prins and Boris Slijper (2002) undertook a discourse analysis of several such arguments (many of their findings have been reiterated in Baukje Prins and Sawitri Saharso's chapter in this volume). They identified five key themes or recurrent theses running through such debates regardless of national context: (1) the clash between cultures (particularly Islam versus Western values), with toleration and unassimilability as basic issues under scrutiny; (2) ethnic diversity and national identity, with separateness or the ostensible unwillingness to assimilate stressed as threats to social cohesion; (3) the socio-economic position of immigrants, pointing to high unemployment, dependence on welfare and juvenile delinquency as failures of integration. Here the question of who is to blame – the system or the victims? – tends to be posed not in terms of structural inequality or deep-set discrimination, but as multicultural policies pandering to immigrants' culture, inherent lack of loyalty to the nation-state and over-reliance on welfare; (4) policies of immigration and asylum, through which debates on multiculturalism and integration are linked directly to debates about immigration, including immigration as over-population, as a breeding ground of disease, as a security threat and liable to produce more failure of integration (especially under conditions of multiculturalism); (5) debates on the debate, meaning the ways in which discussants talk about the issues becomes talked about; this includes controversies about the 'correct' terminology, strategies to counter or demonize opponents, what can and cannot be said, what counts as racism and what does not. Prins and Slijper emphasize that

> in the end, concerning each of the five issues that we discern in the debates on multicultural society ... positions cannot be simply reduced to the classical opposition between right and left, or to more recent distinctions such as those between black and white, immigrant and indigenous, or Muslim and Western.
>
> (Ibid.: 327)

Indeed, they observe, 'in each national debate, we find ample examples of anomalous, of "abnormal" positions, such as xenophobic immigrants, politically incorrect Muslims, and progressive realists' (ibid.). As evidenced by the examples in the preceding section, linking all such discourse is an assumed, sequential logic that (a) multiculturalism fosters accentuated or preserved cultural differences, (b) such differences lead to communal separateness and

(c) separateness deepens socio-economic standing, intensifies the breakdown of social relations and provides an incubator for extremism and possible terrorism. Within this line of thinking, the blame on multiculturalism also entails blame on immigrants/ethnic minorities themselves: as the reasoning goes, it is their own desire to maintain cultural traditions and distinct identities – a desire that multiculturalism supports – which leads to all these negative consequences.

In addition to the typical themes developed within the content of backlash arguments, there is also a common set of stratagems or discursive manoeuvres. In their contribution to this volume, Baukje Prins and Sawitri Saharso examine Dutch public debates around multiculturalism through the 1990s into the late 2000s. Throughout this period they observe the emergence of what they style as the 'new realism'. It is characterized by what its proponents see as the courage to confront taboos, break silence, intervene 'with guts' and speak the truth surrounding societal ills hidden by a (leftist) consensus of political correctness. Prins and Saharso note how the genre of new realism comprises five distinct features. First, the author presents himself or herself as someone who dares face the facts, who speaks frankly about 'truths' that the dominant discourse has supposedly covered up. Second, a new realist sets himself up as the spokesperson of the ordinary people, that is, the autochthonous population (who know what's really going on). A third characteristic of new realism is the suggestion that it is a characteristic feature of national society (in Prins and Saharso's case of the Netherlands, where new realists assert that being Dutch equals being frank). A fourth feature is resistance to the Left, suggesting that progressive elites have dominated the public realm and stifled the possibility of true debate. A final feature of new realism is its gendered discourse, bringing presumed attitudes toward gender and sexuality into the debate as deliberative weapons for their own cause.

Another significant manoeuvre entails the accusation of political correctness. This is often put forward as the ultimate disqualification and weapon of the right (countered by accusations of racism by the Left, which are thrown in order to have the same effect). Anti-multiculturalists declare that by means of controlling language, the 'politically correct' refuse to talk about real issues and social problems; they are therefore untruthful, although presumed to dominate the public sphere. Again, new realist-style critics of multiculturalism subsequently model themselves as intrepid truth-sayers promoting the uncontestable viewpoint that freedom of opinion and open debate is more important than the risk of stigmatization. Yet this manoeuvre only works by first painting the picture of multiculturalism as a dogmatic, debate stifling, separateness fostering, common value refusing, problem denying, overly relativist, terrorist harbouring entity.

Impacts of the backlash

In contexts throughout Europe the discourse attacking multiculturalism has certainly created a certain climate within the public sphere. Broadly, one might say, the term has successfully been associated with the idea of misguided policy. Politicians to the right and left of centre prefer to disassociate themselves from multiculturalism. One telling example came in 2002, when Steven Vertovec was explicitly told by the head speech-writer for the then British Home Secretary, David Blunkett, that 'the minister will never use "the M-word" again'. This conceptual distancing became a significant political trend. When the Home Office (2005) launched its major policy platform, 'Improving Opportunities, Strengthening Society: The Government's Strategy to Increase Race Equality and Community Cohesion', the words 'multicultural' and 'multiculturalism' were nowhere to be found in the document. By the time the UK's Commission on Integration and Cohesion was set up in 2007, its stated approach was that 'we need to update our language to meet the current climate. We therefore intend to avoid using the term "multiculturalism" in our report because of its "catch all" and confusing quality' (CIC 2007: 13). There has not been, however, a complete paradigm shift away from multiculturalism in public debate. In fact, in some quarters the criticism has led to a kind of backlash against the backlash (cf. Eller 1997). This was evident following David Goodhart's 'Too Diverse' article: soon after its original appearance in *Prospect* magazine, the *Guardian* newspaper reprinted the piece and provided a special section with numerous essays and letters strongly disagreeing with Goodhart's assessment; later in 2004, too, on its website *Prospect* itself published critical responses from a range of commentators including Keith Banting and Will Kymlicka, Nathan Glazer, Bhikhu Parekh and Saskia Sassen. As the backlash continued, Anthony Giddens (2006) voiced his concern over the nature of public debate. 'Much of the debate about multiculturalism in this, however, is crass, ignorant and mis-conceived', Giddens said. 'Multiculturalism simply does not mean what most of its critics think'. *The Economist*'s (2007) columnist Bagehot, too, was uneasy about the tone of criticism, noting how 'multiculturalism's detractors tend to concentrate on the easy targets' such as honour killings, forced marriages and the need for national language learning; ultimately the prominent journal came out praising multiculturalism's intents and results.

What effects has the backlash discourse had on actual policies and institu-tional practices? Christian Joppke suggests there has been a 'wholesale retreat' from official multiculturalism policies in Europe. He posits a number of causes for this, including:

(1) the lack of public support for official multiculturalism policies ... , (2) these policies' inherent shortcomings and failures, especially with respect to the socio-economic marginalization and self-segregation of migrants and their children, and (3) a new assertiveness of the liberal state in imposing the liberal minimum on its dissenters.

(2004:244)

These three purported trends sit well with, and are often recapitulated by, backlash discourse. Has there been such a wholesale retreat, and are these causes actual? Below we examine some evidence surrounding each of these claims.

(1) Lack of public support

Joppke nor any other recent observers actually demonstrate a significant public opinion turn against multicultural policies. One should not conflate the appearance, ferocity and ubiquity of backlash discourse in newspapers, by politicians and on talk shows with actual changes of opinion among the general public. To the contrary, one could argue that much of the backlash seems to be but 'sound and fury' rather than a true reflection of public opinion. There have been few polls explicitly about multicultural policies; the closest we can come to evidence is mainly by way of broader opinion polls concerning the accommodation of ethnic diversity.

As with many political issues, quite often public opinion shows itself to be inconsistent or uncertain. This was the situation in August 2005 – one month after the London bombings – when a BBC/MORI poll found the public to be 'confused' about multiculturalism (BBC 2005). At that time, while 58 per cent of the British public who were polled agreed that 'People who come to live in Britain should adopt British values/traditions' and only 35 per cent felt that 'People who come to live in Britain should be free to live by their own values/ traditions', at the same time 62 per cent of these Britons agreed that 'Multi-culturalism makes Britain a better place'. Further, only 32 per cent believed that 'Multiculturalism threatens the British way of life' while just 21 per cent agreed that 'the policy of multiculturalism in Britain has been a mistake and should be abandoned'.

Additionally, a UK government poll found that around this time (when the backlash discourse was steadily growing) measures actually indicated an improvement in already highly positive views toward diversity: it reported that 'Between 2003 and 2005, the percentage of White people in ethnically mixed neighbourhoods who felt that their local area was a place where people respected ethnic differences increased from 79 per cent to 82 per cent' (DCLG 2007: 219). Such findings have been replicated across Europe, too. Euro-barometer is a regular poll of 27,000 people across the European Union. It has examined 'resistance to multicultural society' based on questions such as whether 'It is a good thing for any society to be made up of people from different races, religions or cultures' and whether 'diversity in terms of race, religion or culture adds to [a country's] strengths'. Only 25 per cent of the polled European public indicates such resistance to multicultural society. Certainly in some countries a trend towards more resistance did unfold over time, but a longitudinal analysis of these Eurobarometer measures found that 'Overall, resistance to multicultural society has remained rather stable as a result of a general increase between 1997 and 2000 and a general decrease between 2000 and 2003' (Coenders *et al.* 2003: 43). By 2007 Eurobarometer similarly found that almost three-quarters of EU citizens believe that people with a different ethnic, religious or national background enrich the cultural life of their country (Gallup 2007). Further, 'A remarkably high number (83 per cent) of EU citizens agreed about the benefits of intercultural contacts, and two-thirds were of the opinion that family (cultural) traditions should be kept by the young generations' (ibid.: 4). These findings should not imply that everything's rosy. Racism and xenophobia are rife and discrimination is widespread (see, e.g., FRA 2008). Still, although public opinion polls are not precise nor entirely reliable, these findings seem to suggest that attitudes towards multicultural society and minority culture initiatives have not been drastically affected, despite the backlash barrage.

(2) Policy shortcoming, socio-economic marginalization and self-segregation

There is no doubt that throughout European societies, minorities of recent migrant origin are broadly marked by low educational attainment, poor quality housing conditions, high unemployment or low-grade employment conditions. From context to context, such characteristics have been entrenched through failed policies, to be sure. But have these policies been ones of 'multiculturalism', or just plain failed education, housing and job-creation policies? That is, there is no evidence that policies of cultural accommodation (as mentioned in the first section of this Introduction, such as provision of halal food in hospitals, retraining for culturally sensitive health services, or support of minority media) have led to or worsened these disadvantageous socio-economic traits. Rather than failed multicultural policies, such traits are more likely to have developed and been sustained by sheer discrimination, labour market dynamics and geographies of deprivation.

And what of the claim that migrants and ethnic minorities are, with the help of multiculturalism, retreating into self-segregated enclaves? Again, pockets of ethnic concentration certainly do exist, but data over recent years indicate no particularly alarming patterns or increases. For instance in the UK, where many members of the public believe that Muslims purposely set themselves apart, Deborah Phillips (2006) has studied one well-known context, the city of Bradford. There, she found:

> Discourses of ethnic 'self-segregation' have given rise to the myth that minority ethnic communities live, or wish to live, separate lives and disengage from wider British society. However, neither the evidence on the ground (in terms of residential patterns) nor the diversity of lived experiences and views about social mixing expressed by British Muslims in Bradford would seem to support this conclusion.
> ... The construction of minority ethnic segregation as a 'problem' and British Muslims as alien, inward-looking 'Others' perpetuates, and indeed normalizes, the view that the responsibility for community tensions lies principally with the 'self-segregating' minorities. Yet the evidence from

this research suggests that the radicalization of space in Bradford speaks more loudly of white control and bounded choices, both past and present.
(Ibid.: 36–37)

Looking across Britain, Ludi Simpson (2007) has analysed current data and found that the indices actually show more ethnic mixing and a greater evenness of population distribution in the UK. Therefore, he (ibid.: 423) concludes, 'A doom-laden view of increasing segregation and the threat of ghettos is not supported by the evidence.'

Elsewhere in Europe, there exists a similar mismatch of public rhetoric and actual statistics. Reviewing a number of studies on segregation in the UK, the Netherlands and Sweden, Karen Schönwälder (2007: 6) observes that 'in all three countries, the levels of residential segregation are moderate', especially compared to US levels, and 'the trends seem to be towards decreasing concentration of residential environments rather than towards consolidating ethnic enclaves'. Similarly in Germany, Schönwälder and Jamina Söhn (2007) demonstrate that nowhere are there large-scale concentrations (e.g. over 10 per cent of a city's population) of particularly ethnic groups; there are certainly cities in which over 30–40 per cent of inhabitants are of migrant background, but these areas always comprise a mixture of ethnic groups.

Hence with regard to the assertion of self-segregation – a key tenet of the backlash against multiculturalism – the situation seems to be that 'the anxieties are better seen as ghettos of the mind rather than ghettos of reality' (Simpson 2007: 423).

(3) New assertiveness of liberal state

With regard to the third trend purportedly leading to a wholesale retreat from multiculturalism, Joppke (2004: 249) states, 'The turn from multiculturalism to civic integration reflects a seismic shift not just in the Netherlands, but in other European societies as well.' Over the past few years, there is no doubt that 'integration' (of immigrants and ethnic minorities) has become one of the foremost themes in national domestic policy throughout Europe and at the EU level itself. Most countries of substantial immigration in Europe have, in recent years, rolled out new policy platforms for the integration of immigrants (see Carrera 2005, Süssmuth and Weidenfeld 2005).

In Austria, Belgium (Wallonia and Flanders), France, Germany, Denmark, the United Kingdom, the Netherlands and elsewhere, governments have relatively newly established integration policies and programmes. As described in several chapters in this volume, these often include implementing citizenship courses and mandatory tests for immigrants surrounding knowledge of national civics, dominant cultural norms and values. Increasingly, language requirements for immigrants are being called for in many places too. Newcomers must demonstrate certain standards or levels of competency in the official language, again through compulsory courses and tests – sometimes even prior to entry. Failure to engage or pass such language requirements may threaten secure legal status. In these ways and more, the onus and obligation is being placed on immigrants and ethnic minorities to take up 'host' country values and cultural practices and to actively demonstrate their desire to 'belong'. In Switzerland, for example, such expectations that immigrants should demonstrate their efforts to 'belong' are expressed within a discourse of *fordern* (calling on immigrants' own efforts to integrate) as opposed to *fördern* (supporting immigrants' integration; see D'Amato, this volume). As shown in chapters throughout this volume, such measures are seen by policy-makers as crucial steps to ensure immigrants' and ethnic minorities' own socio-economic mobility, to avoid unrest and to guarantee security.

Joppke's 'seismic shift' would imply that these changes run throughout and deep into policies and public infrastructures. However, apart from an obvious avoidance of the world 'multicultural' within most policy documents across Europe (to the extent it was ever in some), arguably there has not been such a massive change. If so, one would expect a genuine retraction of cultural accommodation measures of the kind listed early in this Introduction. Clearly in most European countries and at EU level there has emerged a pervasive emphasis on so-called integration – but this set of policy reorientations has not emerged with the eradication, nor even much to the detriment, of actual measures, institutions and frameworks for minority cultural recognition.

While 'multicultural' has mostly disappeared from political rhetoric and 'integration' has plainly appeared, continuing support for immigrant and minority cultural difference is evident in the growing use of notions of 'diversity'. For example, while 'multicultural' or 'multiculturalism' are words entirely absent from the key British strategy document 'Improving Opportunities, Strengthening Society' (Home Office 2005), 'diversity' – mostly mentioned in terms of 'promoting diversity' – appears 34 times within a 54-page document; similarly, in the 202-page German national plan for the integration of immigrants (Bundesregierung, 2007), 'diversity' (*Vielfalt*) appears 84 times as something to endorse and encourage.

Multiculturalism by any other name

In national and urban policy, 'diversity' – alongside or alternative to 'multicultural' – is not a particularly new concept. 'Diversity policy', in one form or another, already arose in the late 1990s. 'Diversity' emerged in part as a kind of transference from a corporatist, or 'group-ist', approach to ethnic minority incorporation – indeed criticism of the corporatist model of multiculturalism was widespread in the 1990s (see Ålund and Schierup 1991; Anthias and Yuval-Davis 1993; Vertovec 1996; Baumann 1999) – towards more individual modes of inclusion (Uitermark *et al.* 2005; Bader 2008, Faist 2009). Behind many emergent 'diversity' policies there is the idea that, rather than treating members of ethnic minorities as ever-representative of bounded collectives, institutions should recognize cultural difference as an individual trait. This view has spearheaded the development of 'diversity management' in public administration, corporate structures and industrial workplaces, where 'diversity' calls attention to a range of overall benefits to be gained from recognizing and valuing individuals' cultural differences (see Wrench 2007).

Other uses of 'diversity' in today's policy documents are wholly interchangeable with earlier uses of 'multicultural'. That is, 'diversity' is the term now meant to do much of the work that 'multicultural' used to: as mentioned earlier in this Introduction, this mainly entails measures to reduce discrimination; to promote equality of opportunity and overcome barriers to full participation in society; to allow unconstrained access to public services; to recognize cultural identities (as opposed to assimilation) and open up public spaces to their representation; and to foster acceptance of ethnic pluralism and cultural understanding across all groups. In this way 'multicultural' programs have been replaced by ones concerned with 'diversity'. Examples are now myriad; below we list some selected to indicate variety and range.

On the urban level, across Europe cities such as Copenhagen, Stuttgart, Vienna, Zurich and Dublin have built diversity principles into their current policies and practices (Spencer 2008; D'Amato, this volume; Schönwälder, this volume). At national level, the Belgian government's action plan 2005–7 for developing diversity include the goal of 'respecting differences in the attitudes, values, cultural frameworks, lifestyles, skills and experiences of each member of a group' (ibid.: 7). And at European level, in 2004 the Council of Europe's Congress of Local and Regional Authorities adopted a resolution which included as a key aim 'the use of cultural diversity as a resource, by opening up urban life and public services in an intercultural manner' (ibid.: 12–13). Also at this latter level, an important set of guidelines that emerged as part of the 'integration' trend are the European Union's 'Common Basic Principles for Immigrant Integration Policy in the European Union' (Council of the European Union 2004). The Prelude to this document describes cultural diversity as one of the benefits that member states receive from immigration (acknowledged as 'a permanent feature of European society'; ibid.: 15). Principle No. 7 states that 'Frequent interaction between immigrants and Member State citizens is a fundamental mechanism for integration ... [including] Shared forums, intercultural dialogue, education about immigrants and immigrant cultures ... ' Principle No. 8 notes that 'The practice of diverse cultures and religions is guaranteed under the Charter of Fundamental Rights and must be safeguarded, unless practices conflict with other inviolable European rights or with national law', while the EU promotes 'Constructive social, inter-cultural and inter-religious dialogue, education, thoughtful public discourse, support for cultural and religious expressions that respect national and European values, rights and laws' (ibid.: 23). Such clear statements show that there has not been a real rolling-back of measures to recognize cultural difference – indeed, ever new schemes are being launched (some still using the term 'multicultural', as alternative to or indeed in combination with 'diversity' and 'intercultural'). Illustrations, drawn from the European Commission's (2007) *Third Annual*

Report on Migration and Integration, include: the Swedish government declared 2006 as the 'Swedish Year of Multiculturalism' to create cooperation between different cultural traditions; in Slovenia a 'unit for the cultural rights of minorities and for the development of cultural diversity' was established while the federal government of Belgium set up a Diversity Unit and the French and Flemish Communities created programmes for intercultural communication and awareness raising; Denmark embarked upon various initiatives fostering intercultural dialogue and stressing religious diversity, including dialogue meetings between the Danish Prime Minister and the Minister for Integration and various ethnic minority organizations; in Luxembourg there was a 'festival of migrations, cultures and citizenship' and other 'multicultural initiatives' organized to promote integration; Finland had a 'Multicultural Personality of the Year' award and in Portugal many initiatives are carried out to manage cultural diversity including television and radio programmes, such as the 'Week of Cultural Diversity'; and in France a group of big enterprises drafted a 'Diversity Charter' to commit themselves to create an intercultural environment among their staff (ibid.: 13). Germany has also initiated a Diversity Charter, currently signed by over 500 leading companies such as Daimler, Deutsche Bank, Deutsche BP and Deutsche Telekom. Among its policy goals are:

> to acknowledge the diversity of society in and outside the organization, appreciate its inherent potential and put it to profitable use for the organization; to publicly report on our activities and the progress we have made in promoting diversity and respect for difference on an annual basis; and to inform our employees about diversity and involve them in implementing the Charter.
>
> (www.diversity-charter.org)

In sum, the signatories state that 'We are convinced that embracing and appreciating diversity has a positive impact on society in Germany.'

Still other policy developments show that, despite – or better, alongside – the centrality of 'integration' measures, minority cultural recognition remains prevalent within public policy. In 'Improving Opportunities, Strengthening Society' (Home Office 2005), while community cohesion was flagged as a central tenet, the British government listed among its goals that:

> In health our overall drive to provide greater patient choice will include more tailored services to meet the particular needs of different cultural and ethnic groups ...
>
> (Ibid.: 9)

> As youth services and school partnerships are developed, we will improve opportunities for young people from all backgrounds to learn and socialize together and to develop an inclusive sense of British identity alongside their other cultural identities ...
>
> (Ibid.: 11)

We also expect museums, galleries and community cultural programs to play an increased role in promoting an understanding of, and celebrating, the diverse elements of our local and national society ...

(Ibid.: 12)

More broadly, health services need to be sensitive to the cultural backgrounds of all patients ...

(Ibid.: 18)

Today, Britishness encompasses the collective contribution diverse communities make to the country. People should not need to choose between their British identity and other cultural identities. They can be proud of both.

(Ibid.: 20)

Although now under the rubric of 'integration', these statements and plans were basically the same as those under the rubric 'multiculturalism'.

Other examples demonstrate a reluctance to shift policy strategies. As part of the drive towards fostering community cohesion and being seen to shift from old-style, 'separatist' multiculturalism, in February 2008 the UK government signalled that funding for single ethnic or religious groups would be cut back or phased out altogether. Hazel Blears, the then Communities Secretary, proposed that local councils should not 'risk using public money on projects that might ... unnecessarily keep people apart' (in *The Economist*, 2008a). However, by the end of 2008 the central government dropped such plans, accepting that such funding should be decided on the local level and acknowledging that such single groups themselves often play important roles in building social cohesion.

It is particularly on the local level that cultural accommodation policies are still to be found in number (a point emphasized in several contributions to this volume). Indicative of this fact, in December 2008 *The Economist* (2008b) published a substantial piece pointing to the many ways local governments across Europe are practically and unproblematically accommodating Muslim values and practices, including: approving the building of mosques, providing halal food in schools, regulating facilities for ritual slaughter, consenting to headscarves among Muslim city workers, zoning special areas for Islamic burial in cemeteries and creating times for women-only swimming sessions in public pools. Despite national backlash discourse it seems that, as *The Economist* concludes, 'Local pragmatism works best.'

A crisis of perception

Policies and programmes once deemed 'multicultural' continue everywhere. As Derek McGhee (2008: 145) writes: 'we have entered into a phase of reflexive multiculturalism in which the term 'multiculturalism' has been driven underground, while some of the strategies associated with multiculturalism continue to influence policy and practices at the "local" level'. Yet little public knowledge of the facts around the recognition of minority cultural practices provides fertile ground for backlash discourse to grow. This was notably exemplified in Quebec's recent 'accommodation crisis', a French Canadian version of the backlash against multiculturalism.

In the mid-2000s a growing number of reported cases in Quebec sparked public controversies surrounding the accommodation (or as they came to be portrayed by critics, 'privileges') of migrants' and ethnic minorities' cultural differences. Foremost cases included reported incidents such as when: men who accompanied their spouses to prenatal classes were excluded at the request of Muslim women; female driving instructors were asked to relinquish their places to men when Orthodox Jews were taking their driving tests; customers at a dance hall were expelled so that Muslims could recite prayers; food sectors were told to modify recipes and invest heavily to make products conform to Orthodox Jewish standards; a gym had to frost over windows so that exercising women wouldn't be visible to Hasidic Jews. These kinds of claims – and the sense of majority outrage about them – were all increasingly given press coverage and were exploited by populist politicians in Quebec. This trend became particularly intense between 2002–6, and reached a kind of moral panic by 2006–7.

Therefore the Provincial government set up a Consultation Commission on Accommodation Practices Related to Cultural Differences, headed by sociologist Gérard Bouchard and philosopher Charles Taylor. With a $5 million budget, over the course of a year the Commission gathered the findings of 13 research projects, 31 focus groups, 22 regional forums, 59 meetings with experts and representatives, and 900 written submissions surrounding the issues. After all this, the Commission concluded that the 'accommodation crisis' was a really a 'crisis of perception' in which the media had grossly misrepresented the controversial incidents. 'The negative perception of accommodation often stemmed from an erroneous or partial perception of practices in the field,' say Bouchard and Taylor (2008: 22). 'Had the public been more familiar with such practices, perhaps there would not have been an accommodation crisis.' It seems that this might also be said about the backlash against multiculturalism in Europe.

Trends of opinion, political shifts and crises of perception appear, at first glance at least, common to many countries. However, public debates surrounding multiculturalism should be assessed within existing national contexts and all the distinct political frameworks, historical trajectories of policy and discourse, key incidents and institutional experiences surrounding immigrants and ethnic minorities that such contexts entail. This is the task taken up by the contributors to this volume.

The chapters

In the next chapter, Will Kymlicka takes a global view on multiculturalism not only in relation to immigrants, but also regarding substate national groups and indigenous minorities. He questions the current 'master narrative' of the rise and fall of multiculturalism. By way of various examples, Kymlicka shows that multicultural policy and practice entail what might be called 'citizenization', or overcoming social inequalities by shaping civic and political relations. Kymlicka describes how in various global settings, policies and practices enhancing such civic and political relations have, indeed, been expanded and strengthened rather than weakened, particularly in relation to substate national and indigenous minorities. However, he observes that multiculturalism is, indeed, experiencing a backlash in relation to recent immigrants especially where they are seen as disloyal, illiberal, or a burden to the welfare state. In such contexts, perceptions of the 'death of multiculturalism' can dominate public and political discourse and supersede the forces supporting multiculturalism. By looking at existing multicultural policies from a more global and comparative perspective, Kymlicka challenges the claims of policy failure and retreat. This more optimistic picture is also reflected in other chapters of the book, especially when looking at policies and practices at the local level.

The UK forms one of the classical European examples of long-established multicultural policy and practice, which has recently come under scrutiny in both political and public debates especially since 2001. Ralph Grillo takes a step further back, however, and describes how, since the 1950s, the construction of difference and diversity in Britain has moved from concerns with 'race' during the 1950s and 1960s, to discussions surrounding 'ethnicity', then 'culture' and then 'faith'. More recently 'social cohesion' has since been promoted as the solution to bridge difference and counter segregation, inequality and racism, and to encourage inter-faith dialogue. Towards the end of his chapter, Grillo points to the reality of everyday life in diverse Britain, which is characterized by the co-existence of varying degrees of cultural diversity, assimilation and parallel lives. He reminds us that in many local contexts, people successfully rub along and skilfully adapt to the reality of ever-increasing diversity and changing social circumstances. Again, this is a fact of local life that is overlooked in much backlash discourse.

The Netherlands represents the national case that perhaps gained most media attention across Europe and is often cited as the prime example of the backlash against multiculturalism. Baukje Prins and Sawitri Saharso describe how this shift took place in the context of what they describe as the victory of 'new realism', a particular kind of public discourse which is characterized by the claim to represent the 'ordinary people' and the emphasis on 'facing the facts' in contrast to politically correct left-wing politicians. The emergence of this new kind of discourse in the Netherlands, coupled with events such as the murder of Theo van Gogh, has not only led to political turmoil between parties and individual politicians, but also to an increasing policy emphasis on civic integration and 'Dutch values'. Prins and Saharso trace the complicated entanglement of public discourse, political debates and the role played by specific individuals such as Paul Scheffer and Ayaan Hirsi Ali, who gained a kind of celebrity status within these debates. Despite the Dutch backlash against multiculturalism, Prins and Saharso point out, actual policies regarding immigrants have changed less radically. Rather, such policies seem to be shaping a compromise between individual participation, emancipation and group differences.

While the United Kingdom and the Netherlands are most identified with long-standing multicultural policies, France has usually been portrayed as a prototypical 'assimilationist' country. Patrick Simon and Valérie Sala Pala describe how France moved from a tradition of assimilation and the concealing of societal division along ethnic and racial lines, to the slow recognition of the place of immigrants in society. This recognition was spurred by an increasing awareness of discrimination and the fact that the French principle of equality was not applied to post-colonial migrants and their descendents. However, despite moves towards anti-discrimination, a strong integrationist stance continues to dominate policy discourse. Simon and Sala Pala examine these trends within France's recent public debates surrounding the causes of the urban riots of 2005, the introduction of ethnic categories in statistics, the headscarf affair and the use of religious symbols in public institutions. Such events and debates, Simon and Sala Pala suggest, illustrate the difficulties faced by the French integration model – including the question as to whether the model has constructed an inherently discriminatory system by publicly fostering a negative response to the expression of otherness, and by obfuscating ethnic and racial divisions.

Like France, Denmark has never perceived itself as a multicultural society. Cultural diversity is commonly seen as an un-Danish notion, despite the country's increasingly de-facto ethnic mix. In his contribution to the volume, Ulf Hedetoft observes that this monocultural discourse is no longer just the most prominent, but its current political hegemony is unprecedented. He discusses how, in order to deal with the integration of migrants and the adaptation of the Danish welfare model to the 'immigration challenge', the modernized Danish integration policy consists of a combination of divergent policy approaches: assimilation, integration and pluriculturality. The latter reflects the fact that although assimilation is prioritized as dominant policy, the factual existence of ethnic diversity and the need for economic immigration calls for pragmatism. This is especially so in light of what Hedetoft describes as 'closet, street-level diversity practices', with makeshift multicultural initiatives on the local level. Hedetoft contrasts the Danish example of this combination of interest-based pragmatism and identity-based nationalism with the approach in Sweden, where multiculturalism has been official policy for over 30 years. He thereby demonstrates that small welfare-states based on culturally homogenous histories do not necessarily spawn assimilationist policies.

Despite its similar population size, Switzerland forms a somewhat contrasting example in relation to both Denmark and Sweden because of its historical ethnic and linguistic diversity across four language areas. Regardless of this diversity, and in spite of having the highest immigration rate on the continent during the entire twentieth century, Switzerland refused to consider itself as country of immigration and denied any immigrant policy at federal level until the 1990s. Gianni D'Amato's chapter highlights the controversial academic debate on multiculturalism in Switzerland since the 1990s, and how the concept of 'cultural distance' entered the immigration policy debate. These tendencies were countered by arguments proposing cultural diversity as a pillar of liberal nation-states. Today in Switzerland, multiculturalism remains a topic of ideological combat in both academic debate and public opinion. One outcome is the lack of a consistent multicultural policy. On the other hand, as elsewhere the concept of 'integration' has been advocated by both the left and the right, sometimes alongside an expansion of cultural rights to migrants. This policy blend is due to the political opportunity structures in Switzerland, in particular its federalist structure favouring multifaceted, highly localized policy development.

In Germany, like in Switzerland, an official policy of multiculturalism never existed. Karen Schönwälder describes how, despite significant post-war immigration, the major political parties of both Left and Right only reluctantly accepted the permanent character of immigration. However, this official political acceptance of immigration co-exists with negative attitudes towards ethnic diversity, including the widely held opinion that immigrants should adjust to German ways. At the same time, there is scope for a partial pragmatic acceptance of diversity. While, on the national level, official policies recognizing and promoting ethnic plurality are non-existent, several cities have committed themselves to 'intercultural' policies, and policies that may be regarded as components of a multicultural approach do exist on the local or regional level. Schönwälder questions whether such local initiatives suffice without public commitments to diversity on the federal level, particularly when it comes to influencing public opinion and the wider acceptance of diversity.

Ricard Zapata-Barrero's chapter on Spain exemplifies how policies dealing with cultural and religious diversity are directly linked to discussions surrounding historically established diversities among the different Spanish regions. In this way Zapata-Barrero unpacks the link between immigration and multi-nationalism and raises the question how new processes of diversification are managed alongside already existing diversity, and how far immigrants impact on national, non-state identity constructions. Such questions are particularly relevant in the realm of, for example, minority language acquisition within the Spanish Autonomous Communities. Moreover, in Spain the key debates are less about multicultural accommodation and integration and more about immigration itself, particularly management of migration flows and the control of irregular immigration. According to Zapata-Barrero, attitudes towards the sheer numbers of immigrants are far more negative than attitudes towards those who enter and the religious and cultural diversity they bring.

In the final chapter, David Ley presents a comparative reflection from Canada, where for decades multiculturalism has been positively valued as integral part of national self-perception. Ley suggests that a critical re-assessment of multiculturalism is not particular to Western Europe, but has been evident in most immigrant-receiving countries. Practically everywhere, and exemplified in the European nations represented in this volume, there is now in this post-9/11 era a more visceral and populist attack on multi-culturalism, often associated with the imputed dangers of segregation. In Canada, multiculturalism has moved on from its earlier emphasis on cele-brating cultural difference to a more gritty affirmation of citizenship rights to groups in danger of marginalization. Ley shows how Canada's own public debate has also been agitated by selective media flows from Europe high-lighting points of crisis and ignoring significant differences in national condi-tions. He emphasizes the need to provide a tight, albeit nationally specific, definition of multiculturalism, if for no other reason than to lay out clearly legitimate expectations of multiculturalism both as social ideology and prac-tical policy in immigrant and ethnic integration. Such specificity would also protect multiculturalism from the kind of generic charges that occur whenever a 'failure of integration' is detected in whatever sphere, be it economic, political, social or cultural.

Conclusion

Across a range of countries, there seems to have arisen a kind of convergence of backlash discourse, idioms and stratagems attacking a presumed multi-culturalism. Although each set of public debates has developed within discrete national political contexts, there has subsequently emerged, too, a con-vergence of policy responses. As summarized by Gary Freeman (2004: 945), across Western democracies: 'there is now a clear trend toward a middling form of incorporation – call it integration – that rejects permanent exclusion but neither demands assimilation nor embraces formal multiculturalism'. While focused on ideas of integration, the form this policy strategy takes is practically everywhere permeated with notions of 'diversity', especially sur-rounding the value of ensuring expressions of cultural and religious difference. In public debates – especially when combined with or echoing elements of multicultural backlash discourse – the integration theme might come across as highly proscriptive and based wholly on majority cultural values. But despite the 'integration' banner, when one examines the gamut of local and national policies – now, as before 'ramshackle, multifaceted, loosely con-nected sets of regulatory rules, institutions and practices in various domains of society that together make up the frameworks within which migrants and natives work out their differences' (ibid.: 946) – there does not seem to have materialized a particularly heavy-handed neo-assimilationism or 'new assertiveness' as described by some commentators.

If there was such a hard assimilationist approach re-emergent, one would expect a more manifest cancellation of programmes, restructuring of services, and rolling back of cultural accommodation measures. While the prominent discourse of 'integration' has certainly been placed at centre stage, complete with a number of new policy initiatives, the question remains: why are politicians and policy-makers still making so much effort to 'promote' and 'value' diversity? To answer that it is all meaningless rhetoric just to get votes is simply too flippant and cynical: there is real and extensive public money, political commitment, and institutional activity surrounding the diversity agenda across Europe. A full answer to that question 'why is there still so much attention to diversity?' is beyond the scope of this Introduction; for now, it is important just to raise the question as a way of rebuffing the death-of-multiculturalism/return-of-assimilationism claim.

Again, following the backlash against multiculturalism that has occurred in public discourse since the turn of the millennium, we have seen that at least in policy development and especially on local levels, 'In many ways this retreat from and open hostility to multiculturalism is, on examination, an exercise in avoiding using the term "multiculturalism" rather than moving away from the principles of multiculturalism altogether' (McGhee 2008: 85). This is not to say that the widespread backlash has had no impacts other than killing the 'M-word'. Relentless attacks on multiculturalism – and thereby on basic principles of accommodating cultural and religious difference – might not have changed the basis of policies radically, but they have certainly fomented a negative atmosphere surrounding immigrants, ethnic minorities and particularly Muslims. The backlash discourse has not necessarily been racist in itself, but for those with racist views it provides ample wind to their sails. As Veit Bader (2008: 11) says of anti-multiculturalism pronouncements in the Netherlands:

> Even if they have not been followed by similarly dramatic changes in actual policies ... , they have not been innocent (the 'power of words'). The political climate became increasingly inimical towards 'aliens', 'asylum seekers', 'immigrants' and 'allochtonen' [non-Dutch-born].

Overall public opinion might not have been greatly altered, but the terms in which politicians and media pundits address migration and ethnic minority issues have been reworked. Such changes in terms of public discourse ultimately find their way into everyday discourse. These processes put truth to the adage, 'shit sticks'. That is, if a negative image – no matter how untrue – is persistently directed at something or someone, even after its correction a certain amount of enduring damage is done.

The backlash against multiculturalism in Europe demonstrates how public discourse, policies and public opinion do not form a piece: while certainly touching and even influencing one another from time to time, in effect they move disjointly. The backlash discourse has been strong in its own right; it's fair to say that some political reactions have ensued – but these seem to have mainly taken the form of rhetorical adjustment rather than a significant alteration of course. Public opinion surprisingly does not appear to have profoundly changed in this period either, in spite of the media backlash and even notwithstanding significant events like the London bombings.

The contributions to this volume also underline the nationally specific nature of public debates and policy developments around migration and multiculturalism, and thereby show the absurdity of generalized headlines like 'Europe's Failed Multiculturalism' (*Washington Times* 2004) and 'Europe Backs Away from Multiculturalism' (*Forbes* 2006). A close look at national – and particularly, local or municipal – policies reveals that multicultural principles generally remain intact, and may even be embellished through their incorporation into 'integration' and 'diversity' agendas. In sum, it is fair to conclude (as Will Kymlicka does in his chapter), that 'reports of multiculturalism's death are very much exaggerated'.

Acknowledgements

We wish to thank Thijs Bogers, Marcel Maussen, Bettina Voigt and Annekatrin Kühn for their assistance in preparing and gathering materials for this volume. Also, we are grateful to the EU Framework 6 Programme and its Network of Excellence International Migration, Integration and Social Cohesion in Europe (IMISCOE) for funding the research cluster and conference leading to this publication.

References

Ålund, A. and Schierup, C. (1991) *Paradoxes of Multiculturalism: Essays on Swedish Society*, Aldershot: Avebury.

Anthias, F. and Yuval-Davis, N. (1993) *Racialized Boundaries: Race, Nation, Gender, Colour and Class and the Anti-Racist Struggle*, London: Routledge.

Bader, V. (2008) 'Associational governance of ethno-religious diversity in Europe: The Dutch case', conference paper presented at the Penn Program on Democracy, Citizenship, and Constitutionalism.

Barry, B. (2001) *Culture and Equality: An Egalitarian Critique of Multiculturalism*, Cambridge: Polity Press.

Baumann, G. (1999) *The Multicultural Riddle: Rethinking National, Ethnic, and Religious Identities*, New York: London: Routledge.

BBC/British Broadcasting Corporation (2005) 'UK majority back multiculturalism'. Online. Available HTTP: http://www.news.bbc.co.uk/2/hi/uk_news/4137990.stm (accessed 10 August 2005).

Bennett, D. (1998) 'Introduction.' In D. Bennett (ed.), *Multicultural States: Rethinking Difference and Identity*, London: Routledge.

Bild (2006a) 'Polizei bewacht härteste Schule Deutschlands, 1 April.

——(2006b) 'Multi-Kulti ist gescheitert', 5 April.

Blunkett, D. (2002) *Integration with Diversity: Globalization and the Renewal of Democracy and Civil Society*, London: Foreign Policy Centre.

Bouchard, G. and Taylor, C. (2008) *Building the Future: A Time for Reconciliation* [Report of the Consultation Commission on Accommodation Practices Related to Cultural Differences], Montreal: Government of Quebec.

Bundesregierung, Die [Deutschland] (2007) *Der Nationale Integrationsplan: Neue Wege – Neue Chancen*, Berlin: Presse-und Informationsamt der Bundesregierung.

Carrera, S. (2005) 'A typology of different integration programs in the EU', Brussels: Centre for European Policy Studies Briefing Paper IP/C/LIBE/OF/2005-2167.

Chicago Cultural Studies Group (1994) 'Critical multiculturalism', in D.T. Goldberg (ed.) *Multiculturalism: A Critical Reader*, Oxford: Blackwell, 114–39.

CIC, Commission on Integration and Cohesion (2007) *Our Interim Statement*. Online. Available HTTP: http://www.integrationandcohesion.org.uk.

Cliteur, P. (2001) 'Niet alle culturen zijn gelijkwaardig', *NRC Handelsblad*, 16 October.

Coenders, M., Lubbers, M. and Scheepers, P. (2003) 'Majorities' attitudes towards minorities in the European Union Member States: Results from the Standard Eurobarometers 1997–2000–2003', Vienna: Report 2 for the European Monitoring Centre on Racism and Xenophobia.

Council of the European Union (2004) 'The Hague Programme: Strengthening freedom, security and justice in the European Union', 'Brussels: Council Document 16054/04'. Annex 'Common Basic Principles for Immigrant Integration Policy in the European Union'.

Daily Express (2007a) 'We should abandon failed policy of multiculturalism', 2 July.

——(2007b) 'Multiculturalism has let terror flourish in Britain', 7 July.

Daily Mail (2006) 'Kelly condemns multiculturalism', 24 August.

——(2007) 'Multiculturalism "drives young Muslims to shun British values"', 29 January.

——(2008a) 'Multiculturalism is making Britain "a soft touch for terrorists"', 15 February.

——(2008b) ' "Sharia law will undermine British society," warns Cameron in attack on multiculturalism', 26 February.

Daily Telegraph (2005) 'Multicultural Britain is not working, says Tory chief', 4 August.

DCLG/Department for Communities and Local Government (2007) *Improving Opportunities, Strengthening Society – Two Years On. Statistical Annex – Race Equality in Public Services*, London: The Stationery Office.

Delanty, G. (2003) *Community*, London: Routledge.

Economist, The (2007) 'Bagehot: In praise of multiculturalism', 16 June.

——(2008a) 'The search for social glue', 23 February.

——(2008b) 'When town halls turn to Mecca', 6 December.

Eller, J.D. (1997) 'Anti-anti-multiculturalism', *American Anthropologist*, 99(2): 249–56.

European Commission (2007) *Third Annual Report on Migration and Integration*, Brussels: COM(2007)512 Final.

Faist, T. (2009) 'Diversity – a new mode of incorporation?', *Ethnic and Racial Studies*, 32(1): 171–90.

Focus (2004) 'Angst vor ungebildeten Moslems', 24 October.

Forbes (2006) 'Europe backs away from multiculturalism'. Online. Available HTTP: http://www.forbes.com/2006/11/17/multiculturalism-assimilation-europe-biz-cx_1120 oxford.html (accessed 20 October 2006).

FRA/European Union Agency for Fundamental Rights (2008) *Annual Report*, Vienna: European Union Agency for Fundamental Rights.

Freeman, G.P. (2004) 'Immigrant incorporation in Western democracies', *International Migration Review*, 38(3): 945–69.

Gallup Organization, The (2007) 'Intercultural dialogue in Europe', Flash Euro-barometer 217 for the European Commission.

Gerard, J. (2006) 'Be clear, this is Asian apartheid', *Sunday Times,* 27 August.

Giddens, A. (2006) 'Misunderstanding multiculturalism', *Guardian,* 14 October.

Giroux, H.A. (1994) 'Insurgent multiculturalism and the promise of pedagogy', in D.T. Goldberg (ed.) *Multiculturalism: A Critical Reader,* Oxford: Blackwell, pp. 325–43.

Goodhart, D. (2004) 'Too diverse?', *Prospect,* February.

Grillo, R. (2005) 'Backlash against diversity? Identity and cultural politics in European cities', Oxford: Centre on Migration, Policy and Society [COMPAS] Working Paper WP-05–14.

Hall, S. (2001) 'The multicultural question', Milton Keynes: Open University Pavis Papers in Social and Cultural Research no. 4.

Halstead, H. (1988) *Education, Justice and Cultural Diversity: an Examination of the Honeyford Affair, 1984–5,* London: The Falmer Press.

Heitmeyer, W. (1996) 'Für türkische Jugendliche in Deutschland spielt der Islam eine wichtige Rolle', *Die Zeit,* 23 August.

Home Office (2001) *Community Cohesion: A Report of the Independent Review Team* (aka the *Cantle Report*), London: Home Office.

——(2005) *Improving Opportunities, Strengthening Society: The Government's Strategy to increase race equality and community cohesion,* London: Her Majesty's Stationery Office.

Joppke, C. (2004) 'The retreat of multiculturalism in the liberal state: theory and policy', *British Journal of Sociology,* 55(2): 237–57.

Kymlicka, W. (1995) *Multicultural Citizenship: A Liberal Theory of Minority Rights,* Oxford: Oxford University Press.

Lewis, P. (2002) *Islamic Britain: Religion, Politics and Identity Among British Muslims,* London: I.B. Taurus, 2nd edn.

Lust, S. (2008) *Abschied von Multikulti: Wege aus der Integrationskrise,* Munich: Resch-Verlag.

Martiniello, M. (1998) *Multicultural Policies and the State: A Comparison of Two European Societies,* Utrecht: ERCOMER.

McGhee, D. (2008) *The End of Multiculturalism? Terrorism, Integration and Human Rights,* Maidenhead: Open University Press.

Modood, T. (2007) *Multiculturalism,* Cambridge: Polity.

O'Sullivan, J. (2007) 'Social acid has burnt the heart of Britain', *Daily Telegraph,* 16 August.

Parekh, B. (2000) *Rethinking Multiculturalism: Cultural Diversity and Political Theory,* Basingstone: Palgrave.

Phillips, A. (2007) *Multiculturalism without Culture,* Princeton: Princeton University Press.

Phillips, D. (2006) 'Parallel lives? Challenging discourses of British Muslim self-segregation', *Environment and Planning D: Society and Space,* 24: 25–40.

Phillips, M. (2005) 'This lethal moral madness', *Daily Mail,* 14 July.

——(2006a) *Londonistan: How Britain is Creating a Terror State Within,* London: Gibson Square.

——(2006b) 'The Londonistan mindset', *New York Post,* 4 June.

——(2006c) 'The country that hates itself', *Canada National Post,* 16 June.

Prins, B. and Slijper, B. (2002) 'Multicultural society under attack: Introduction', *Journal of International Migration and Integration*, 3(3/4): 313–28.

Rogers, A. and Tillie, J. (eds) (2001) *Multicultural Policies and Modes of Citizenship in European Cities*, Aldershot: Ashgate.

Scheffer, P. (2000) 'Het multiculturele drama', *NRC Handelsblad*, 29 January 2000.

Schönwälder, K. (ed.) (2007) 'Residential segregation and the integration of immigrants: Britain, the Netherlands and Sweden', Berlin: Wissenschaftszentrum (WZB) Discussion Paper Nr. SP IV 2007–2602.

Schönwälder, K. and J. Söhn (2007) 'Siedlungsstrukturen von Migrantengruppen in Deutschland: Schwerpunkte der Ansiedlung und innerstädtische Konzentrationen', Berlin: Wissenschaftszentrum (WZB) Discussion Paper Nr. SP IV 2007–2601.

Shohat, E. and Stam, R. (1994) *Unthinking Eurocentrism: Multiculturalism and the Media*, New York: Routledge.

Simpson, L. (2007) 'Ghettos of the mind: The empirical behavior of indices of segregation and diversity', *Journal of the Royal Statistical Society Series A*, 170(2): 405–24.

Slack, J. (2006) 'Why the dogma of multiculturalism has failed Britain', *Daily Mail*, 7 July.

Spencer, S. (2008) *Equality and Diversity in Jobs and Services: City Policies for Migrants in Europe*, Dublin: European Foundation for the Improvement of Living and Working Conditions/Cities for Local Integration Policy (CLIP) Network.

Süssmuth, R. and Weidenfeld, W. (eds) (2005) *Managing Integration: The European Union's Responsibilities towards Immigrants*, Washington, DC: Migration Policy Institute and Bertelsman Foundation.

Tagesspiegel (2008) 'Multikulti ist gescheitert', 17 January.

Taylor, C. (1992) *Multiculturalism and the Politics of Recognition*, Princeton: Princeton University Press.

Uitermark, J., Rossi, U. and van Houtum, H. (2005) 'Reinventing multiculturalism: Urban citizenship and the negotiation of ethnic diversity in Amsterdam', *International Journal of Urban and Regional Research*, 29(3): 622–40.

Turner, T. (1993) 'Anthropology and multiculturalism: What is anthropology that multiculturalists should be mindful of it?', *Cultural Anthropology*, 8: 411–29.

Verma, G.K. (ed.) (1989) *Education for All: A Landmark in Pluralism*, London: Routledge.

Vertovec, S. (1996) 'Multiculturalism, culturalism and public incorporation', *Ethnic and Racial Studies*, 19(1): 49–69.

——(1998) 'Multi-multiculturalisms', in M. Martiniello (ed.) *Multicultural Policies and the State*, Utrecht: ERCOMER, pp. 25–38.

Washington Times (2004) 'Europe's failed multiculturalism', 10 December.

Wheatcroft, P. (2006) 'Multiculturalism hasn't worked: let's rediscover Britishness', *Daily Telegraph*, 8 October.

Wrench, J. (2007) *Diversity Management and Discrimination: Immigrants and Ethnic Minorities in the EU*, Aldershot: Ashgate.

2 The rise and fall of multiculturalism?

New debates on inclusion and accommodation in diverse societies[1]

Will Kymlicka

Ideas about the legal and political accommodation of ethnic diversity have been in a state of flux for the past 40 years around the world. A familiar way of describing these changes is in terms of the "rise and fall of multiculturalism." Indeed, this has become a kind of "master narrative," widely invoked by scholars, journalists, and policy-makers alike to explain the evolution of contemporary debates about diversity. Although people disagree about what comes "after multiculturalism," there is a surprising consensus that we are indeed in a "post-multicultural" era.

My goal in this chapter will be to explore and critique this master narrative, and to suggest an alternative framework for thinking about the choices we face. In order to make progress, I will suggest, we need to dig below the surface of the master narrative. Both the rise and fall of multiculturalism have been very uneven processes, depending on the nature of the issue and the country involved, and we need to understand these variations if we are to identify a more sustainable model for accommodating diversity.

In its simplest form, the master narrative goes like this:[2]

- From the 1970s to mid-1990s there was a clear trend across the Western democracies towards the increased recognition and accommodation of diversity through a range of multiculturalism policies and minority rights. These policies were endorsed both at the domestic level in various states and by international organizations, and involved a rejection of earlier ideas of unitary and homogenous nationhood.
- Since the mid-1990s, however, we have seen a backlash and retreat from multiculturalism, and a re-assertion of ideas of nation-building, common values and identity, and unitary citizenship—even a "return of assimilation."
- This retreat is partly driven by fears amongst the majority group that the accommodation of diversity has "gone too far" and is threatening their way of life. This fear often expresses itself in the rise of nativist and populist right-wing political movements, such as the Danish People's Party, defending old ideas of "Denmark for the Danish."
- But the retreat also reflects a belief amongst the centre-left that multiculturalism has failed to help the intended beneficiaries—namely,

minorities themselves—because it has failed to address the underlying sources of their social, economic, and political exclusion, and may indeed have unintentionally contributed to their social isolation. As a result, even the centre-left political movements that had initially championed multiculturalism, such as the social democratic parties in Europe, have backed away from it, and shifted to a discourse that emphasizes ideas of "integration," "social cohesion," "common values," and "shared citizenship."[3]

- The social-democratic discourse of national integration differs from the radical right discourse in emphasizing the need to develop a more inclusive national identity, and to fight racism and discrimination, but nonetheless distances itself from the rhetoric and policies of multiculturalism. The term "post-multiculturalism" has often been invoked to signal this new approach, which seeks to overcome the perceived limits of a naïve or misguided multiculturalism while avoiding the oppressive reassertion of homogenizing nationalist ideologies.[4]

This, in brief, is the master narrative of the "rise and fall of multiculturalism." It helpfully captures important features of our current debates. Yet in some respects it is misleading, and may obscure the real challenges and opportunities we face.

In the rest of this chapter, I will argue that the master narrative (a) mischaracterizes the nature of the experiments in multiculturalism that have been undertaken over the past 40 years, (b) exaggerates the extent to which they have been abandoned, and (c) misidentifies the genuine difficulties and limitations they have encountered.

What is multiculturalism?

In much of the post-multiculturalism literature, multiculturalism is characterized as a feel-good celebration of ethnocultural diversity, encouraging citizens to acknowledge and embrace the panoply of customs, traditions, music, and cuisine that exist in a multi-ethnic society. Alibhai-Brown calls this the "3S" model of multiculturalism in Britain—saris, samosas, and steel drums (Alibhai-Brown 2000). Multiculturalism takes these familiar cultural markers of ethnic groups—clothing, cuisine, and music—and treats them as authentic cultural practices to be preserved by their members, and safely consumed as cultural spectacles by others. So they are taught in multicultural school curricula, performed in multicultural festivals, displayed in multicultural media and museums, and so on.

In my view, as I will explain below, this is a caricature of multiculturalism. But it is an influential caricature, and as such has been the focus of many critiques. To list the most obvious criticisms:

- It entirely ignores issues of economic and political inequality. Even if all Britons come to enjoy Jamaican steel drum music or Indian samosas, this by itself would do nothing to address the real problems facing Caribbean and south Asian communities in Britain—problems of unemployment, poor educational outcomes, residential segregation, poor English language skills, and political marginalization. These economic and political issues cannot be solved simply by celebrating cultural difference.

- Even with respect to the (legitimate) goal of promoting greater understanding of cultural difference, the focus on celebrating discrete "authentic" cultural practices that are "unique" to each group is potentially dangerous and misleading. First, not all customs that may be traditionally practiced within a particular group are worthy of being celebrated, or even of being legally tolerated, such as forced marriage. To avoid this risk, there's a tendency to choose safely inoffensive practices as the focus of multicultural celebrations—such as cuisine or music—practices that can be enjoyably consumed by members of the larger society. But this runs the opposite risk of the trivialization or Disneyfication of cultural difference (Bissoondath 1994), ignoring the real challenges that differences in cultural values and religious doctrine can raise.

- Second, the 3S model of multiculturalism can encourage a conception of groups as hermetically sealed and static, each reproducing its own distinct authentic practices. Multiculturalism may be intended to encourage people to share their distinctive customs, but the very assumption that each group has its own distinctive customs ignores processes of cultural adaption, mixing and mélange, and renders invisible emerging cultural commonalities, and thereby potentially reinforces perceptions of minorities as eternally "Other."

- Third, this model can end up reinforcing power inequalities and cultural restrictions within minority groups. In deciding which traditions are "authentic," and how to interpret and display them, the state generally consults the traditional elites within the group—typically older males—while ignoring the way these traditional practices (and traditional elites) are often challenged by internal reformers, who have different views about how, say, a "good Muslim" should act. It can therefore imprison people in "cultural scripts" that they are not allowed to question or dispute.

According to post-multiculturalists, it is the gradual recognition of these flaws that explains the retreat from multiculturalism, and the search for new post-multicultural models of citizenship that emphasize the priority of political participation and economic opportunities over the symbolic politics of cultural recognition, the priority of human rights and individual freedom over respect for cultural traditions, the priority of building inclusive common national identities over the recognition of ancestral cultural identities, and the priority of cultural change and cultural mixing over the reification of static cultural differences.

If indeed multiculturalism was fundamentally about celebrating cultural difference in the form of discrete folk-practices, then the post-multiculturalist critique would certainly be justified. In my view, however, this is a caricature of the reality of multiculturalism as it has developed over the past 40 years in the Western democracies, and a distraction from the real issues that we need to face.

I cannot rehearse the full history of multiculturalism here, but I think it is important to situate it in its historical context. In one sense, "multi-culturalism" is as old as humanity—different cultures have always found ways of co-existing, and respect for diversity was a familiar feature of many historic empires, such as the Ottoman Empire. But the sort of multiculturalism that is said to have had a "rise and fall" is a much more specific historic phenom-enon, emerging first in the Western democracies in the late 1960s. This timing is important, for it helps us situate multiculturalism in relation to larger social transformations of the post-war era.

More specifically, multiculturalism can be seen as part of a larger "human rights revolution" in relation to ethnic and racial diversity. Prior to World War II, ethnocultural and religious diversity in the West was characterized by a range of illiberal and undemocratic relations—including relations of con-queror and conquered; colonizer and colonized; master and slave; settler and indigenous; racialized and unmarked; normalized and deviant; orthodox and heretic; civilized and primitive; ally and enemy. These relationships of hier-archy were justified by racialist ideologies that explicitly propounded the superiority of some peoples and cultures, and their right to rule over others. These ideologies were widely accepted throughout the Western world, and underpinned both domestic laws (e.g., racially-biased immigration and citizenship policies) and foreign policies (e.g., in relation to overseas colonies).

After World War II, however, the world recoiled against Hitler's fanatical and murderous use of such ideologies, and the UN decisively repudiated them in favor of a new ideology of the equality of races and peoples. And this new assumption of human equality has generated a series of political movements designed to contest the lingering presence or enduring effects of older hier-archies. We can distinguish three "waves" of such movements: (a) the struggle for decolonization, concentrated in the period 1947 to 1965; (b) the struggle against racial segregation and discrimination, initiated and exemplified by the African-American civil rights movement from 1955 to 1965; and (c) the struggle for multiculturalism and minority rights, which has emerged from the late 1960s.

Each of these movements draws upon the human rights revolution, and its foundational ideology of the equality of races and peoples, to challenge the legacies of earlier ethnic and racial hierarchies. Indeed, the human rights revolution plays a double role here: not just as the inspiration for struggle, but also as a constraint on the permissible goals and means of that struggle. Insofar as historically excluded or stigmatized groups struggle against earlier hierarchies in the name of equality, they too have to renounce their own tra-ditions of exclusion or oppression in the treatment of, say, women, gays, people of mixed race, religious dissenters, and so on. The framework of human rights, and of liberal-democratic constitutionalism more generally, provides the overarching framework within which these struggles are debated and addressed.

Each of these movements, therefore, can be seen as contributing to a process of democratic "citizenization"—that is, turning the earlier catalogue of hierarchical relations into relationships of liberal-democratic citizenship, both in terms of the vertical relationship between the members of minorities and the state, and the horizontal relationships amongst the members of different groups. In the past, it was often assumed that the only way to engage in this process of citizenization was to impose a single undifferentiated model of citizenship on all individuals. But the ideas and policies of multiculturalism that emerged from the 1960s start from the assumption that this complex history inevitably and appropriately generates group-differentiated ethnopolitical claims. The key to citizenization is not to suppress these differential claims, but to filter and frame them through the language of human rights, civil liberties and democratic accountability. And this is what multiculturalist movements have aimed to do.

The precise character of the resulting multicultural reforms varies from group to group, as befits the distinctive history that each has experienced. They all start from the anti-discrimination principle that underpinned the second wave, but go beyond it to challenge other forms of exclusion or stigmatization. In most Western countries, explicit state-sponsored discrimination against ethnic, racial or religious minorities had largely ceased by the 1960s and 1970s, under the influence of the second wave of human rights struggles. Yet evidence of ethnic and racial hierarchies remained, and continues to be clearly visible in many societies, whether measured in terms of economic inequalities, political under-representation, social stigmatization or cultural invisibility. Various forms of multiculturalism have been developed to help overcome these lingering inequalities.

We can broadly distinguish three patterns of multiculturalism that have emerged in the Western democracies. First, we see new forms of empowerment of indigenous peoples, such as the Maori in New Zealand; Aboriginal peoples in Canada and Australia; Native Americans; Sami in Scandinavia, or Inuit of Greenland. These new models of multicultural citizenship for indigenous peoples often include some combination of the following nine policies:[5]

1   recognition of land rights/title
2   recognition of self-government rights
3   upholding historic treaties and/or signing new treaties
4   recognition of cultural rights language; hunting/fishing, sacred sites
5   recognition of customary law
6   guarantees of representation/consultation in the central government
7   constitutional or legislative affirmation of the distinct status of indigenous peoples
8   support/ratification for international instruments on indigenous rights
9   affirmative action.

Second, we see new forms of autonomy and power-sharing for substate national groups, such as the Basques and Catalans in Spain, Flemish and Walloons in Belgium, Scots and Welsh in Britain, Quebecois in Canada, Germans in South Tyrol, Swedish in Finland, and so on. These new forms of multicultural citizenship for national minorities typically include some combination of the following six elements:

1   federal or quasi-federal territorial autonomy
2   official language status, either in the region or nationally
3   guarantees of representation in the central government or on Constitutional Courts
4   public funding of minority language universities/schools/media
5   constitutional or parliamentary affirmation of "multinationalism"
6   according international personality e.g., allowing the substate region to sit on international bodies, or sign treaties, or have their own Olympic team.

And, finally, we see new forms of multicultural citizenship for immigrant groups, which may include a combination of the following eight policies:

1   constitutional, legislative or parliamentary affirmation of multiculturalism, at the central and/or regional and municipal levels
2   the adoption of multiculturalism in school curriculum
3   the inclusion of ethnic representation/sensitivity in the mandate of public media or media licensing
4   exemptions from dress-codes, Sunday-closing legislation etc. either by statute or by court cases
5   allowing dual citizenship
6   the funding of ethnic group organizations to support cultural activities
7   the funding of bilingual education or mother-tongue instruction
8   affirmative action for disadvantaged immigrant groups.

While there are important differences between these three modes of multiculturalism, each of them has been defended as a means to overcome the legacies of earlier hierarchies, and to help build fairer and more inclusive democratic societies.

In my view, therefore, multiculturalism is first and foremost about developing new models of democratic citizenship, grounded in human rights ideals, to replace earlier uncivil and undemocratic relations of hierarchy and exclusion. Needless to say, this account of multiculturalism-as-citizenization differs dramatically from the "3S" account of multiculturalism as the celebration of static cultural differences. Whereas the 3S account says that multiculturalism is about displaying and consuming differences in cuisine, clothing and music, to the neglect of issues of political and economic inequality, the citizenization account says that multiculturalism is precisely about constructing new civic and political relations to overcome the deeply-entrenched inequalities that have persisted after the abolition of formal discrimination.

It is obviously important to determine which of these accounts provides a more accurate description of the Western experience with multiculturalism. Before we can decide whether to celebrate or lament the fall of multi-culturalism, or to replace it with post-multiculturalism, we need first to make sure we know what multiculturalism has in fact been. I have elsewhere tried to give a fuller defense of my account (Kymlicka 2007: chaps. 3–5), so let me here just note three ways in which the 3S account is misleading.

First, the claim that multiculturalism is solely or primarily about symbolic cultural politics depends on a complete misreading of the actual policies. If we look at the three lists of policies above, it is immediately apparent that they combine economic, political, social, and cultural dimensions. Take the case of land claims for indigenous peoples. While regaining control of their traditional territories certainly has cultural and religious significance for many indigenous peoples, it also has profound economic and political significance. Land is the material basis for both economic opportunities and political self-government. Or consider language rights for national minorities. According official language status to a minority's language is partly valued as a form of symbolic "recog-nition" of a historically-stigmatized language. But it is also a form of economic and political empowerment: the more a minority's language is used in public institutions, the more its speakers have access to employment opportunities and decision-making procedures. Indeed, the political and economic dimensions of the multiculturalist struggles of indigenous peoples and national minorities are obvious: they are precisely about restructuring state institutions, including redistributing political control over important public and natural resources.

The view that multiculturalism is about the apolitical celebration of ethnic folk-customs, therefore, only has any plausibility in relation to immigrant groups. And indeed representations of cuisine, dress and music are often the most visible manifestations of "multiculturalism" in the schools and media. It is not surprising, therefore, that when post-multiculturalists discuss multi-culturalism, they almost invariably ignore the issue of indigenous peoples and national minorities, and focus only on the case of immigrant groups, where the 3S account has more initial plausibility.

But even in this context, if we look back at the list of eight multiculturalism policies adopted in relation to immigrant groups, we will quickly see that they too involve a complex mixture of economic, political, and cultural elements. While immigrants are (rightly) concerned to contest the historic stigmatiza-tion of their cultures, immigrant multiculturalism also includes policies that are centrally concerned with access to political power and to economic opportunities—for example, policies of affirmative action, mechanisms of political consultation, funding for ethnic self-organization, or facilitated access to citizenship.

All three familiar patterns of multiculturalism, therefore—for indigenous peoples, national minorities, and immigrant groups—combine cultural recognition, economic redistribution, and political participation. In this respect, the post-multiculturalist critique of multiculturalism as ignoring economic and political inequality is simply off the mark.

Second, the post-multiculturalists' claim that multiculturalism ignores the importance of universal human rights is equally misplaced. On the contrary, as we've seen, multiculturalism is itself a human rights-based movement, inspired and constrained by principles of universal human rights and liberal-democratic constitutionalism. Its goal is to challenge the sorts of traditional ethnic and racial hierarchies that have been discredited by the post-war human rights revolution. Understood in this way, multiculturalism-as-citizenization offers no support for protecting or accommodating the sorts of illiberal cultural practices within minority groups that have also been discredited by this human rights revolution. The same human rights-based reasons we have for endorsing multiculturalism-as-citizenization are equally reasons for rejecting cultural practices that violate human rights. And indeed, this is what we see throughout the Western democracies. Wherever multiculturalism has been adopted, it has been tied conceptually and institutionally to larger human rights norms, and has been subject to the overarching principles of the liberal-democratic constitutional order. No Western democracy has exempted immigrant groups from constitutional norms of human rights in order to maintain practices of, say, forced marriage, criminalization of apostasy, or cliterodectomy. Here again, the post-multiculturalist claim that human rights should take precedence over the recognition of cultural traditions simply reasserts what has been integral to the theory and practice of multiculturalism.

And this in turn points out the flaws in the post-multiculturalists' claim that multiculturalism ignores or denies the reality of cultural change. On the contrary, multiculturalism-as-citizenization is a deeply (and intentionally) transformative project, both for minorities and majorities. It demands both dominant and historically subordinated groups to engage in new practices, to enter new relationships, and to embrace new concepts and discourses, all of which profoundly transform people's identities and practices.

This is perhaps most obvious in the case of the historically-dominant majority nation in each country, which is required to renounce fantasies of racial superiority, to relinquish claims to exclusive ownership of the state, and to abandon attempts to fashion public institutions solely in its own national (typically white/Christian) image. In fact, much of multiculturalism's "long march through the institutions" consists precisely in identifying and attacking those deeply rooted traditions, customs, and symbols that have historically excluded or stigmatized minorities. Much has been written about the transformations in majority identities and practices this has required, and the backlash it can create.

But multiculturalism is equally transformative of the identities and practices of minority groups. Many of these groups have their own histories of ethnic and racial prejudice, of anti-Semitism, of caste and gender exclusion, of religious triumphalism, and of political authoritarianism, all of which are delegitimized by the norms of liberal-democratic multiculturalism and minority rights. Moreover, even where the traditional practices of a minority group are free of illiberal or undemocratic elements, they may involve a level of cultural closure that becomes unattractive and unsustainable under multiculturalism. These practices may have initially emerged as a response to earlier experiences of discrimination, stigmatization, or exclusion at the hands of the majority, and may lose their attractiveness as that motivating experience fades in people's memories. For example, some minority groups have developed distinctive norms of self-help, endogamy, and internal conflict resolution because they have been excluded from or discriminated within the institutions of the larger society. Those norms may lose their rationale as ethnic and racial hierarchies break down, and as group members feel more comfortable interacting with members of other groups and participating in state institutions. Far from guaranteeing the protection of the traditional ways of life of either the majority or minorities, multiculturalism poses multiple challenges to them. Here again, the post-multiculturalists' claim about recognizing the necessity of cultural change simply reasserts a long-standing part of the multicultural agenda.

In short, I believe that the post-multiculturalist critique is largely off-target, primarily because it misidentifies the nature and goals of the multiculturalism policies and programs that have emerged over the past 40 years during the "rise" of multiculturalism.

The retreat from multiculturalism?

But this then raises a puzzle. If post-multiculturalist claims about the flaws of multiculturalism are largely misguided, then what explains the fall of multiculturalism? If, as I claim, multiculturalism is inspired by human rights norms, and seeks to deepen relations of democratic citizenship, why has there been such a retreat from it?

Part of the answer is that reports of multiculturalism's death are very much exaggerated. Here again, we need to keep in mind the different forms that multiculturalism takes, only some of which have faced serious backlash. For example, there has been no retreat from the commitment to new models of multicultural citizenship for indigenous peoples. On the contrary, the trend towards enhanced land rights, self-government powers and customary law for indigenous peoples remains fully in place across the Western democracy, and has just been reaffirmed by the UN's General Assembly through the adoption of the Declaration of the Rights of Indigenous Peoples in 2007. Similarly, there has been no retreat from the commitment to new models of multicultural citizenship for national minorities. On the contrary, the trend towards enhanced language rights and regional autonomy for substate national groups remains fully in place in the Western democracies.[6] Indeed, these two trends are increasingly firmly entrenched in law and public opinion, backed by growing evidence that the adoption of multicultural reforms for indigenous peoples and national minorities has in fact contributed to building relations of democratic freedom and equality.[7] Few people today, for example, would deny that regional autonomy for Catalonia has contributed to the democratic consolidation of Spain, or that indigenous rights are helping to deepen democratic citizenship in Latin America.

So it is only with respect to immigrant groups that we see any serious retreat. Here, without question, there has been a backlash against multiculturalism policies relating to postwar migrants in several Western democracies. And there is also greater scholarly dispute about the impact of these policies. For example, while studies have shown that immigrant multiculturalism policies in Canada have had strongly beneficial effects in relation to citizenization (Bloemraad 2006), other studies suggest that immigrant multiculturalism in the Netherlands has had deleterious effects (Koopmans et al. 2005; Sniderman and Hagendoorn 2007).[8]

It is an important question why immigrant multiculturalism in particular has been so controversial, and I will return to this below. But we can begin by dismissing one popular explanation. Various commentators have suggested that the retreat from immigrant multiculturalism reflects a return to the traditional liberal and republican belief that ethnicity belongs in the private sphere, and that citizenship should be unitary and undifferentiated. On this view, the retreat from immigrant multiculturalism reflects a rejection of the whole idea of multiculturalism-as-citizenization (e.g., Brubaker 2001; Joppke 2004).

But this cannot be the explanation. If Western democracies were rejecting the very idea of multicultural citizenship, they would have rejected the claims of substate national groups and indigenous peoples as well as immigrants. After all, the claims of national groups and indigenous peoples typically involve a much more dramatic insertion of ethnocultural diversity into the public sphere, and a more dramatic degree of differentiated citizenship, than is demanded by immigrant groups. Whereas immigrants typically seek modest variations or exemptions in the operation of mainstream institutions, historic national minorities and indigenous peoples typically seek a much wider level of recognition and accommodation, including such things as land claims, self-government powers, language rights, separate educational systems, and even separate legal systems. These claims involve a much more serious challenge to ideas of undifferentiated citizenship and the privatization of ethnicity than is involved in accommodating immigrant groups. Yet Western democracies have not retreated at all from their commitment to accommodating these historic minorities.

Western democracies are, in fact, increasingly comfortable with claims to differentiated citizenship and the public recognition of difference, when these claims are advanced by historic minorities. So it is not the very idea of multicultural citizenship per se that has come under attack.[9] The problem, rather, is specific to immigration. What we need to sort out, therefore, is why multiculturalism has proven so much more controversial in relation to this particular form of ethnocultural diversity.

But even that way of phrasing the question is too general. The retreat from immigrant multiculturalism is not universal—it has affected some countries more than others. Public support for immigrant multiculturalism in Canada, for example, remains at an all-time high. And even in countries that are considered the paradigm cases of a retreat from immigrant multiculturalism, such as the Netherlands or Australia, the story is more complicated. The Dutch military, for example, which in the 1990s had resisted ideas of accommodating diversity, has recently embraced the idea of multiculturalism, even as other public institutions are now shying away from it. And in Australia, while the federal government has recently backed away from multiculturalism, the state governments have moved in to adopt their own new multiculturalism policies. What we see, in short, is a lot of uneven advances and retreats in relation to immigrant multiculturalism, both within and across countries.

So the post-multiculturalists' narrative of a "retreat" from multiculturalism is overstated, and misdiagnosed. Many new forms of multicultural citizenship have taken root, and not faced any significant backlash or retreat. This is true of the main reforms relating to both national minorities and indigenous peoples, backed by evidence of their beneficial effects. Even with respect to immigrant multiculturalism, claims of policy failure and retreat are overstated, obscuring a much more variable record in terms of policy outcomes and public support.

I will discuss some possible explanations for the distinctive fate of immigrant multiculturalism below. But notice that we cannot start to identify these factors until we set aside the post-multiculturalists' assumption that what is being rejected is multiculturalism as such. What is happening here is not a general or principled rejection of the public recognition of ethnocultural diversity. On the contrary, many of the countries that are retreating from immigrant multiculturalism are actually strengthening the institutionalization of other ethnocultural differences. For example, while the Netherlands is retreating from immigrant multiculturalism, it is strengthening the rights of its historic Frisian minority; while France is retreating from immigrant multiculturalism, it is strengthening recognition of its historic minority languages; while Germany is retreating from immigrant multiculturalism, it is celebrating the 50th anniversary of the special status of its historic Danish minority; while Britain is retreating from immigrant multiculturalism, it has accorded new self-government powers to its historic nations in Scotland and Wales; and so on. None of this makes any sense if we explain the retreat from immigrant multiculturalism as somehow a return of orthodox liberal or republican ideas of undifferentiated citizenship and the privatization of ethnicity.

In short, contrary to the post-multiculturalists' narrative, the ideal of multiculturalism-as-citizenization is alive and well, and remains a salient option in the "tool-kit" of democracies, in part because we now have 40 years of experience to show that it can indeed contribute to citizenization. However, particular uses of this approach, in relation to particular forms of diversity in particular countries, have run into serious obstacles. Not all attempts to adopt new models of multicultural citizenship have taken root, or succeeded in achieving their intended effects of promoting citizenization.

The crucial question, therefore, is why multicultural citizenship works in some times and places and not others. This is a crucial question not only for explaining the variable fate of multicultural citizenship in the West, but also for exploring its potential role as a model for thinking about diversity in post-colonial and post-communist societies. Unfortunately, the post-multiculturalist debate is largely unhelpful in answering this question. Since post-multiculturalists ignore the extent to which multiculturalism ever aspired to citizenization, and also over-generalize the retreat from multiculturalism, they do not shed light on the central question of why multicultural citizenization has flourished in some times and places, and failed elsewhere.

The preconditions of multicultural citizenship

In my view, we do not yet have a systematic account of the preconditions for successful experiments in multicultural citizenship, and so a certain degree of caution is required when making judgments and recommendations in this area. However, if we explore the varying fate of multiculturalism across different types of groups and different countries, we can gain some preliminary indications about the preconditions for a sustainable model of democratic multiculturalism.

The theory and practice of multiculturalism suggests that multiculturalism can contribute to citizenization, but the historical record suggests that certain conditions must be in place for it to have its intended effects. Multicultural citizenship cannot be built (or imposed) out of thin air: certain sources and preconditions must be present. In a recent book (Kymlicka 2007, chap. 4), I discuss a number of these conditions, but let me focus here on two: the desecuritization of state-minority relations; and the existence of a human rights consensus.

Desecuritization: Where states feel insecure in geo-political terms, fearful of neighboring enemies, they are unlikely to treat fairly their own minorities. More specifically, states are unlikely to accord powers and resources to minorities that they view as potential collaborators with neighboring enemies.

In the past, this has been an issue in the West. For example, prior to World War II, Italy, Denmark, and Belgium feared that their German-speaking minorities were more loyal to Germany than to their own country, and would support attempts by Germany to invade and annex areas of ethnic German concentration. These countries worried that Germany might invade in the name of liberating their co-ethnic Germans, and that the German minority would collaborate with such an invasion.

Today, this is a non-issue throughout the established Western democracies with respect to historic national minorities and indigenous peoples, although it remains an issue with respect to certain immigrant groups, particularly Arab/Muslim groups after 9/11. It is difficult to think of a single Western democracy where the state fears that a national minority would collaborate with a neighboring enemy and potential aggressor.[10] This is partly because Western states do not have neighboring enemies who might invade them. NATO has removed the possibility of one Western country invading its neighbors. As a result, the question of whether national minorities and indigenous peoples would be loyal in the event of invasion by a neighboring state is moot.

Of course, Western democracies do have long-distance potential enemies— such as Soviet Communism in the past, Islamic jihadism today, and perhaps China in some future scenario. But in relation to these long-distance threats, national minorities and indigenous peoples are on the same side as the state. If Quebec gains increased powers or even independence, no one in the rest of Canada worries that Quebec will start collaborating with Al Qaeda or China to overthrow the Canadian state. An autonomous or independent Quebec would be an ally of Canada, not an enemy.

In most parts of the world, however, minority groups are still seen as fifth columns collaborating with neighboring enemies. This is particularly true where the minority is related to a neighboring state by ethnicity or religion, or where a minority is found on both sides of an international border, so that the neighboring state claims the right to protect "its" minority. Consider the ethnic Serbs in Bosnia, or Kashmiris in India.

Under these conditions, ethnic relations become "securitized." Relations between states and minorities are seen, not as a matter of normal democratic debate and negotiation, but as a matter of state security, in which the state has to limit the democratic process to protect itself. Under conditions of securitization, minority political mobilization may be banned, and even if minority demands can be voiced, they will be rejected by the larger society and the state. After all, how can groups that are disloyal have legitimate claims against the state? So the securitization of ethnic relations erodes both the democratic space to voice minority demands, and the likelihood that those demands will be accepted.

In most Western countries, however, ethnic politics have been "desecuritized." Ethnic politics is just that—normal, day-to-day politics. Relations between the state and minority groups have been taken out of the "security" box, and put in the "democratic politics" box. This is one essential precondition for multicultural citizenship to emerge and take root.

Human rights protection: A second precondition concerns the security, not of the state, but of individuals who would be subject to self-governing minority institutions. States are unlikely to accept minority self-government if they fear it will lead to islands of local tyranny within a broader democratic state.

This too has been a worry in the past in the West, where some long-standing minorities were seen as carriers of illiberal political cultures.

And this fear persists in relation to some recent immigrant groups. But at least in relation to national minorities, it is now widely assumed that there is a deep consensus across ethnic lines on basic values of liberal democracy and human rights. As a result, it is assumed that any self-government powers granted to national minorities will be exercised in accordance with shared standards of democracy and human rights. Everyone accepts that minority self-government will operate within the constraints of liberal-democratic constitutionalism, which firmly upholds individual rights. Where minorities have gained autonomy in the West, their self-governing institutions are subject to the same constitutional constraints as the central government, and so have no legal capacity to restrict individual freedoms in the name of cultural authenticity, religious orthodoxy or racial purity. Not only is it legally impossible for national minorities in the West to establish illiberal regimes, but they have no wish to do so. On the contrary, all of the evidence suggests that members of national minorities are at least as strongly committed to liberal-democratic values as members of dominant groups, if not more so.[11]

This removes one of the central fears that dominant groups have about minority autonomy. In many parts of the world, there is the fear that once national minorities or indigenous peoples acquire self-governing power, they will use it to persecute, dispossess, expel or kill anyone who does not belong to the minority group. In Western democracies, this is a non-issue. Where there is a strong consensus on liberal-democratic values, people feel confident that however issues of multiculturalism are settled, their own civil and political rights will be respected. No matter how the claims of ethnonational and indigenous groups are resolved—no matter what language rights, self-government rights, land rights, or multiculturalism policies are adopted—people can rest assured that they won't be stripped of their citizenship, fired from their jobs, subjected to ethnic cleansing, jailed without a fair trial, or denied their rights to free speech, association and worship. Put simply, the consensus on liberal-democratic values ensures that debates over accommodating diversity are not a matter of life and death. As a result, dominant groups will not fight to the death to resist minority claims. This, too, is a precondition for the successful adoption of multicultural citizenship.

There are other factors that underpin the rise of multiculturalism in the West, including demographic changes, but desecuritization and human rights are pivotal. Where these two conditions are absent, multiculturalism is unlikely to emerge, except perhaps as the outcome of violent struggle or external imposition. These two factors not only help explain the rise of multiculturalism, but also help explain the partial retreat from multiculturalism in some countries in relation to recent Muslim immigrants, who are often seen as both disloyal and illiberal. There are other factors at play as well in the backlash against immigrant multiculturalism, including concerns about illegal immigration, and about the economic burden of supporting unemployed immigrants, as well as old-fashioned racial prejudice.[12] For many people, the latter is the key factor. But of course prejudice is found in all countries—indeed its existence is part of the justification for adopting multi-culturalism—and so cannot explain the variation across countries (or over time) in support for multiculturalism. And if we try to understand why this latent prejudice and xenophobia sometimes coalesces into powerful political movements against multiculturalism, the answer I believe lies in perceptions of threats to geo-political security, human rights, and economic security. Where such perceptions are lacking, as they are in relation to most immigrant groups in North America, then support for multiculturalism can remain quite strong.

Conclusion: the future of multiculturalism in the West

If this analysis is correct, it has important implications for the future of multiculturalism in the West. On the one hand, despite all the talk about the retreat from multiculturalism, it suggests that multiculturalism in general has a bright future. There are powerful forces at work in modern Western societies pushing in the direction of the public recognition and accommodation of ethnocultural diversity. Public values and constitutional norms of tolerance, equality, and individual freedom, underpinned by the human rights revolution, all push in the direction of multiculturalism, particularly when viewed against the backdrop of a history of ethnic and racial hierarchies. These factors explain the ongoing trend towards the recognition of the rights of sub-state national groups and indigenous peoples. Older ideas of undifferentiated citizenship and neutral public spheres have collapsed in the face of these trends, and no one today seriously proposes that these forms of minority rights and differentiated citizenship for historic minorities could be abandoned or reversed.[13] That minority rights, liberal democracy, and human rights can comfortably co-exist is now a fixed point in both domestic constitutions and international law. There is no credible alternative to multiculturalism in these contexts.

The situation with respect to immigrant groups is more complex. The same factors that push for multiculturalism in relation to historic minorities have also generated a willingness to contemplate multiculturalism for immigrant groups, and indeed such policies seem to have worked well under "low-risk" conditions. However, immigrant multiculturalism has run into difficulties where it is perceived as carrying particularly high risks. Where immigrants are seen as predominantly illegal, as potential carriers of illiberal practices or movements, and/or as net burdens on the welfare state, then multiculturalism poses perceived risks to both prudential self-interest and moral principles, and this perception can override the forces that support multiculturalism.

On the other hand, one could also argue that these very same factors also make the rejection of immigrant multiculturalism a high-risk move. It is precisely when immigrants are perceived as illegitimate, illiberal, and burdensome that multiculturalism may be most needed. Without some proactive policies to promote mutual understanding and respect, and to make immigrants feel comfortable within mainstream institutions, these factors could quickly lead to a situation of a racialized underclass, standing in permanent opposition to the larger society. Indeed, I would argue that, in the long term, the only viable response to the presence of large numbers of immigrants is some form of liberal multiculturalism, regardless of how these immigrants arrived, or from where. But we need to accept that the path to immigrant multiculturalism in many countries will not be smooth or linear. Moreover, we need to focus more on how to manage the risks involved. In the past, defenders of immigrant multiculturalism have typically focused on the perceived benefits of cultural diversity and inter-cultural understanding, and on condemning racism and xenophobia. Those arguments are sound, I believe, but they need to be supplemented with a fuller acknowledgement of the prudential and moral risks involved, and with some account of how those risks will be managed.

If we still have only a sketchy understanding of the preconditions of multicultural citizenship in the West, this is even more true in relation to the post-communist or post-colonial world. The analysis above suggests that efforts to diffuse multicultural citizenship will be difficult, and perhaps even counter-productive, in parts of the world where regional security and human rights protections are absent. Where minorities are potential pawns in unstable regional geo-politics, and where human rights guarantees are weak, attempts to transplant Western models of multiculturalism may exacerbate pre-existing relations of enmity and exclusion, rather than contribute to citizenization. And yet here again there are often no feasible alternatives to multiculturalism. Attempts to replicate the nineteenth-century French model of assimilationist nation-building in twenty-first century post-communist or post-colonial states are almost certainly doomed to failure, not least because minorities today are more conscious of their rights, better organized, and more connected to international networks. The fact that there are grave obstacles to multiculturalism does not mean that there are viable alternatives to it.

Notes

1 This chapter is an edited version of a Background Paper commissioned for the UNESCO World Report on Cultural Diversity, and will appear in a forthcoming special issue of the *International Social Science Journal*.

2 For influential academic statements of this "rise and fall" narrative, claiming that it applies across the Western democracies, see Brubaker 2001; Joppke 2004; cf. Baubock 2002. There are also, of course, many accounts of the "decline", "retreat," or "crisis" of multiculturalism in particular countries, such as the Netherlands (Entzinger 2003; Koopmans 2006; Prin and Slijper 2002), Britain (Hansen 2007; Back *et al.* 2002; Vertovec 2005); Australia (Ang and Stratton 2001), and Canada (Wong *et al.* 2005).

3 For an overview of the attitudes of European social democratic parties to these issues, see Cuperus *et al.* 2003.

4 For references to "post-multiculturalism" by progressive intellectuals and academics, who distinguish it from the radical right's "anti-multiculturalism", see

Alibhai-Brown 2000, 2004 (re the UK); Jupp 2007 (re Australia); King 2004; Hollinger 2006 (re the US).

5 This and the following lists of multicultural policies are taken from the "Index of Multicultural Policies" developed in Banting and Kymlicka 2006.

6 There has however been a retreat from attempts to formulate the rights of national minorities at the level of international law: see Kymlicka 2007: chap. 6.

7 I survey the evidence in Kymlicka 2007: chapter 5.

8 I discuss and criticize these Dutch studies in a review of the Sniderman/ Hagendoorn book (Kymlicka 2008).

9 Commentators who argue that Western democracies are rejecting multicultural citizenship per se typically simply ignore the obvious counter-examples of national minorities and indigenous peoples – see, e.g., Joppke 2004; Barry 2001.

10 If we move outside Western Europe, Cyprus and Israel are consolidated democracies which still exhibit this dynamic of viewing their historic Turkish and Arab minorities as potential collaborators with external enemies, and not coincidentally have been unable to agree on minority autonomy.

11 The situation with respect to some indigenous groups is more complicated, since they are sometimes perceived as falling outside the liberal-democratic consensus. But since indigenous self-government rarely involves the exercise of power over non-members, unlike the regional autonomy accorded to national minorities, there is less concern that indigenous self-government may harm the rights of non-members. Moreover, the evidence suggests that indigenous peoples are increasingly accepting of broader liberal-democratic principles (Schouls 2003).

12 For a more detailed discussion of these factors, see Kymlicka 2004.

13 Even a fierce critic of multiculturalism like Brian Barry (2001) makes no attempt to apply his ideas to the case of substate national groups and indigenous peoples.

References

Alibhai-Brown, Y. (2000) *After Multiculturalism*, London: Foreign Policy Centre.

——(2003) "Post-Multiculturalism and Citizenship Values," presented to Immigrant Council of Ireland Conference on Immigration, Ireland's Future, 11 December 2003.

——(2004) "Beyond multiculturalism," *Canadian Diversity/Diversité Canadienne*, 3 (2): 51–54.

Ang, I. and Stratton, J. (2001) "Multiculturalism in crisis: The new politics of race and national identity in Australia," in I. Ang (ed.) *On Not Speaking Chinese: Living Between Asia and the West*, London: Routledge: 95–111.

Back, L., Keith, M., Khan A., Shukra K. and Solomos, J. (2002) "New Labour's white heart: Politics, multiculturalism and the return of assimilation," *Political Quarterly*, 73: 445–54.

Banting, K. and Kymlicka W. (eds.) (2006) *Multiculturalism and the Welfare State: Recognition and Redistribution in Contemporary Democracies*, Oxford: Oxford University Press.

Barry, B. (2001) *Culture and Equality: An Egalitarian Critique of Multiculturalism*, Cambridge: Polity Press.

Baubock, R. (2002) "Farewell to multiculturalism? Sharing values and identities in societies of immigration," *Journal of International Migration and Immigration*, 3: 1–16.

Bissoondath, N. (1994) *Selling Illusions: The Cult of Multiculturalism in Canada*, Toronto: Penguin.

Bloemraad, I. (2006) *Becoming a Citizen: Incorporating Immigrants and Refugees in the United States and Canada*, Berkeley: University of California Press.

Brubaker, R. (2001) "The Return of Assimilation?" *Ethnic and Racial Studies*, 24/4: 531–48.

Cuperus, R., Duffek, K. and Kandel, J. (eds.) (2003) *The Challenge of Diversity: European Social Democracy Facing Migration, Integration and Multiculturalism*, Innsbruck: Studien Verlag.

Entzinger, H. (2003) "The Rise and Fall of Multiculturalism in the Netherlands," in C. Joppke and E. Morawska (eds.) *Toward Assimilation and Citizenship: Immigrants in Liberal Nation-States*, London: Palgrave, 59–86.

Hansen, R. (2007) "Diversity, integration and the turn from multiculturalism in the United Kingdom," in K. Banting, T. Courchene, and L. Seidle (eds.) *Belonging? Diversity, Recognition and Shared Citizenship in Canada*, Montreal: Institute for Research on Public Policy, 35–86.

Hollinger, D. (2006) *Post-ethnic America: Beyond Multiculturalism*, revised edition, New York: Basic Books.

Joppke, C. (2004) "The retreat of multiculturalism in the liberal state: Theory and policy," *British Journal of Sociology*, 55/2: 237–57.

Jupp, J. (2007) *From White Australia to Woomera: The Story of Australian Immigration*, 2nd edition, Cambridge: Cambridge University Press.

King, D. (2004) *The Liberty of Strangers: Making the American Nation*, Oxford: Oxford University Press.

Koopmans, R., Statham P., Guigni M., and Passy F. (2005) *Contested Citizenship: Immigration and Cultural Diversity in Europe*, Minneapolis: University of Minnesota Press.

Koopmans, R. (2006) "Trade-offs between equality and difference: the crisis of Dutch multiculturalism in cross-national perspective," Brief, Danish Institute for International Affairs, December.

Kymlicka, W. (2004) "Marketing Canadian Pluralism in the International Arena," *International Journal*, 59/4: 829–52.

——(2007) *Multicultural Odysseys: Navigating the New International Politics of Diversit*, Oxford: Oxford University Press.

——(2008) "Review of Paul Sniderman and Louk Hagendoorn's *When Ways of Life Collide: Multiculturalism and its Discontents*," *Perspectives on Politics*, 6(4): 804–7.

Prins, B. and Slijper, B. (2002) "Multicultural Society Under attack," *Journal of International Migration and Integration*, 3(3): 313–328.

Schouls, T. (2003) *Shifting Boundaries: Aboriginal Identity, Pluralist Theory, and the Politics of Self-Government*, Vancouver: UBC Press. 2005 in text.

Sniderman, P. and Hagendoorn, L. (2007) *When Ways of Life Collide*, Princeton University Press.

Vertovec, S. (2005) "Pre-, high-, anti- and post-multiculturalism," ESRC Centre on Migration, Policy and Society, University of Oxford.

Wong, L., Garcea J., and Kirova A. (2005) "An analysis of the 'anti- and post-multiculturalism' discourses: The fragmentation position," Prairie Centre for Excellence in Research on Immigration and Integration.

3   British and others

From 'race' to 'faith'

Ralph Grillo

Introduction

Since 2001 the governance of the UK as a multi-ethnic, multi-cultural society has seemed increasingly problematic, with principles which underpinned that governance from the 1960s widely questioned. Yet the trajectory of the post-millennium period also presents a paradox. For despite misgivings about the growing diversity of British society, and often open hostility towards multi-culturalism, government policy has, in a complex dialectical relationship with the reality of everyday lives, emphasized religion as a mode of recognizing and working with minorities. Thus the construction of difference and diversity in Britain has moved from 'race' (as in 'race relations' in the 1950s and 1960s), to 'ethnicity', to 'culture', and thence 'faith'.

Drawing on anthropology, sociology and history, this chapter explores these discursive shifts from a documentary, rather than normative, perspective. There is enough of the latter in political philosophy and in speeches by political and religious leaders; indeed, in public debates on difference and diversity there is often little else. By focusing on the UK the chapter has the advantage of looking in depth at one nation-state. The disadvantage is that public debates on multiculturalism cannot be fully comprehended without taking into account the wider context in which they are embedded. There is a cross-national interweaving of political, academic and popular discourse, embracing a skein of vocabulary, sources, tropes, ideas, instances and paradigms, but this intertextuality cannot be addressed here.

Integration plus

> The West Indian or Asian does not, by being born in England become an Englishman. In law he becomes a United Kingdom citizen by birth; in fact he is a West Indian or an Asian still. Unless he be one of a small minority – for number, I repeat again and again, is of the essence – he will by the very nature of things have lost one country without gaining another, lost one nationality without acquiring a new one.
>
> (Enoch Powell, in Smithies and Fiddick 1969: 77)

The Parekh Report on The Future of Multi-Ethnic Britain (2000: 38) argued, mistakenly in the view of the media, that 'Britishness, as much as Englishness, has systematic, largely unspoken, racial connotations. Whiteness nowhere features as an explicit condition of being British, but it is widely understood that Englishness, and therefore by extension Britishness, is racially coded.' The phrasing, like that of the maverick, populist Conservative politician, Enoch Powell, cited above, demonstrates the slippery way in which 'English' metonymically may mean 'British', and illustrates how in the multi-national UK no single term unproblematically encompasses everyone. Indeed, with some justification this chapter could be entitled 'English and others',[1] assimilating Welsh, Scots and Irish to the latter, as happened in the past, and to a degree still does. Controversially and problematically, 'England'/'English' is sometimes used metonymically to stand for 'Britain'/'British', a practice which some take as reflecting a past colonial attitude of the English to the rest of the British Isles.[2]

If, historically, internal colonialism (Hechter 1975) defined the relationship between English, British and others, so did religion. In the eighteenth century, Britishness, as a Protestant identity, emerged against a background of internal difference and external conflict with Catholic France, the image of alterity par excellence (Colley 1992). Additionally there were the Jews, subject to expulsion in 1290, and later one of the objects of the first modern British legislation to regulate the entry of foreigners (Aliens Act 1905). The markers distinguishing the British/English from such others were not inherently racial, but were readily reworked as such by designating them as stemming from some naturally inferior 'stock', and by the nineteenth century this was commonplace, especially with respect to another group, those with origins in Britain's external colonies.

After 1945 there were three main sets of arrivals in the UK: refugees from Europe displaced by war and Cold War (e.g. Poles, Hungarians); migrant workers and their families especially from Southern Europe (e.g. Italians); Empire/Commonwealth immigrants from the Caribbean and South Asia[3]. Despite some hostility (in John Osborne's play *The Entertainer*, 1957, the hero's father complains about 'Poles and Irish'), the first two rarely posed difficulties for the governance of diversity. The third did, evidenced by 'race riots' in the late 1950s in London and elsewhere directed against the Afro-Caribbean population (for pre-war riots see Fryer 1984). Antipathy towards the latter, and the newly arriving Asians, also characterized the 1960s, especially in the West Midlands. In 1968, Enoch Powell infamously 'look[ed] ahead' and was 'filled with foreboding; like the Roman, I seem to see "the River Tiber foaming with much blood"' (in Smithies and Fiddick 1969: 43). Not for the first or last time in British public life, speeches like Powell's denied the possibility of such others ever becoming British (or English), even if born and bred in the UK. Racism of a traditional kind, therefore, was a key issue for the governance of diversity in a period of rapid decolonization.

Official response was two-fold: legislation restricting and controlling entry to Britain, and redefining British nationality; and regulating 'race relations', so-called, with laws to combat discrimination. These latter embodied a move towards a form of integration defined by Home Office advisers under the then minister, Roy Jenkins, not as a 'flattening process of assimilation but as equal opportunity, coupled with cultural diversity, in an atmosphere of mutual tolerance' (Jenkins 1967: 267). The future for immigrants and the next generation was within a common public sphere of shared norms and values with equal opportunity in employment, housing, education, health and welfare, equality before the law, and protection from racism, with distinctive beliefs, values, practices, religion, language, in private. Immigrant and minority ethnic groups would be 'here but different'.

This compromise pervaded public policy in a remarkably consistent way from the mid-1960s, irrespective of the political complexion of the government. It constituted a 'weak' multiculturalism (the term gains purchase from the late 1960s), recognizing cultural diversity (to varying extent and up to a point), but promoting acculturation in many areas of life and attempting to tackle inequalities in access to employment, housing, education, health and welfare. Major public institutions, national and local, gave these policies reality by addressing the daily difficulties faced by those dealing with culturally, linguistically and religiously diverse populations in large, ethnically mixed cities. What happened in education illustrated this. With increasing numbers of children from minority ethnic backgrounds, and classes in which there was often considerable tension, teachers had to think in new ways, promoting anti-racist initiatives and a curriculum emphasizing minority ethnics as bearers of other cultures, a multicultural perspective considered a desirable Education for All (Swann Report 1985).

Between 1960–2000, therefore, policies emanating principally from two ministries (Home Office and Education) sought to control immigration while accepting that most immigrants were here to stay. There was a widespread desire to address discrimination and disparities of achievement (especially between children), growing recognition of the legitimacy of cultural difference, and greater willingness to allow the expression of such difference in the private sphere, and to some degree the public sphere too. This might seem a rose-tinted view, and certainly progress was neither uniform nor uncontested. Rightly, the Parekh Report, and the Commission for Racial Equality (2007), documented the many problems that minority ethnic groups still faced (police, criminal justice, education, the media, health and welfare, employment, political representation). Limits to what had been achieved were apparent in disturbances in the mid-1980s, and in racist murders in the 1990s. Yet the outcome was a gradual move towards a plural Britain. Since he first came to Britain, says Amartya Sen, 'The distance travelled has been, in many ways, quite extraordinary' (2006: 152). As broadcaster George Alagiah, put it: 'A country in which John Sentamu helps to run the Church of England and where Shami Chakrabati is one of the most eloquent defenders of our hard-won liberties is vastly different from the one I came to in 1967' (2006: 265).[4]

Incompatible values, parallel lives

> It seems very likely that cultural pluralism will represent official govern-
> ment policy ... for the foreseeable future.
>
> (Poulter 1998: 18)

> Respect for cultural difference has limits, marked out by fundamental
> human rights and duties. Some of these boundaries are very clear. [Some]
> practices are clearly incompatible with our basic values.
>
> (Labour Home Secretary, David Blunkett, 2002: 76)

Although British society generally became more open to diversity, there remained doubters. Far-right parties campaigned against turning Britain into a multicultural (sc. 'multiracial') society, but there were sceptics in the mainstream, too, notably among Conservative ministers, and belief in the value of diversity was severely tested by the Rushdie affair (1989). By the turn of the millennium, however, reservations about multiculturalism could be found across the political spectrum. Opposition took many forms.[5] Among academics, multiculturalism was criticized for transgressing principles of liberal democracy; for essentialism; for treating cultures as static, finite and bounded ethnolinguistic blocs; for privileging patriarchy and disempowering women; for allowing a concern with 'culture' to override traditional social issues; or alternatively for tokenism and condescension. Politicians stressed the need to reassert 'core values' against those thought at odds with them: patriarchy and the segregation and suppression of women, forced/arranged marriages, the power of religious as opposed to secular authorities. There was alarm about ghettoization, communal separatism and exclusion, and demands that immigrants learn English and declare their loyalty to the nation-state in which they reside, rather than the one whence they came, and with which many retained significant ties. There were earnest discussions of 'Britishness'.

The year 2001 was critical in mobilizing opinion, first as a result of disturbances in the ethnically-mixed northern cities of Britain which occasioned heart-searching about the alienation of minorities, especially young Muslims, then because of 9/11. The latter, along with the July 2005 London bombings ('7/7'), shaped debate by focusing attention on Islam, the second largest religion in Britain with some two million adherents, principally though not exclusively from South Asia. Muslims, many of whom are long-term migrants or born and bred in the UK, constitute a visible public presence, symbolized by the widespread building of mosques, and often by their dress, and by claims for the recognition of Islamic-specific needs. A report into the 2001 disturbances recorded that 'many communities operate on the basis of a series of parallel lives' (Cantle Report 2001, Section 2.1), a phrase that achieved wide currency and led to the view that Britain was 'sleepwalking to segregation', as Trevor Phillips (2005), then Chairman of the Commission for Racial Equality, put it. What the government concluded, says McGhee (2005a: 64), was that 'Britain cannot allow "migrant communities" in the UK to establish themselves as separate and distinct cultural groupings that proceed to live in isolated enclaves segregated from "mainstream British society" '.

Against this background, and growing belief in multiculturalism's divisive character, the government sought to re-orient policy in a series of initiatives concerned with 'cohesion', which, while continuing to celebrate ethnic and cultural 'diversity', eschewed 'difference' (Grillo 2007a; see also Cantle Report 2001, McGhee 2003, 2005a, Blunkett 2004, Cantle 2005, Robinson 2005, Ballard 2007). In 2006 a new Department of Communities and Local Government was established, whose terms of reference included reducing race inequalities and building community cohesion.[6] The Department immediately formed a 'Commission on Integration and Cohesion', to 'examin[e] the issues that raise tensions between different groups in different areas, and that lead to segregation and conflict', and to consider 'how local areas themselves can play a role in forging cohesive and resilient communities'.[7] In doing so, they were to emphasize 'practical solutions ... based on the best existing practice'. In a speech introducing the Commission, headed by a British Sikh, Darra Singh, a prominent figure in local government, the then Secretary of State, Ruth Kelly, declared:

> I believe that we should celebrate and clearly articulate the benefits that migration and diversity have brought – but while celebrating that diversity we should also recognize that the landscape is changing ... And we should not shy away from asking ... some of the more difficult questions that arise. I believe it is time now to engage in a new and honest debate about integration and cohesion in the UK ... we have moved from a period of uniform consensus on the value of multiculturalism, to one where we can encourage that debate by questioning whether it is encouraging separateness.
>
> (Kelly 2006)

Shortly afterwards, at the Labour Party Annual Conference, Gordon Brown, who later succeeded Tony Blair as Prime Minister, argued that 'if for too long we overvalued what makes us different, it is time to also value what we believe in common' (Brown 2006), a theme taken up by Tony Blair himself (2006) in a lecture on 'Our Nation's Future: Multiculturalism and Integration':

> Christians, Jews, Muslims, Hindus, Sikhs and other faiths have a perfect right to their own identity and religion, to practice their faith and to conform to their culture. This is what multicultural, multi-faith Britain is about ... But when it comes to our essential values – belief in democracy, the rule of law, tolerance, equal treatment for all, respect for this country and its shared heritage – then that is where we come together, it is what we hold in common; it is what gives us the right to call ourselves British.

At that point no distinctive culture or religion supersedes our duty to be part of an integrated United Kingdom ... Being British carries rights. It also carries duties. And those duties take clear precedence over any cultural or religious practice.

The mountain gives birth

The conclusion drawn by the media from these interventions was that they amounted to a 'rejection of multiculturalism as an approach to fostering inter-ethnic relations' (*Financial Times*, 26 September 2006), and this was underlined by the Commission's report entitled 'Our Shared Future' (2007a: 46), in which multiculturalism is mentioned only to dismiss it:

In our conversations with a wide range of people, we have heard concern about how the multiculturalism of the past at times placed an emphasis on the different routes that brought people into local communities in the UK, rather than keeping sight of the shared concerns that matter to everyone.

Instead, the report stressed 'a new definition of integration and cohesion':

the process by which new individuals and groups take their place within the majority community, achieving and being accorded their full rights as citizens. Integration can be full or partial and can take a long time, perhaps generations, to happen. Cohesive communities are ones that are able to exist together in a state of harmony and peaceful relationships, characterized by a climate of mutual understanding and respect.

(Commission on Integration and Cohesion 2007b: 4)

'Shared futures', said the Commission's press release (2007c), is about 'articulating what binds communities together – rather than the differences that might divide them'. This grand vision, supported by analysis of the contemporary situation influenced by commissioned studies (e.g. Vertovec 2007), contrasted with recommendations which were permeated with the managerial language of contemporary local government: local authorities were advised that they should 'Mainstream integration and cohesion into their Sustainable Community Strategies, LSP [Local Strategic Partnership] management and wider service delivery, particularly for youth provision' (Commission on Integration and Cohesion 2007a: 52). Indeed, speeches launching the report stressed a limited number only of practical proposals: nationally sponsored community weeks, citizenship ceremonies for students who pass an appropriate examination, and a national school linking programme.[8] There were also detailed recommendations concerning language. Arguing that lack of English constituted a barrier to integration the Report proposed abandoning the commitment to provide translations and translators in favour of provision for learning English as a second language, and this was the message picked up by the media: ' "Learn lingo" order', said the *Sun* (11 June 2007).[9] 'Until recently', commented a well-known critic of multiculturalism,

> integration was a dirty word, almost as sinister as assimilation ... multiculturalism has suddenly and rather sneakily been dumped. Late in the day ministers are discovering what should have been blindingly obvious. The dogma of multiculturalism has made immigration and race relations much more painful and difficult than they need have been. The social policies based on it have kept people in ghettos and bred mistrust and suspicion.
>
> (Marrin 2007)

White backlash?

> We didn't recognize the limits of multiculturalism early enough. And we weren't brave enough to talk honestly about the fragmentation and differences emerging within and between our communities. The sense of insecurity and instability that many people feel as their communities change. The familiar becoming the unfamiliar.
>
> (Amos 2006)

The distance travelled since Jenkins is apparent. After 2001, many politicians, intellectuals and the media came to believe that multiculturalism institutionalized 'difference' and exacerbated the governability of what, in a neoliberal, transnationalized world, are increasingly fragmented societies. Popular opinion was similarly hostile, for other reasons. Two publications (Hewitt 2005, Dench *et al.* 2006; see also Alagiah 2006) explored this in the context of the evolution of British 'white' working-class communities in London. Although their approach is different, as are the boroughs they studied (Tower Hamlets and Greenwich, adjacent across the River Thames), both tell a story of economic restructuring dislocating local lives.

In Tower Hamlets, the transformation of the docklands into a financial centre around Canary Wharf offered employment for upwardly mobile professionals, and housing to suit, while destroying the basis of working-class life (extended families living close together and offering each other mutual support), documented in a classic sociological study (Willmott and Young 1957). At the same time, the area, which had always attracted immigrants (notably Jews in the early twentieth century), received increasing numbers of families from Bangladesh. Dench *et al.* 2006 argue (controversially) that hostility to immigrants stemmed from policies which allocated housing accorded to universalistic criteria (need) whereas previously they had been governed by a 'sons and daughters' principle, and a 'housing ladder' whereby residents progressed steadily to larger accommodation. Dench *et al.* assert that such particularistic principles reflected 'communitarian values ... considered fair in traditional working-class morality' (p. 47), but

Descendants of members of former dependencies now compete for opportunities and national welfare resources on equal terms with white Britons who see themselves as indigenous to the area ... [middle-class liberals] have promoted a swathe of political measures and institutions which consolidate the rights of minorities while multiplying the sanctions against indigenous whites who object to this.

(2006: 6)

The system, they continue, is 'dominated by a political class, drawing power from its operation of state services and mobilized around the ideology of cultural tolerance and social and economic inclusiveness' (ibid). Their analysis echoes closely their white working-class informants' hostile perceptions of their Bangladeshi neighbours. Similarly, in 1990s Greenwich, Hewitt describes 'an essentially disunited and politically powerless white working-class backlash to equalities policies and to the emergence of an increasingly confident multiculturalism began to take shape' (2005: 34), adding: 'Part "underclass", part the political and economic forgotten, the homes where school failure was the norm and job expectations low were the site of grievances festering away in a political no-man's-land.' They were, he says, 'at odds with the local political order in which, to them, minority concerns were given greater precedence' (2005: 55).

This white working-class 'backlash' is often read as racism, and certainly far-right groups readily exploit local tensions. Those concerned would deny it, and popular responses are often complex. McGhee's account of anti-asylum seeker protests in Glasgow and Wrexham, and the 'culture of resentment' within poor white working class communities they represent, makes this point (2005a: 82–87). Nonetheless, popular anxieties about the erosion of traditional values and the presumed threat represented by immigrants and ethnic and religious minorities, are of great concern to mainstream politicians, not least in the Labour Party, as they endanger their own heartlands. The mainstream backlash thus partly reflects fears of a reaction by a disaffected, anxious and xenophobic electorate, mobilized by populist parties. And all are responding to a growing Islamic presence with an implicit, sometimes explicit, Islamophobia, which 9/11 and 7/7 greatly exacerbated (Runnymede Trust 1997, Commission on British Muslims and Islamophobia 2004, Ansari 2004, Abbas 2005).

'Race' to 'faith'

Our major faith traditions – all of them more historic and deeply rooted than any political party or ideology – play a fundamental role in supporting and propagating values which bind us together as a nation.

(Blair 2001)

Yet despite questioning multiculturalism, government policy has assigned an important role to 'faith communities' as channels for representation, consultation and dialogue in the major conurbations. There has emerged a faith-based multiculturalism, evident in the favouring of 'faith schools', and measures making religious hatred, or so-called 'racism by [religious] proxy', a crime (Racial and Religious Hatred Act, 2006, see Grillo 2007b). This faith-based multiculturalism is in accord with both government policy, based on communitarian theories, and claims by minorities increasingly defining themselves in religious terms.

'British discourse on racialized minorities', says Peach (2005: 18), 'has mutated from 'colour' in the 1950s and 1960s, to 'race' in the 1960s–1980s, 'ethnicity' in the 1990s, and 'religion' in the present period' (see also Gilroy 1993: 86, Raj 2000, Back *et al.* 2002, Statham *et al.* 2005, Beckford *et al.* 2006, Hundal 2007). During the 1970s and 1980s, while activists and academics sought to articulate a unity of people of Afro-Caribbean and South Asian origin around the all-embracing class-race term 'black', dominant discourse shifted towards ethnic and cultural specificities. This re-focusing led to, and partly explains, a subsequent shift towards religious specificity, symbolized by the question asking for religious affiliation in the 2001 UK census. Allen (2005) interprets this as cultural racism, with religion the latest marker through which xenophobia is expressed. It is rather that the terms of debate have 'mutated', as Peach (2005) puts it, in a dialectical relationship between three sets of actors: the state, faith institutions and believers. Modood (2003) stresses the part played by the Rushdie affair and contends that the shift was not solely or even principally top-down, but reflected the increasing tendency for minority ethnic groups to stress religious faith as a key element of public and private identity. And not just Muslims. In the mid-1990s a swathe of Hindu societies emerged among students in British post-secondary education institutions (Raj 2000), with, after 9/11, an accelerating rejection of 'Asian' as an all-embracing ethnic identity in favour of ones specifying religion; Hindus and Sikhs rallied to their faiths, seeking to differentiate themselves from Muslims (Hindu Forum of Britain 2006).

As Raj (2000) points out, British multiculturalism creates space for this form of identification.[10] Furbey and Macey (2005) note the way in which policy initiatives linking religion, community, urban neighbourhood and social cohesion, which date from the formation in 1992 of the Inner Cities Religious Council (see also Smith 2004), were favoured by the 1997 Labour government drawing on 'communitarian' ideas. Successful collaboration with faith communities in the millennium and Queen's Golden Jubilee celebrations (2002), at a time when faith communities themselves were seeking a fresh direction, was also influential (Clegg and Rosie 2005, Barrow 2006). After 2001 government turned its attention decisively to 'faith', with David Blunkett in the Home Office accepting a central role for faith communities in civic renewal (Blunkett 2003, Smith 2004: 194), and establishing a 'Faith Communities Unit' to interface with religious bodies. Inter alia the government attributed great importance to enrolling Muslims in the fight against extremism (McGhee 2005b: 5.2), and to this end looked for appropriate community representation.[11] Indeed, an earlier Home Office initiative (set in train by a Conservative Home Secretary in the mid-1990s) had sought a single Muslim body with which to dialogue (Ansari 2004, Birt 2005). From this emerged the Muslim Council of Britain (MCB) whose chairman, Iqbal Sacranie, was subsequently knighted. After 9/11, however, the MCB found itself increasingly squeezed between the demands of its Muslim constituents and those of government (Birt 2005: 104), and other organizations came to prominence, including the Muslim Association of Britain, founded in 1997, and a Sufi Council (created in 2006) which criticized the MCB for failing to confront extremism.

Another route to community representation is via inter-faith groups and networks (Beckford 1998, 1999, Farnell *et al.* 2003, Beckford *et al.* 2006). While some are debating societies (the Cambridge Inter-Faith Group's pro-gramme of activities for 2006 included a discussion on 'Who or what is God?'),[12] others are more pro-active. The East of England Faith Council,[13] which includes representatives of nine faiths, prepared 'position papers' on agriculture, health, education, and so on, and is the nominating body for the 'faiths' seat on the East of England Regional Assembly. Inter alia it partici-pated in consultations regarding regional strategies for the economy, plan-ning, and culture. Inter-faith groups also offer opportunities beyond the local or regional level. Thus, the (Sikh) chairman of Leicester Council of Faiths attended a meeting at 10 Downing Street, addressed by the Archbishop of Canterbury, on 'Belief, unbelief and religious education',[14] and faith commu-nities were formally consulted on entry requirements for religious ministers coming from abroad and on religious hatred legislation; the Home Office provide a chart guiding civil servants through the consultation process (2004: 15). Faith groups and networks are supported by the 'Faith Commu-nities Capacity Building Fund', which in 2005 made 578 grants, including £49,510 to the Birmingham Council of Sikh Gurdwaras to 'build the capacity of the organization itself, and enable the organization to recruit a develop-ment worker [to] establish a professional office, submit fundraising bids, manage key projects and develop a sustainable funding strategy'.[15]

The religious shift has been reinforced by the encouragement of 'faith schools' (Department for Children, Schools and Families 2007). Initiatives in multicultural education responded to the perceived needs of pupils, and to pressure from the parents of minority ethnic children and their religious and political leaders (Halstead 1988). In the 1980s these became increasingly vocal, calling for single-sex education, for the inclusion of 'mother-tongue' teaching within mainstream education, and state support for schools for Muslims, Sikhs and others (Parker-Jenkins *et al.* 2004). There had long been a 'voluntary-aided' sector of schools run by the Church of England, Catholics, Methodists and Jews, overseen by the state, and through the 1980s there were bids for voluntary-aided status for Muslim and Sikh schools in Bradford, Glasgow and London (Halstead 1988; see also Ansari 2004: 324–34, Parker-Jenkins *et al.* 2004: 43 ff.). None were successful, despite the backing, on equity grounds, of the Commission for Racial Equality (1990), and the Runnymede Trust (1997).

In 1997, however, the Labour government accepted the argument and a small number of state-aided non-Christian, non-Jewish schools have opened – seven Muslim and two Sikh, with a Hindu school scheduled for 2008. In addition there are over a hundred private 'Muslim schools', with pedagogy based on Islamic principles, many insufficiently resourced (Parker-Jenkins *et al.* 2004: 46). Such schools, which are poorly studied (Kucukan 1998, Lawson 2005), should not be confused with state schools whose intake is predominantly Muslim (because of catchment areas), and which are often deemed symbolic of parallel lives (Modood 2003: 111–12; see also AMSS 2004; Commission on British Muslims and Islamophobia, 2004).

Many dispute this promotion of faith schools (Gardner *et al.* 2005). It has been criticized on pedagogic grounds (Bell 2005, Ofsted 2005), because it is potentially divisive (Gillard 2001, Parker-Jenkins *et al.* 2004), or because religion should be excluded from education (Humanist Philosophers' Group 2001). In a House of Lords debate (Hansard 2006, 8 February, Column 720), Lord Taverne argued that faith schools 'promote particular faiths, not Enlightenment values [and] over-emphasize religious identity'. They are 'introspective, ghettoized and a nucleus for the fomenting of violence' (Viscount Bridgeman); 'agents of social division and social exclusion' (Lord Lucas); 'damag[e] social cohesion' (Baroness Turner); and we should learn lessons from Northern Ireland (Lord Dubs). Teaching unions have on several occasions debated motions calling for an end to their state funding.

Some Christians oppose any aid for other faiths. The commentator Patrick Sookhdeo (2006), discussing a survey which found 44 per cent of Londoners wanting to ban faith schools, argued that the problem was Muslim schools which 'nurture values that are radically different from those of the prevailing society ... Christian denominational schools as well as Jewish schools continue to play an important role in community cohesion. Whether Islamic schools can fill such a role is highly questionable. Has the time come to say no to Islamic schools, whilst allowing the others to exist, even though this may seem unjust?'

'A naïve multiculturalism', he added, 'leads not to a mosaic of cultures living in harmony, but to one threatened by Islamic extremism.' The Commission on British Muslims and Islamophobia (2004), however, rejected the view that Muslim schools were responsible for division, as did the Association of Muslim Social Scientists who offered a robust defence against critics of faith schools in general and Muslim schools in particular. Faith schools, it claimed, are generally very successful in terms of examination results and pupil discipline, and are not 'seed-beds where individuals grow to become incompatible with wider society' (AMSS 2004: 30–31; Barker and Anderson 2005 and Halstead and McLaughlin 2005 offer contrasting views). 'Rarely', the AMSS added, 'is the word 'separate' used negatively in respect of Christian or Jewish faith schools'. Indeed, Trevor Phillips (2006), referring to the debate about the compatibility of faith schools with integration, conceded that Muslim, Jewish and Sikh schools were often 'monoethnic', but argued that opposition was hypocritical and discriminatory.

More generally, while some Christians are concerned about the promotion of other religions (one bishop complained that Britain had become a 'multi-faith mish-mash', Ekklesia 2006) secularists are dismayed by any importance attached to religion (Sen 2006). Moreover, there is, according to Smith (2004: 199–200), a 'naïve optimism about religious diversity, and the benevolent contribution of faiths towards the common good'. Simplistic views of community homogeneity abound (Furbey and Macey 2005). Moreover, the promotion of faith, says Singh (2004) has 'legitimized rotten multiculturalism, where culture has long given way to religion, particularly if it is capable of delivering ethnic minority votes'. Policy and practice, it is argued, respond to, but through recognition heighten, the public profile of faith leaders encouraged to pursue their own ends. The manifest of New Generation Network (2006), a pressure group of intellectuals and activists, many of minority ethnic background, roundly criticized government's 'entrusting power to so-called community leaders and other umbrella groups who claim to be the voice of minority groups'. This, it said, was a 'throwback to the colonial era'.

'Londonistan'?

> [Our laws] are decided on by one group of people, members of Parliament, and that's the end of the story. Anybody who lives here has to accept that's the way we do it. If you want to have laws decided in another way, you have to live somewhere else.
>
> (Trevor Phillips in BBC News 2006)

There is an apocalyptic air to some reactions to this shift to faith, the expectation of imminent catastrophe apparent in vocabulary such 'Londonistan' (to portray the UK capital as a haven for Islamic fundamentalists, Melanie Philips 2006) and 'dhimmitude' (the status of being a dhimmi, a non-Muslim in an Islamic society). Scare stories that UK Muslims want, and will soon achieve, the implementation of Sharia law, illustrate this. 'In a decade', averred Sookhdeo (in Palmer 2006), 'you will see parts of English cities which are controlled by Muslim clerics and which follow, not the common law, but aspects of Muslim sharia law'. This was in response to a poll which reported that 40 per cent of Muslims would welcome the introduction of Sharia in predominantly Muslim areas in Britain.

In February 2008 there was a furore over a lecture at the Royal Courts of Justice by the Archbishop of Canterbury, Dr Rowan Williams, on 'Civil and Religious Law in England' (Williams 2008). Speaking about Sharia, the Archbishop carefully considered the advantages and disadvantages of permitting 'supplementary jurisdictions' within the British legal system, arguing: 'If we are to think intelligently about the relations between Islam and British law, we need a fair amount of "deconstruction" of crude oppositions and mythologies, whether of the nature of Sharia or the nature of the Enlightenment.' A high-powered speech to a high-powered legal audience, but the reaction to what he said, or was imagined to have said, was extra-ordinary, with widespread calls through the press and the media (nationally and internationally) for his resignation, if not his impeachment for treason. A nine-day wonder, perhaps, but it generated a lively journalistic debate and burgeoning academic literature (e.g. Bano 2008), illustrating the tensions surrounding the presence of 'Others' in contemporary Britain.

In fact, there have been calls for the availability of Muslim family law in Britain since the 1970s (Poulter 1998: 201 ff.), though many Muslims oppose such measures. When, in 2006, delegates met Ruth Kelly to discuss tackling extremism, it was widely reported that they had advocated adopting the Sharia, though the proposal was made by one member only (from the Union of Muslim Organisations), and opposed by the Muslim Council of Britain. It was, commented Osama Saeed (2006), a 'godsend for those who love bashing Muslims', adding: 'This call for sharia needs to be framed in terms of what exactly Muslims are asking for ... civil matters like divorce, inheritance and custody. No one is calling for beheadings or stonings.' 'Of course lots of Muslims would like to live their lives by the Sharia', said a representative of Hizb-ut-Tahrir, but this means living 'in a more Islamic way', with Islamic bank accounts and halal meat (in Meehan 2006). Indeed there already exists (among other such bodies) the Islamic Sharia Council, established in 1982, through which UK Muslims can obtain advice on the application of Sharia principles, and have disputes settled (Poulter 1998: 234–35, Ansari 2004: 386–87, Césari *et al.* 2004: 38–42). Its objectives are:

> To advance the Islamic Religion by fostering and encouraging the prac-tice of the Muslim faith according to the Quran and the Sunnah; pro-viding advice and assistance in the operation of Muslim family; establishing a bench to operate as court of Islamic Shari'a and to make decisions on matters of Muslim Family law referred to it; doing all such other lawful things as may be in the interest of promoting the proper practice of the Muslim faith in the United Kingdom.[16]

It deals mostly with family matters (guidance on appropriate practices around marriage, divorce, the custody of children, inheritance), and the religious propriety of issues ranging from intravenous fertilization to trading in shares (Césari, Caeiro and Hussain 2004: 38 ff., Bano 2007, Keshavjee 2007). For Muslims, the Jewish Beth Din provides an example of what can be achieved within the framework of the existing legal order (Shah 2007).[17] Some would consider this separatism, but neither 'parallel lives', let alone 'Londonistan', adequately characterize contemporary Britain.

Or 'Londonstani'?

Early studies of minority ethnicity spoke of youngsters as 'between two cultures' (Watson 1977). In the 1980s, however, it emerged that in streets and playgrounds there was a greater degree of linguistic and cultural 'mixity' than previously supposed. Hewitt (1986), Jones (1988), Rampton (1995), Baumann (1996) and Back (1996), have shown that the language, gestures and music of the street-wise Afro-Caribbean became powerful icons for many young white and Asian Britons who 'appropriate some of the blazonry of black youth style' (Hewitt 1986: 47), using so-called 'Multicultural London English', combining elements from Afro-Caribbean Creole, African-American speech and the South London black vernacular.

This socio-linguistic milieu is explored in Gautam Malkani's novel, ironically entitled *Londonstani* (2006), which, incidentally was included in the holiday reading of the head of the Commission on Integration and Cohesion (Benjamin 2006). 'Perhaps', said Hebdige, 'there is another nation being formed for the future beyond the boundaries of race' (Hebdige 1987: 158). This was premature, but it could be argued that in contemporary London street-level negotiations are producing 'syncretic cultures', which are 'neither simply black nor simply white [but] simultaneously black and white' (Back 1996: 159).

The picture is confusing. Multiculturalism is under pressure across the political spectrum, in a climate dominated by the events of 2001 and much tension around the Islamic presence. But faith communities are promoted, and in sites where hybridity is produced (schools, playgrounds, mixed marriages, the arts, music) there is a multiplicity of voices, languages, dialects, registers, joking, playing, crossing, engaging in dialogues through which new identities and relationships emerge. British society is highly heterogeneous and fragmented with different things happening at the same time in different places, and at different times in the same place. Many trajectories are apparent: hybridity, yes, but also integration, with varying degrees of cultural diversity; assimilation and 'parallel lives'. It is also changing rapidly, the populations with which governments, national and local, are confronted in the 2000s are different from what they were in the 1960s or earlier: in 1900, Jews, Irish and Italians; in the 1950s immigrants from the Caribbean; in the 1960s and 1970s, from South Asia, with their distinctive cultures and languages; in the 1990s and 2000s refugees and asylum seekers from all over the world, and economic migrants from Eastern Europe. A city like London is experiencing a new 'super-diversity' (Vertovec 2007), though this does not mean that challenges posed by 'old' diversities have disappeared.

Conclusion

Since the 1960s, the governance of diversity has involved setting boundaries, pragmatically negotiating complex issues with no obvious solution: hijabs and turbans, yes, jilbabs, niqabs and burqas, perhaps not; freedom of expression, yes, incitement to racial or religious hatred, no; arranged marriages, perhaps, forced marriages, by no means; mother-tongue maintenance, yes, except in schools. Yet the multiculturalism of the critics is often an imagined 'strong' multiculturalism (Grillo 2007a), and they overlook the multiplicity of practical accommodations on issues such as providing halal meals or issuing health guidance leaflets in strange languages, and the quotidien, 'demotic' (Baumann 1996) multiculturalism, built on 'conviviality' (Gilroy 2004), which hopefully remains intact.

In some cases, opposition is simply xenophobia. In others, it is the fear that outsiders are getting an unfair share of resources when neo-liberal reforms impact on welfare. For others again, the sticking point is the clash with principles of liberal democracy and secular (enlightenment) values. McGhee (2005a; 164) argues, somewhat sanguinely, that the 1997 Labour government sought to promote a new model of 'cosmopolitan citizenship' which replaced 'loyalty and commitment to communities, cultures, traditions and identities which are not open, not flexible, and that are detached and hostile to others' with 'dialogue between groups and across boundaries'. Inflexible multiculturalism would be incompatible with such ideals, and, post-2001, increasingly seen as an obstacle to governance in an era of tension. The promotion of faith, which reflects the espousal of communitarian principles by a devout prime minister, the everyday lives of British minorities[18] and the current global climate, apparently encourages such dialogue, and provides a means of taming diversity, making multiculturalism manageable through a form of 'indirect rule'. No paradox, then, though the outcome might just be the opposite of what was intended.

Notes

1 'Other' here should not be taken to indicate a psychoanalytical approach. There is need for an account of alterity beyond the fatuities of Lacanian-influenced cultural and post-colonial theories (Baumann and Gingrich 2004). As Young argues (2003: 456), such theories 'depict othering ... as a cultural universal, a product of ever-present problems of human psychology or group formation,' whereas what is needed is the 'when, why, who, what, how and whether' (see also McGhee 2005a: 3).

2 The distinction between 'UK citizen', 'British', and 'English' is sometimes as obscure to the natives as it is to outsiders. Technically the 'United Kingdom of Great Britain and Northern Ireland' consists of four 'home countries': England, Wales, Scotland and Northern Ireland (the six counties in the island of Ireland which form part of the province of 'Ulster,' the other part being in the Republic of Ireland). All but England now have some form of devolved government.

3 On post-war immigration to the UK, see, among others, Rose *et al.* 1969, Watson 1977, Fryer 1984, Gilroy 1987, Holmes 1988, Hiro 1991; Layton-Henry 1992, Ballard 1994, Goulbourne 1998, Phillips and Phillips 1998, Parekh Report 2000, Ansari 2004, Winder 2004, Modood 2005.

4 John Sentamu, Archbishop of York, comes from Uganda; Shami Chakrabarti, Director of the National Council for Civil Liberties, was born in London – her family came to Britain from India in the 1950s; Indian-born Amartya Sen is the Nobel Prize-winning economist who among many other distinctions was Master of Trinity College, Cambridge. George Alagiah himself was born in Sri Lanka.

5 Parekh (2000), Grillo (2005, 2007a); Giddens (2006) and Modood (2007) offer a robust defence.

6 A further re-organization of institutions concerned with race and ethnicity was implemented in 2007. The Commission for Racial Equality, which in 2006 celebrated 30 years of work, became part of a 'Commission for Equality and Human Rights', headed by Trevor Phillips.

7 < http://www.integrationandcohesion.org.uk/terms_of_reference.aspx > (accessed 8 June 2007).

8 Many of the proposals, including those on language, were accepted by the government which agreed to invest £50 million in community cohesion (< http://www.communities.gov.uk/news/corporate/500395 >, (accessed 6 October 2007).

9 The media also leapt on remarks that problems of integration and cohesion were not confined to inner cities, but found in (relatively affluent) rural areas beginning to experience diversity through the arrival of migrants from Eastern Europe. The *Daily Star* headlined: 'RACE riots are set to erupt in Britain's countryside towns' (8 June 2007).

10 Foley and Hodge (2007) describe immigrant faith organizations in the USA.

11 In another initiative, the government recruited 100 prominent Muslims as a 'task force' to tackle the issue of young people and extremism. They made sixty-four detailed recommendations. The government response was tepid (Home Office 2005).

12 < http://www.cam.net.uk/home/interfaith > (accessed 11 August 2007).

13 < http://www.eefaithscouncil.org.uk > (accessed 31 August 2007).

14 < http://www.leicestercounciloffaiths.org.uk/LCoFNewsArchive.htm > (accessed 18 July 2006).

15 < http://www.cdf.org.uk/SITE/UPLOAD/DOCUMENT/Projects/Round1WEST MIDLANDSregion.pdf > (accessed 31 August 2007).

16 <http://www.islamic-sharia.co.uk/main.html > (accessed 31 August 2007).

17 Shah (2007) records the hostile media response to a BBC programme discussing informal minority ethnic arbitration tribunals such as the *Beth Din* and a 'court' (*gar*) organized by Somalis in East London. On Sharia banking in the UK; see http://www.islamic-bank.com/islamicbanklive/VisionAndValues/1/Home/1/Home.jsp (accessed 8 October 2007). Poulter (1998: 210 ff) discusses obstacles to making Muslim family law available in Britain.

18 This oversimplifies a complex set of issues. The existing literature points this way, but the significance of religion in the everyday lives of minorities deserves further research.

References

Abbas, T. (ed.) (2005) *Muslim Britain: Communities Under Pressure*, London: Zed Books.

Alagiah, G. (2006) *A Home from Home: From Immigrant Boy to English Man*, London: Little, Brown.

Allen, C. (2005) 'From Race to Religion: the New Face of Discrimination', in T. Abbas (ed.) *Muslim Britain: Communities Under Pressure*, London: Zed Books.

Amos, V. (2006) 'Labour is an Inclusive Party'. Online. Available HTTP: http://www.labour.org.uk/index.php?id=news2005&ux—news[id]=inclusiveparty&cHash=e756947a16 (accessed 26 September 2006).

AMSS (2004) *Muslims on Education: A Position Paper*, Richmond: Association of Muslim Social Scientists UK.

Ansari, H. (2004) *The 'Infidel Within': Muslims in Britain since 1800*, London: Hurst.

Back, L. (1996) *New Ethnicities and Urban Culture: Racisms and Multiculture in Young Lives*, London: UCL Press.

Back, L., Keith, M., Khan, A., Shukra, K. and Solomos, J. (2002) 'The Return of Assimilationism: Race, Multiculturalism and New Labour', *Sociological Research Online*, 7(2). Online. Available HTTP: http://www.socresonline.org.uk/7/2/back.html (accessed 23 April 2006).

Ballard, R. (ed.) (1994) *Desh Pardesh: The South Asian Presence in Britain*, London: Hurst & Co.

—— (2007) 'Living with Difference: A Forgotten Art in Urgent Need of Revival?', in J. Hinnells (ed.) *Religious Reconstruction in the South Asian Diasporas*, London: Palgrave Macmillan.

Bano, S. (2007) 'Muslim Family Justice and Human Rights: The Experience of British Muslim Women', *Journal of Comparative Law*, 1(4): 1–29.

—— (2008) 'In Pursuit of Religious and Legal Diversity: A Response to the Archbishop of Canterbury and the "Sharia Debate" in Britain', *Ecclesiastical Law Journal*, 10(3): 283–309.

Barker, R. and Anderson, J. (2005) 'Segregation or Cohesion: Church of England Schools in Bradford', in R. Gardner, J. Cairns and D. Lawton (eds) *Faith Schools: Consensus or Conflict*, London: Routledge.

Barrow, S. (2006) 'Redeeming Religion in the Public Square'. Online. Available HTTP: http://www.ekklesia.co.uk/oldsite/content/article–060724redeeming. shtml (accessed 31 August 2007).

Baumann, G. (1996) *Contesting Culture: Ethnicity and Community in West London*, Cambridge: Cambridge University Press.

Baumann, G. and Gingrich, A. (2004) *Grammars of Identity/Alterity*, Oxford: Berghahn Books.

BBC News (2006) 'Muslims 'Must Accept' Free Speech', http://news.bbc.co.uk/1/hi/uk/4752804.stm (accessed 26 February 2006).

Beckford, J.A. (1998) 'Three Paradoxes in the Relations Between Religion and Politics in an English City', *Review of Religious Research*, 39(4): 344–59.

——(1999) 'The Management of Religious Diversity in England and Wales with Special Reference to Prison Chaplaincy', *Journal on Multicultural Societies*, 1(2): 56–66.

Beckford, J.A., Gale, R., Owen, D., Peach, C. and Weller, P. (2006) *Review of the Evidence Base on Faith Communities*, London: Office of the Deputy Prime Minister.

Bell, D. (2005) 'Hansard Society/OFSTED Lecture'. Online. Avalaible HTTP: http://www.ofsted.gov.uk/assets/3821.doc (accessed 31 August 2007).

Benjamin, A. (2006) 'Unifying Force', *Guardian*, 26 July.

Birt, J. (2005) 'Lobbying and Marching: British Muslims and the State', in T. Abbas (ed.) *Muslim Britain: Communities Under Pressure*, London: Zed Books.

Blair, T. (2001) 'PM's speech to the Christian Socialist Movement'. Online. Available HTTP: http://www.number-10.gov.uk/output/Page3243.asp .(accessed 29 March 2001).

——(2006) 'Our Nation's Future: Multiculturalism and Integration'. Online. Available HTTP: http://www.number-10.gov.uk/output/Page10563.asp (accessed 8 December 2006).

Blunkett, D. (2002) 'Integration with Diversity: Globalisation and the Renewal of Democracy and Civil Society', in P. Griffith and M. Leonard (eds) *Reclaiming Britishness*, London: Foreign Policy Centre.

——(2003) 'One Nation, Many Faiths. The Heslington Lecture, 2003'. Online. Available HTTP: http://www.york.ac.uk/admin/presspr/pressreleases/blunkettspeech.htm (accessed 28 October 2003).

——(2004) 'New Challenges for Race Equality and Community Cohesion in the 21st Century'. Online. Available HTTP: http://www.ippr.org.uk/uploadedFiles/events/Blunkettspeech.pdf (accessed 31 August 2007).

Brown, G. (2006) 'Speech to Labour Party Conference, 2006', *Guardian*, 25 September 2006.

Cantle Report (2001) *Community Cohesion: A Report of the Independent Review Team*, London: Home Office.

Cantle, T. (2005) *Community Cohesion: A New Framework for Race and Diversity*, London: Palgrave Macmillan.

Césari, J., Caeiro, A. and Hussain, D. (2004) *Islam and Fundamental Rights in Europe. Final Report*, Brussels: European Commission, Directorate-General Justice and Home Affairs.

Clegg, R. and Rosie, M. (2005) *Faith Communities and Local Government in Glasgow*, Edinburgh: Scottish Executive Social Research.

Colley, L. (1992) *Britons: Forging the Nation 1707–1837*, London: Pimlico.

Commission for Racial Equality (1990) *Schools of Faith: Religious Schools in a Multicultural Society*, London: CRE.

——(2007) *A Lot Done, A Lot to Do: Our Vision for an Integrated Britain*, London: CRE.

Commission on British Muslims and Islamophobia (2004) *Islamophobia: Issues, Challenges and Action*, Stoke on Trent: Trentham Books.

Commission on Integration and Cohesion (2007a) *Our Shared Future*, London: Commission on Integration and Cohesion.

——(2007b) *Themes, Messages and Challenges: A Summary of Key Themes from the Commission for Cohesion and Integration Consultation*, London: Commission on Integration and Cohesion.

——(2007c) 'Building United and Resilient Communities – Developing Shared Futures'. Online. Available HTTP: http://www.integrationandcohesion.org.uk/news/Building_united_and_resilient_communities-developing_shared_futures.aspx (accessed 14 June 2007).

Dench, G., Gavron, K. and Young, M. (2006) *The New East End*, London: Profile Books.

Department for Children, Schools and Families (2007) *Faith in the System*, London: Department for Children, Schools and Families.

Ekklesia (2006) 'Bishop Opens Debate with Christian Society Claims'. Online. Available HTTP: http://www.speroforum.com/site/article.asp?idCategory=34&idsub=?127&id = 3902 (accessed 5 June 2006).

Farnell, R., Furbey, R., Shams al-Haqq Hills, S., Macey, M. and Smith, G. (2003) *'Faith' in Urban Regeneration? Engaging Faith Communities in Urban Regeneration*, Policy Press: Bristol.

Foley, M.W. and Hoge, D. (2007) *Religion and the New Immigrants: How Faith Communities Form our Newest Citizens*, Oxford/New York: Oxford University Press.

Fryer, P. (1984) *Staying Power: The History of Black People in Britain*, London: Pluto.

Furbey, R. and Macey, M. (2005) 'Religion and Urban Regeneration: A Place for Faith?', *Policy and Politics*, 33(1): 95–116.

Gardner, R., Cairns, J. and Lawton, D. (2005), *Faith Schools: Consensus or Conflict*, London: Routledge.

Giddens, A. (2006) 'Misunderstanding Multiculturalism', *Guardian*, 14 October 2006.

Gillard, D. (2001) 'Glass in their Snowballs – The Faith Schools Debate'. Online. Available HTTP: http://www.dg.dial.pipex.com/articles/educ22.shtml (accessed 31 August 2007).

Gilroy, P. (1987) *There Ain't No Black in the Union Jack: The Cultural Politics of Race and Nation*, London: Hutchinson.

——(1993) *Black Atlantic: Modernity and Double Consciousness*, London: Verso.

——(2004) *After Empire: Melancholia or Convivial Culture?* London: Routledge.

Goulbourne, H. (1998) *Race Relations in Britain since 1945*, Basingstoke: Macmillan.

Grillo, R.D. (2005) *Backlash Against Diversity? Identity and Cultural Politics in European Cities*, Oxford: COMPAS, Working Paper No.14.

——(2007a) 'An Excess of Alterity? Debating Difference in a Multicultural Society', *Ethnic and Racial Studies*, 30(6): 979–98.

——(2007b) 'Artistic Licence, Free Speech and Religious Sensibilities in a Multicultural Society', in P. Shah (ed.) *Law and Ethnic Plurality: Socio-Legal Perspectives*, Leiden: Brill/Martinus Nijhoff.

Halstead, J.M. and McLaughlin, T. (2005) 'Are Faith Schools Divisive', in R. Gardner, J. Cairns and D. Lawton (eds) *Faith Schools: Consensus or Conflict*, London: Routledge.

Halstead, M. (1988) *Education, Justice and Cultural Diversity: An Examination of the Honeyford Affair, 1984–85*, London: Falmer Press.

Hansard (2006) *Faith Schools*. Online. Available HTTP: http://www.publications.parliament.uk/pa/ld200506/ldhansrd/vo060208/text/60208–21.htm (accessed 31 August 2007).

Hebdige, D. (1987) *Cut'n'Mix: Culture, Identity and Caribbean Music*, London: Routledge.

Hechter, M. (1975) *Internal Colonialism: The Celtic Fringe in British National Development 1536–1966*, London: Routledge and Kegan Paul.

Hewitt, R. (1986) *White Talk, Black Talk: Interracial Friendship and Communication Amongst Adolescents*, Cambridge: Cambridge University Press.

——(2005) *White Backlash and the Politics of Multiculturalism*, Cambridge: Cambridge University Press.

Hindu Forum of Britain (2006) *Connecting British Hindus: An Enquiry into the Identity and Public Engagement of Hindus in Britain*, London: Department for Communities and Local Government.

Hiro, D. (1991) *Black British, White British* (3rd Edition), London: Grafton Books.

Holmes, C. (1988) *John Bull's Island: Immigration and British Society, 1871–1971*, London: Macmillan.

Home Office (2004) *Working Together: Co-operation between Government and Faith Communities*, London: Home Office.

——(2005) *Preventing Extremism Together: Response to Working Group Reports*, London: Home Office.

Humanist Philosophers' Group (2001) *Religious Schools: The Case Against*, London: Humanist Philosophers' Group.

Hundal, S. (2007) 'Multiculturalism and Citizenship: Responses to Tariq Modood'. Online. Available HTTP: http://www.opendemocracy.net/faith-terrorism/response_madood_4630.jsp#hundal (accessed 21 May 2007).

Jenkins, R. (1967) *Essays and Speeches*, London: Collins.

Jones, S. (1988) *Black Culture, White Youth: The Reggae Tradition From JA To UK*, Basingstoke: Macmillan Foundation.

Kelly, R. (2006) 'Launch of the Commission on Integration and Cohesion'. Online. Available HTTP: http://www.communities.gov.uk/speeches/corporate/commission-integration-cohesion (accessed 31 August 2007).

Keshavjee, M. (2007) 'Alternative Dispute Resolution in a Diasporic Muslim Community', in P. Shah (ed.) *Law and Ethnic Plurality: Socio-Legal Perspectives*, Leiden: Martinus Nijhoff.

Kucukan, T. (1998) 'Community, Identity and Institutionalisation of Islamic Education: The Case of Ikra Primary School in North London', *British Journal of Religious Education*, 21(1): 30–41.

Lawson, I. (2005) *Leading Islamic Schools in the UK: A Challenge for Us All*, Nottingham: National College for School Leadership.

Layton-Henry, Z. (1992) *The Politics of Immigration: Immigration, 'Race' and 'Race Relations' in Post-war Britain*, Oxford: Blackwell.

Malkani, G. (2006) *Londonstani*, London: Fourth Estate.

Marrin, M. (2007) 'Should We Limit Immigrants to Europeans?', *Sunday Times*, 17 June.

McGhee, D. (2003) 'Moving to "Our" Common Ground: A Critical Examination of Community Cohesion Discourse in Twenty-first Century Britain', *Sociological Review*, 51(3): 376–404.

——(2005a) *Intolerant Britain? Hate, Citizenship and Difference*, Milton Keynes: Open University Press.

——(2005b) 'Patriots of the Future? A Critical Examination of Community Cohesion Strategies in Britain', *Sociological Research Online*, 10(3). Available HTTP: http://www.socresonline.org.uk/10/3/mcghee.html.

Meehan, S. (2006) 'Sharia in the UK'. Online. Available HTTP: http://www.voice-online.co.uk/content.php?show=8757 (accessed 17 March 2006).

Modood, T. (2003) 'Muslims and the Politics of Difference', *Political Quarterly*, 74(1, Supplement 1): 100–115.

——(2005) *Multicultural Politics: Racism, Ethnicity and Muslims*, Minneapolis: University of Minnesota Press.

——(2007) *Multiculturalism: A Civic Idea*, Cambridge: Polity.

New Generation Network (2006) 'Race and Faith: A New Agenda'. Online. Available HTTP: http://www.new-gen.org/manifesto (accessed 31 August 2007).

Ofsted (2005) *Annual Report of Her Majesty's Chief Inspector of Schools 2003/4*, London: Oftsed.

Osborne, J. (1957) *The Entertainer: A Play*, London: Faber.

Palmer, A. (2006) ' "The day is coming when British Muslims form a state within a state" ', *Sunday Telegraph*, 19 February 2006.

Parekh, B. (2000) *Rethinking Multiculturalism: Cultural Diversity and Political Theory*, Basingstoke: Macmillan.

Parekh Report (2000) *The Future of Multi-Ethnic Britain*, London: Runnymede Trust/ Profile Books.

Parker-Jenkins, M., Hartas, D. and Irving, B. (2004) *In Good Faith: Schools, Religion and Public Funding*, Aldershot: Ashgate.

Peach, C. (2005) 'Muslims in the UK', in T. Abbas (ed.) *Muslim Britain: Communities Under Pressure*, London: Zed Books.

Phillips, Melanie. (2006) *Londonistan: How Britain Is Creating a Terror State Within*, London: Gibson Square Books.

Phillips, Mike and Phillips, Trevor (1998) *Windrush: The Irresistible Rise of Multiracial Britain*, London: HarperCollins.

Phillips, Trevor (2005) 'After 7/7: Sleepwalking to Segregation'. Online. Available HTTP: http://www.cre.gov.uk/Default.aspx.LocID-0hgnew07s.RefLocID-0hg00900c 002.Lang-EN.htm/ (accessed 22 September 2005).

——(2006) 'Speech to the Royal Geographical Society'. Online. Available HTTP: http://www.cre.gov.uk/Default.aspx.LocID-0hgnew0jl.RefLocID-0hg00900c002. Lang-EN.htm (accessed 30 August 2006).

Poulter, S. (1998) *Ethnicity, Law and Human Rights: The English Experience*, Oxford: Clarendon Press.

Raj, D.S. (2000) ' "Who the hell do you think you are?" Promoting Religious Identity Among Young Hindus in Britain", *Ethnic and Racial Studies*, 23(3): 535–58.

Rampton, B. (1995) *Crossing: Language and Ethnicity among Adolescents*, London: Longman.

Robinson, D. (2005) 'The Search for Community Cohesion: Key Themes and Dominant Concepts of the Public Policy Agenda', *Urban Studies*, 42(8): 1411–27.

Rose, E.J.B. *et al.* (1969) *Colour and Citizenship: A Report on British Race Relations*, London: Oxford University Press.

Runnymede Trust (1997) *Islamophobia, Its Features and Dangers*, London: Runnymede Trust.

Saeed, O. (2006) 'Multiculturalism, Terror and Sharia'. Online. Available HTTP: http://www.osamasaeed.org/osama/2006/08/multiculturalis.html#more (accessed 31 August 2006).

Sen, A. (2006) *Identity and Violence*, London: Allen Lane.

Shah, P. (2007). 'Between God and the Sultana? Legal Pluralism in the British Muslim Diaspora', paper presented to the conference Sharia as Discourse, University of Copenhagen.

Singh, G. (2004) 'Sikhs are the Real Losers from *Behzti*', *Guardian*, 24 December.

Smith, G. (2004) 'Faith in Community and Communities of Faith', *Journal of Contemporary Religion*, 19(2): 185–204.

Smithies, B. and Fiddick, P. (1969) *Enoch Powell on Immigration*, London: Sphere Books.

Sookhdeo, P. (2006) 'The Schools that Divide the Nation', *Evening Standard*, 4 September 2006.

Statham, P., Koopmans, R., Giugni, M. and Passey, F. (2005) ' "Resilient or Adaptable Islam? Multiculturalism, Religion and Migrants" Claims-Making for Group Demands in Britain, The Netherlands and France', *Ethnicities*, 5(4): 427–59.

Swann, R. (1985) *Education for All. Report of the Committee of Inquiry into the Education of Children from Ethnic Minority Groups. Cmnd 9453*, London: Her Majesty's Stationery Office.

Vertovec, S. (2007) *New Complexities of Cohesion in Britain: Super-Diversity, Transnationalism and Civil-Integration. Think Piece for the Commission on Integration and Cohesion*, Oxford: COMPAS.

Watson, J.L. (1977) *Between Two Cultures*, Oxford: Basil Blackwell.

Williams, R. (2008) "Archbishop's Lecture – Civil and Religious Law in England: a Religious Perspective", 7 February. Available at http://www.archbishopofcanterbury. org/1575 (accessed 11 November 2008).

Willmott, P. and Young, M. (1957) *Family and Kinship in East London*, London: Routledge.

Winder, R. (2004) *Bloody Foreigners: The Story of Immigration to Britain*, London: Little, Brown.

Young, J. (2003) 'To These Wet and Windy Shores: Recent Immigration Policy in the UK', *Punishment and Society*, 5(4): 449–62.

4 From toleration to repression

The Dutch backlash against multiculturalism

Baukje Prins and Sawitri Saharso

Before the murder of Pim Fortuyn shocked the country, it was widely believed that the Dutch cherished no nationalistic sentiments outside politically innocent happenings like football matches, skating championships and Queen's Day. Only a couple of years and two political murders later, a majority of the population had rejected the European Constitution, intellectuals emphasized the need for a Dutch Leitkultur, while the value of cultural diversity and the loyalty of the Muslim population to Dutch society were widely questioned.

On 6 May 2002, ten days before the national elections, with pollsters predicting that the Lijst Pim Fortuyn (LPF) could well become the largest party in the country, Fortuyn was shot dead by a radical environmentalist. In the weeks following his death many mourners indicated how 'Pim' had 'said what we were not allowed to say', i.e. that they feared how foreigners 'invaded' the country. On election day, the governing 'purple' coalition of Social Democrats, Conservative Liberals and Social Liberals suffered great losses, and the Lijst Pim Fortuyn, suddenly the second largest political party, was to become part of the next cabinet, headed by the Christian Democrat Jan Peter Balkenende.

This political landslide, signifying the beginning of a serious backlash against multiculturalism in the Netherlands, did not appear out of the blue. Fortuyn's popularity can be understood in terms of the growing appeal of a particular genre of discourse that has become increasingly dominant in Dutch public discourse, the genre of new realism. Fortuyn, we will argue, did not so much break with previous approaches to multicultural society as radicalize a genre of discourse that, at the time of his arrival on the political scene, had already gained considerable respectability.

In this chapter we will trace the gradual rise and eventual victory of new realism through an analysis of a series of public debates, starting with the 'national minorities debate' initiated by Frits Bolkestein in 1991 and ending with the controversies raised by the extreme-right politicians Rita Verdonk and Geert Wilders in 2008. These significant moments of public debate will be linked with five stages in which Dutch policies regarding immigrants embraced respectively a model of assimilation (1950s–82), pillarization (1982–94), multiculturalism (1994–2002), new realism (2002–6) and civic integration (since 2007).

Assimilation (1950s–82)

After World War II, the first migration flow to the Netherlands consisted of inhabitants of the former Dutch East Indies, who arrived after the independence of Indonesia in 1949. During the 1950s and 1960s, they were joined by guest workers from Mediterranean countries, Yugoslavia, Morocco and Turkey. In 1970, the Netherlands counted about 63,600 guest workers from non-western origin, 0.5 per cent of a population of 13 million (CBS Statline 2009). At the time an influential governmental advisor, the sociologist Hilda Verwey-Jonker, assumed that 'allochthones' would eventually integrate or even assimilate to the wider society, to the point that 'the alien group as such' would become unrecognizable.[1]

Between 1975 and 1980, the yearly number of newcomers reached a first culmination point. The prospect of Surinamese independence (1975) and the expiry of an immigration treaty between the two countries (1980) started a large-scale process of migration from Surinam. Together with family reunifications of Turkish and Moroccan workers, this led to the rise of the percentage of non-western immigrants in 1980 to nearly 3 per cent (around 400,000) of a population of 14 million (CBS Statline 2009). The assumption that most guest workers would eventually return to their country of origin proved increasingly unrealistic. At the end of the seventies, moreover, Dutch society was startled by violent protests by second-generation Moluccans who harboured strong feelings of frustration about the way Dutch government had betrayed their fathers, former soldiers of the KNIL (the Royal Dutch East Indies Army). The devastating finale of a train hijack in 1977, during which the Dutch military killed two hostages and six hijackers, made the ruling elite aware of the necessity to develop specific policies to improve the economic and social position of immigrants. It marked the beginning of the Dutch 'minorities policy' (*minderhedenbeleid*) which in subsequent periods followed different models of dealing with diversity.

Pillarization (1982–94)

During the first phase, the policy motto was: 'integration with preservation of identity'. It summarized the well-tried Dutch way of accommodating differences through institutionalized 'pillarization'. The right to organize oneself publicly in order to maintain one's religion was laid down in the Dutch constitution in 1917. Since then, Dutch consociational democracy got firmly established on the four religious-ideological pillars of Calvinism, Catholicism, Socialism and Liberalism. It was generally acknowledged that the pillarized system had furthered the emancipation of Dutch religious minorities (Lijphart 1975). Following this insight, policies regarding immigrant integration targeted not individuals, but (ethnic minority) groups. Their emancipation was believed to be executed best via the establishment of so-called 'self-organizations' and participatory boards (*inspraakorganen*) (see

Minderhedennota 1983). Immigrant communities have since made active use of the constitutional rights of consociational society, for example by founding Hindu and Muslim schools. Since 1985, moreover, after at least five years of legal residence, immigrants have the active and passive right to vote in Dutch municipal elections.

Apart from family reunification and postcolonial immigration, this period also saw a dramatic increase in the number of refugees and asylum seekers. Thus, in 1992, 15.1 per cent of the population of 15 million were officially marked as 'allochthone', 6.1 per cent were from non-Western descent (SCP 1996: 16).

The national minorities debate

In 1991, Frits Bolkestein, then leader of the Conservative Liberals, caused quite a stir when he proclaimed that 'the integration of minorities should be handled with guts' (Bolkestein 1991a). His lecture launched what came to be known as the 'national minorities debate'. Bolkestein's intervention involved a determined defence of the achievements of European civilization such as the universal values of secularization, freedom of speech and the principle of nondiscrimination, against 'the world of Islam' in which these values did not flourish. It should be made crystal clear to Muslims living in the Netherlands that any kind of bargaining about the principles of Western liberalism was out of the question.

Bolkestein challenged the dominant Dutch discourse, which defined ethnic minorities as groups who occupied a marginal socioeconomic position and were in need of support. He claimed that the attitude of the government had become too lenient and permissive. The urge to help ethnic minority groups emancipate themselves had made them more rather than less dependent on the welfare state, allowing them to withdraw into their own group rather than integrate into the larger society.

The newly emerging genre of public discourse of new realism, of which Bolkestein was one of the first influential representatives, has five distinct features. First, the advocates of this discourse present themselves as people who dare face the facts, who speak frankly about 'truths' that the dominant discourse has supposedly covered up. Thus Bolkestein (1991a) spoke firmly about the 'guts' and 'creativity' needed to solve the problem of integration and how this would leave no room for 'compromise', 'taboos' or 'disengagement'. Second, a new realist sets himself up as the spokesperson of the ordinary people, that is, the 'autochthonous' population. Bolkestein observed that 'below the surface a widespread informal national debate, which was not held in public, was already going on' (Bolkestein *et al.* 1992).

Why listen to the vox populi? On the one hand, ordinary people deserve to be represented because they are realists par excellence: they know from day-to-day experience what is really going on; they are not blinded by politically correct ideas: 'Voters find that politicians do not take sufficient notice of their problems' (Bolkestein 1991b).

On the other hand, one should take the complaints of the ordinary people seriously in order to keep their emotions under control and channel them in the right direction: 'Someone who ignores the anxiety, nourishes the resentment he intends to combat' (Bolkestein 1992). A third characteristic is the suggestion that realism is a characteristic feature of national Dutch identity: being Dutch equals being frank, straightforward and realistic. This is particularly manifest in the publications of another new realist, the journalist Herman Vuijsje. In *Murdered Innocence* (1986) Vuijsje elaborated the view that, after World War II, the Dutch had collectively developed a guilty conscience about the fate of the Dutch Jews, the majority of whom did not survive the holocaust. Ever since, the Dutch had become overcautious: wary of being accused of racism whenever they treated people differently because of their ethnicity. Vuijsje appealed to an authentic Dutchness, to be found in the pre-war days when 'our country distinguished itself for its preeminently matter-of-fact like treatment of ethnic difference' (Vuijsje 1986: 7). A fourth feature of new realism is its resistance to the left. New realists find it is high time to break the power of the progressive elite that dominates the public realm with its politically correct sensibilities regarding fascism, racism and intolerance. This supposedly left-wing censorship of public discourse is also criticized because it is accompanied by a highly relativistic approach to the value of different cultures.

Finally, new realism is a highly gendered discourse. When participants in the debate on multiculturalism want to prove the relevance of the issue at hand, they refer to issues of gender and sexuality, such as the headscarf, forced marriage, female genital mutilation, honour killing, domestic violence and homophobia. Within the new realist discourse, gender also seeps in in more subtle ways. Thus, in cases where immigrants are called to leave behind their cultural and religious inheritance and submit to the laws and customs of Dutch society, implicitly it is only male immigrants who are addressed. The assumption is that Dutch laws and customs particularly conflict with the privileges of immigrant (i.e. Muslim) men. Immigrant (i.e. Muslim) women, on the other hand, are depicted as victims of their own culture, and as having a self-evident interest in their integration into Dutch society (Prins 2004).

Multiculturalism (1994–2002)

Although the national minorities debate suggested otherwise, by the end of the 1980s, the Dutch government already started to discard the perspective of collective rights and care, and to put more emphasis on individual responsibilities and obligations (Fermin 1997). This was inspired by a change in political outlook, but also compelled by a long-term economic recession. Cutbacks in social welfare could no longer be avoided. This reorientation was further extended by the two consecutive 'purple' coalitions, in power since 1994, from which the Christian Democrats, traditionally the champions of pillarization, were excluded.

The bulk of policy measures regarding ethnic minorities aimed at improving the school achievements of immigrant children and at promoting labour participation. But there was a growing feeling that the lack of socioeconomic integration of immigrants was also due to their insufficient familiarity with Dutch language and society. As a consequence, since 1998, every newly arrived immigrant from outside the European Union was obliged to attend a newly launched programme of language- and civic integration (*inburgering*) courses. A memorandum by the newly established Ministry for Metropolitan Affairs and Integration sketched the outlines of a policy finely balanced between taking care of people and urging them to take initiative (Kansen pakken, kansen krijgen 1998). At the same time Minister Rogier van Boxtel declared the Netherlands to be an immigration country and a multicultural society.

A multicultural drama

In public discourse the position of non-western migrants remained a recurrent issue. People expressed concern about the emergence of so-called 'black' and Muslim schools, about the ongoing 'flood' of immigrants and refugees, and about the questionable role of Islam. In January 2000, publicist and social democrat Paul Scheffer castigated the Dutch for closing their eyes to 'the multicultural drama' that was developing right before their eyes. Although rates of unemployment, criminality and school drop-out among ethnic minorities were extremely high, the Dutch, according to Scheffer, mistakenly held onto their good old strategies of peaceful coexistence through deliberation and compromise. They ignored the fundamental differences between the new situation and the earlier days of pillarized society. Presently, Scheffer argued, there existed fewer sources of solidarity, while Islam, with its refusal to accept the separation of church and state, could not be compared to modernized Christianity. Teaching Dutch language, culture and history should be taken much more seriously. Only then would immigrant residents acquire a clear view of the basic values of Dutch society (Scheffer 2000).

Scheffer accused politicians of 'looking the other way', causing 'a whole nation to lose sight of reality'. His rhetoric perfectly complied with the genre of new realism. Here again was someone who dared to break taboos. Several commentators were pleased that it was finally possible to have a 'frank' and 'candid' conversation without 'politically correct reflexes' taking the upper hand. Scheffer too claimed that what happened to ordinary people, the stories told 'below the surface', remained unseen and unheard, although his reference was not to the autochthonous population, but to the feelings of anger and frustration among the children of migrants. Yet Scheffer showed a similar ambivalence as to why these feelings should be taken seriously: on the one hand, these youngsters were frustrated for a legitimate reason, that is, for remaining stuck at the bottom of the social ladder; on the other, government should do more to prevent these frustrations from turning into social upheaval. Scheffer recommended the affirmation of Dutch culture and identity as an important remedy for the problems of multicultural society, although his ideal Dutchman was not the romanticized 'ordinary' man or woman in the street, but the decent and politically knowledgeable citizen who was finely aware of the good and bad sides of Dutch identity.

Nevertheless, Scheffer shared with his predecessors an impatience with the cultural relativism of the progressive elite, which in his view had developed into an attitude of moral indifference. Resisting the growing leniency and laxity in the execution of laws and regulations, the typically Dutch culture of toleration (*gedogen*), Scheffer emphasized that it was high time to draw clear lines on what people were and were not allowed to do. What irritated him was not so much the toleration of anti-Western values and practices (although this surely should be tackled too), but the incomprehensible indifference of the left to the ever-widening gap between a (mostly *autochthonous*) majority of the well-off and a (mostly *allochthone*) minority that remained stuck in a situation of deprivation. Scheffer's new realism had adopted a social face.

The Fortuyn revolt

In the atmosphere of crisis following the attacks of 11 September 2001, Pim Fortuyn entered the Dutch political scene as the elected leader of Leefbaar Nederland. An ex-Marxist sociologist, in the 1990s Fortuyn had left his job at the university to start a consultancy in political strategic decision-making. In his weekly columns for the liberal-conservative magazine *Elsevier*, he expressed his aversion to the welfare state, European unification, Islam, the policy of toleration, the 'left church' and the continual influx of immigrants and asylum seekers (Fortuyn 2001a).

Fortuyn's rhetoric showed all the characteristics of the genre of new realism. On one occasion his face was pictured on the cover of a magazine gagged with his necktie, accompanied by the caption: 'Are you allowed to say everything you think? Dutch taboos' (De Jong 2000). And notwithstanding his aristocratic manners and appearance, Fortuyn prided himself on knowing what was going on in the poor neighbourhoods and fully understanding the concerns of ordinary people. Like the new realists before him, Fortuyn's attitude toward his constituency remained ambiguous. On the one hand, the ordinary Dutchman was a new realist like himself. If people living on welfare illegally took jobs on the black market, their choice was entirely understandable, for 'The poor are not at all the pitiful people the left church wants them to be. Most of them are just like us: emancipated, individualized, independent citizens' (Fortuyn 2001a: 105). On the other hand, the Dutch people were in need of a true leader, someone who could act both as their father and mother: 'the father as the one who lays down the law, the mother as the binding element of the herd' (Het Fenomeen Fortuyn 2002: 40). The third element of new realism, the affirmation of national identity, was shown both in Fortuyn's insistence on the preservation of national sovereignty against the ever-expanding influence of the EU and in his warnings about the imminent 'Islamization' of Dutch society (Fortuyn 2001b). His contempt for the progressive elite pervaded almost every aspect of his writings, resulting in his last book in which he wiped the floor with the 'purple' governments (Fortuyn 2002). Finally, because of his outspoken homosexuality, Fortuyn challenged conservative views of gender and sexuality. His dandy-like performance made a mockery of traditional ideas of masculinity and his frankness about his own love life made him the ultimate embodiment of the sexual revolution of the sixties (Pels 2003: 247–54)

Fortuyn further radicalized the new realist discourse. Freedom of opinion, even for an imam who deemed homosexuals like himself lower than pigs, was more important than legal protection against discrimination. In the interview that cost him the leadership of Leefbaar Nederland, he claimed that the Netherlands was a 'full country', Islam 'a backward culture' and it would be better to abolish 'that weird article of the constitution: thou shalt not discriminate (Het Fenomeen Fortuyn 2002: 61, 63). People were asked to put their trust in Fortuyn more on account of his guts than on the basis of his actual political programme. And so they did, as was evident in the massive outburst of grief and anger following his murder and at his funeral. Fortuyn's particular style, an odd mixture of aristocratic appearance and tough talk, was his strongest political weapon. One of the main ingredients of Fortuyn's attractiveness had been his 'frank' speech on immigrants. Having the courage to speak freely about problems and how they should be solved was turned into simply expressing yourself, giving vent to your feelings. Fortuyn thus managed to radicalize new realism to such an extent that it turned into its opposite, into hyperrealism. Frankness was no longer practised for the sake of truth, but for its own sake. References to reality and the facts had become mere indicators of the strong personality of the speaker, proof that a 'real leader' had entered the stage.

New realism (2002–06)

The murder of Fortuyn meant a huge blow to all those who had defended the ideal of multiculturalism. His followers accused left-wing politicians and the progressive press of having demonized Fortuyn and concluded that 'the bullet came from the left'. Combined with juridical charges and death threats, this resulted in an unprecedented atmosphere of (self-)censorship. Arguments in favour of multiculturalism were considered politically incorrect, and many critics of Fortuyn's views found themselves stunned into speechlessness. In the mainstream media, multiculturalism was self-evidently taken as a hopelessly outmoded and politically disastrous ideology, and firm talk about the need to reanimate Dutch norms and values attested to a more hostile and unwelcome atmosphere for (especially Muslim) immigrants.

Thanks to the immense electoral victory in May 2002 of the Christian Democrats and the LPF, these parties formed a coalition with the conservative-liberal VVD, presided over by the Christian Democrat Jan Peter Balkenende. This Cabinet fell within 87 days, due to blunders by and conflicts among LPF politicians. After new elections the Social Liberal party D66 (Democrats 66) replaced the LPF as coalition partner. This second Balkenende government was to remain in power until June 2006, when the Social Liberals pulled the plug. The outgoing minority government Balkenende III remained in office until the beginning of 2007. During this period, the backlash against multiculturalism reached its peak and got a clear translation in public policies.

In this period a parliamentary commission was installed to evaluate the effect of thirty years of integration policy. When it presented its findings, in particular its conclusion that the integration was a partial success (Blok 2004) met with disapproval among members of the Second Chamber. The general opinion among politicians was that integration had failed. Rather than a precondition for socioeconomic integration, culture now came to be considered as a problem in its own right. Cultural differences were associated with Islamic terrorism and with the undermining of social cohesion and national identity. 'The integration of ethnic minorities into Dutch society has grown into ... the "social question" of the 21st century', so the Cabinet started its response to the contested report of the commission Blok (*Regeringsreactie op 'Bruggen Bouwen'* 2004). Referring to (inter)national terrorism, the document continued that 'these events have raised doubts about the loyalty of parts of the minority population to the central values of Dutch society' (p. 2). Former integration policies were criticized fosr putting too much emphasis on the acceptance of differences. The alternative was 'shared citizenship', meaning that every inhabitant keeps to the same basic (Dutch) norms. These include

> doing one's best to be able to support oneself ... caring for one's environment, respecting the physical integrity of others, also in marriage, acceptance of every person's right to express his opinion, acceptance of the sexual preferences of others, the equality of women and men.
>
> (pp. 8–9)

Not the government but immigrants themselves were responsible for their successful integration (p. 9). Integration exams were compulsory, but individual immigrants carried the responsibility for organizing and financing their preparation for the exam, for instance by following integration courses. This trajectory was supposed to ensure immigrant citizens' loyalty to central Dutch values. More generally, civic education was introduced as a new and compulsory discipline in schools in 2006. Equal treatment of men and women was to be explicitly addressed as one of the core values of Dutch society – especially 'parts of the minority population' needed to be educated on this point urgently (*Brief Onderwijs, integratie en actief burgerschap* 2003). This shift is also reflected in the public debate on the Islamic veil. In this period the veil came to be more frequently framed as a signifier that stood for a lack of identification with the nation and a lack of integration of Muslim women (Saharso and Lettinga 2008).

Ayaan Hirsi Ali and the murder of Theo van Gogh

The elections of January 2003 may have been a letdown for the List Pim Fortuyn, but Fortuyn's ideas had found a new and charismatic spokesperson in the Dutch-Somali Ayaan Hirsi Ali. In autumn 2002, after her appearance on a couple of TV talk shows, Hirsi Ali had become known to the wider public as a fierce critic of Islam. When she was forced to go into hiding because of death treats from angry Muslims, the Conservative Liberal party convinced her to stand for a seat in parliament. This was not a bad bet: Hirsi Ali gathered over 30,000 preferential votes. During the era of the Balkenende II and III Cabinets, Hirsi Ali (or 'Ayaan', as her admirers liked to call her) became one of the most contoversial public figures of the country.

Like Fortuyn, Hirsi Ali sought confrontation. Initially she exclusively attacked leftwing intellectuals and multiculturalists for their relativistic attitude and their indifference to the fate of Muslim women. But she quickly turned against her former fellow believers too. In her first publication, in November 2001, her rhetoric about Islam had still been inclusive: 'We Muslims have lost sight of the balance between religion and reason' (Hirsi Ali 2002: 42). But in a later, more outspoken feminist essay she no longer identified herself as a Muslim, but as someone 'with knowledge of and experience with the Islamic religion' (Hirsi Ali 2002: 47) In one of her first television appearances she 'came out' as a former Muslim who deemed Islam to be a 'backward culture'. Her public criticism of Islam was completed when in a newspaper interview she put Mohammed to the pillory as a 'tyrant' and a 'perverse man' (Visser 2003). Throughout the time of her public presence in the Netherlands, Hirsi Ali showed the same guts as her new realist predecessors to attack Islam and the 'left church', and to put issues of gender and sexuality squarely on the public agenda. Although she was neither a populist nor a nationalist – her position being inspired by the high minded and cosmopolitan ideals of Enlightenment rather than the feelings of the ordinary man in the street – her radical opinions did fall on the fertile breeding grounds of Islamophobia and nationalistic sentiments.

Her views left Dutch feminists (Muslim and non-Muslim) severely divided. Some (white) feminists celebrated her as a brave woman who, in the best tradition of feminist activism, dared to be controversial and speak up against patriarchal traditions. Others criticized her for stirring up the latent racism and xenophobia among the Dutch population, and for wanting to liberate Muslim women without taking into account their own ideas on liberation. Whereas Hirsi Ali suggested that women's emancipation could only be achieved through the adoption of secular liberal values, many Muslim women insisted on the viability of their attempt to combine Islamic faith with their struggle for emancipation.

Dutch Muslims accused her of 'fouling her own nest' and behaving like 'a bounty'. Hirsi Ali was not impressed. In the summer of 2004, together with filmmaker Theo van Gogh, she made a short movie, Submission, part I, broadcast on national Dutch television in August 2004. It is a dramatic staging of the difficulties many Muslim women face in the form of a prayer to Allah. Texts from the Koran are inscribed on the skin of the women, whose bodies shiver from the wounds inflicted upon them by being beaten up, flogged and raped by their father, brother or husband.[2] Because of the inscribed Koranic texts, the film was extremely blasphemous in the eyes of Muslims, and it soon showed that to some it had indeed exceeded all bounds. On 2 November 2004, Van Gogh, while biking to his work in Amsterdam, was brutally slaughtered. His murderer, the 26 year old Dutch-Moroccan Mohammed Bouali, had knifed a letter into Van Gogh's body, which made it clear that his deed was actually meant as a warning to Hirsi Ali (Buruma 2006). She was forced to go underground again, while Dutch government responded with a series of arrests and stricter measures to fight Muslim terrorism. When some months later she returned to the scene of Dutch politics, she proved determined to hold on to her mission to stimulate Muslims to make a 'shortcut to Enlightenment' – as she announced the title of her next book would be. In the meantime, Van Gogh's murder had put Hirsi Ali in the spotlight of the international media (Caldwell 2004). She received numerous awards in different countries, was celebrated by Time-Magazine as one of the 100 most influential people of 2005, and her texts were translated into several languages.

Immigrant women in the spotlight

While in the previous governments problems of integration fell under the jurisdiction of the Ministry of Internal Affairs, and (legal and illegal) immigrants were the concern of the Ministry of Justice, after the Fortuyn revolt, both were to be dealt with by the Ministry of Justice. Rita Verdonk, in office as the Minister of Alien Affairs and Integration since 2003, soon came to be known as 'iron Rita' for her rigid implementation of immigration and integration policies. She for instance decided that homosexuals from Iran could safely be returned to their homeland (a decision she later had to recall), and she defended decisions of the Immigration and Naturalization Services to deport refugees which afterwards proved to be unlawful. In 2006 the Netherlands was condemned by the European Council and Human Rights Watch for violating the basic human rights of asylum seekers and immigrants.

Verdonk was also responsible for the integration policy, which in this period, also due to the influence of Ayaan Hirsi Ali, strongly focused on the position of immigrant women. Two of the four aims articulated in the long-term emancipation plan of 2005, for instance, were actually geared to non-western, immigrant women, i.e. the prevention and combat of violence against women and girls (the plan referred to honor killings, female genital mutilation, trafficking in women) and the prevention of the social exclusion of 'vulnerable and deprived women' (Emancipatie 2005).

A high profile commission was installed (PaVEM, Participation of Women from Ethnic Minority groups) whose aim was to improve immigrant women's mastery in Dutch language, their access to paid work and their social parti- cipation. The plan was inspired by the motto 'If you educate a women, you educate a family' (PaVEM 2005). Immigrant women's education and partici- pation were hence not only meant to stimulate their own personal develop- ment, it was also expected that as wives and mothers they would pass on Dutch values and norms to their husbands and children, and thus have what was described as a 'benevolent' influence on their own community.

Critics often warned that Hirsi Ali's attacks on Islam would hinder Muslim and immigrants' organizations in recognizing family violence as a problem in their communities. It seems however, that their effect was precisely the oppo- site: they created the opportunity and the financial means (as government was prepared to invest in the issue) for these organizations to act against it. Like- wise, while the dominant public discourse insisted on legal prosecution, practitioners in the field opted for the soft approach of information and per- suasion. And while the official policy line was to target the individual immi- grant, practitioners chose for close collaboration with immigrants' organizations. On the local level, the entire approach was very much phrased in terms of the practices to be combated; the cultural background of some of these practices was only alluded to in-between the lines. Domestic violence, for instance, was conceptualized as a general problem of the violence of men against women rather than the problem of a different culture. Hence, whereas during this heyday of the backlash against multiculturalism, the culture card was drawn frequently in public debate, policymakers and practitioners in the field were careful not to link up certain problematics too quickly with a par- ticular cultural or religious background. They rather found a fruitful and effective way to negotiate the tension between the value of gender equality and the value of respecting cultural diversity by developing culture sensitive measures, but naming them in culture blind terms (Prins and Saharso 2008).

'Saint' Ayaan contra 'iron' Rita

The downfall of the second Balkenende government was ushered in by a clash between Ayaan Hirsi Ali and Rita Verdonk, Minister of Alien Affairs and Integration, fellow party member and personal friend. Due to their tough talk and uncompromising attitude toward Muslims and immigrants, both women were extremely popular among a significant part of the Dutch population.

Rita Verdonk prided herself on following an unequivocal and impartial style of ruling, not surrendering to emotional considerations or subjective reasoning. She also regularly claimed that asylum seekers should not pri- marily be perceived as victims: many of them were not really political refu- gees, but economic 'fortune-hunters'. Hirsi Ali had always agreed with

Verdonk that integration into Dutch society required immigrants to express full loyalty to liberal values and to the Dutch nation. And she agreed that asylum seekers should not be handled with too much pity – especially Somali refugees, she once conceded, were prone to fraudulent practices. But Hirsi Ali had been an asylum seeker herself. And she had been publicly open about the fact that she herself had committed fraud when applying for asylum back in 1992. In an early interview she related how she had given a false name and a false date of birth, that she had lied about the country from which she had fled and the reasons for her flight (Hirsi Ali 2002: 7–18). However, when a television documentary in May 2006 supposedly 'revealed' those lies of 'saint Ayaan', as she was cynically referred to (Zembla 2006), a member of parliament asked critical questions. Within just a few days Verdonk announced that, formally speaking, Hirsi Ali had never acquired Dutch citizenship – which implied that her membership of Dutch parliament was unlawful too. Hirsi Ali responded with a press conference, during which she announced her immediate departure from the Netherlands to take up a position at the American Enterprise Institute, a conservative Washington D.C. think-tank with close ties to the Bush administration (Hirsi Ali 2007).

The tragic irony of this affair was that both heroines fell on their own swords. The unflinching Somali 'war lord' (as Hirsi Ali once called herself) felt forced to leave the country that she held so dear, the country that had taught her about the value of freedom, while 'iron Rita' was openly put under the guardianship of prime minister Balkenende to ensure that she would execute motions by parliament insisting on more thorough research regarding Hirsi Ali's status.[3] A month later, controversies concerning Verdonk's functioning led to the fall of the second Balkenende government. However, whereas Hirsi Ali fell out of favour with the public that scolded her for being a fraudulent asylum seeker who had taken on starlike airs, opinion polls showed that the majority of the Dutch stood squarely behind Verdonk and had little qualms in seeing Hirsi Ali leave the country. When push came to shove, xenophobic feelings among the Dutch proved stronger than their (feminist) commitment to Muslim women.

Civic integration (since 2007)

The national elections of November 2006 resulted in a progressive majority in Dutch Parliament. In February 2007, the Balkenende IV Cabinet, a coalition of Christian Democrats, Labour Party and Christian Union was installed. The latter, a small orthodox-protestant party, had been consistently critical of the previous government for its incompassionate policies regarding asylum seekers and its ill-disposed attitude vis-à-vis religion. It also was the only party that withstood the backlash against multiculturalism by remaining committed to the model of pillarization and recognizing the significance of collective identity for immigrant groups (Spijkerboer 2007). The new government replaced the individualistic, neoliberal approach of its predecessor with a more communitarian outlook emphasizing the importance of social cohesion, civic duties and family values. Its first Policy Programme (Samen werken, samen leven 2007) avoided notions such as 'autochthone', 'allochthonous' or 'ethnic minority', and contained not a single reference to Islam. Instead, when addressing immigrant issues, the programme used ethnically neutral terms like persons, citizens or inburgeraars (literally: someone who is becoming a citizen).

Asylum and integration policies have since 2007 clearly acquired a more human face. Government immediately granted a general pardon for the aforementioned group of 26,000 asylum seekers, and while immigration and asylum remained under the jurisdiction of the Department of Justice, issues concerning immigrant integration (inburgering) moved to the Ministry of Housing, Spatial Planning and the Environment. The Cabinet wished to put a stop to the ongoing process of separation and polarization between 'autochthones' and 'allochthones': by stimulating the emancipation of the latter with the help of better education and equal job opportunities. Its other aim is integration, interpreted as 'active citizenship': the acceptance of the core values of the constitutional state, knowledge of each other's backgrounds, willingness to fight discrimination, and participation in communal activities (Zorg dat je erbij hoort! 2007: 7). The Cabinet also launched the 'Deltaplan civic integration' to stimulate more immigrants to follow integration courses, and it invested in educational projects for children of immigrants. In line with its communitarian perspective, the Minister of Housing, Communities and Integration, Ella Vogelaar, started a project to improve the quality of the 40 poorest neighborhoods in the country, where many immigrants live.

It would be too much to suggest that these recent initiatives form a clear break with the previous period. Many strict measures introduced earlier remain firmly in place. People who want to immigrate to the Netherlands are still required to do a basic Dutch language proficiency exam in their home country (and pay €350 for it), the costs of visa are among the highest in Western Europe (€833 when visiting relatives, €433 for students or jobholders), income and age requirements for marriage with a partner from abroad remain relatively high, and integration trajectories are still leaning towards the model of cultural assimilation.

Much of the tough phraseology of new realism, moreover, has nowadays become commonplace. Although in official policy documents there is much talk of reciprocity, common interests and equal treatment, the afore quoted governmental memorandum on integration opens with much understanding for 'autochthonous' feelings of fear and alienation by the 'growing visibility' of Islam, while 'allochthones' (i.e. Muslims) are expected ('just like autochthones', it is added) that they do their best to secure a place in society, by learning the language, to follow and finish an education, to obtain an income, to take responsibility for the education of their children' (Zorg dat je erbij hoort! 2007: 6). But the requirements go further than this. Immigrants are also expected 'to be curious about the ins and outs of Dutch society and the lifeworld of (autochthonous) fellow citizens, in particular about Dutch culture and history' (p. 6). Hence, integration does not only involve economic and social participation, but also a considerable immersion in, if not identification with Dutch culture. And integration comes not just with rights, but first and foremost with responsibilities and duties. Several integration aims are captured under the heading of 'safety'. Government does not only offer positive support to well-meaning newcomers, but in order to 'restore' feelings of safety among the (autochthonous) population, it will also adopt a 'firm repressive approach' against derailed youngsters, criminality, radicalization and the infringement of fundamental rights. While in the models of pillarization and multiculturalism, commitment to one's own community was considered a source of strength for the economic and social integration into the larger society, the recent policy document speaks of 'withdrawing' or 'reverting' to one's own group, which it considers as a sign of separation and estrangement from Dutch society.

Against Islam: the rise of the Freedom Party

The elections of 2006 seemed a victory for the moderate forces. Yet, in terms of the number of seats in parliament, the winners were those at the nationalistic extremes of the political spectrum: the extreme-right Freedom Party (PVV) established by Geert Wilders (expelled from the VVD for his radical views on Islam and immigration), went from 1 to 9 seats, the Socialist Party, led by the (former Maoist) populist Jan Marijnissen, sky-rocketed with 16 seats to a total of 25, while Rita Verdonk won over 620,000 votes for the VVD (the party as a whole losing 6 of its 28 seats). The socialists, admittedly, did not brand immigrants as scapegoats. But each of these parties, in line with new realism, tapped into the fears of the 'ordinary people' regarding Dutch sovereignty and identity.

In the first years of her career in parliament, Verdonk's popularity rose to unprecedented heights, but the party establishment of the VVD had grown wary of her lack of team spirit. It pressurized her to resign her party membership. In October 2007 Verdonk launched her own political movement, TON ('Proud of the Netherlands'). In the course of time, she lost the competition for the populist vote to Geert Wilders, who clearly is the better manipulator of 'autochthonous' resentment. In March 2007, when the new Cabinet was introduced, Wilders had caused uproar by publicly questioning the loyalty of the Ministers Albayrak and Aboutaleb because of their double nationality. His motion demanding that they either hand in their 'other' passport or resign, was rejected by a large majority. But Wilders, triumphant because of the many Dutch who welcomed his debating style, coolly announced: 'They should prepare for the worst, I haven't even started yet. Whoever cannot stomach it, should look for another profession.'

No wonder, also given the wave of anti-western riots and boycotts during the Danish cartoon affair in 2006, that when Wilders announced the making of a critical film against the Koran, the Cabinet called all hands on deck. Wilders was asked to behave responsibly, the Minister of the Interior instructed police and fire brigades throughout the country to prepare for calamities after the release, and prime minister Balkenende anticipated 'a substantial crisis'. When Fitna, the movie came out (on the internet) in March 2008, it appeared to be a compilation of incidences of worldwide Islamic extremism, followed by a series of images and quotes meant to prove that the 'Islamization' of Dutch society was imminent. The movie ends with the call to defeat Islamic ideology, just as the West has defeated the ideologies of Nazism and Communism. The calm and almost indifferent response of Dutch Muslims caused somewhat of an anti-climax. Still, Wilders reaps the fruits of his crusade against Islam. These are bitter fruits, in so far as he can't go anywhere without several bodyguards following his heels, he also runs the risk that Jordan will shortly issue an international warrant for his arrest, and in January 2009, the court of Amsterdam ordered the Public Prosecutor to start criminal proceedings against him for inciting hatred and the discrimination of Muslims and their religion. But there are also sweet fruits, like awards and applause by adherents of radical freedom of speech (at home and abroad), and ever higher scores for his Freedom Party in Dutch opinion polls. In January 2009, the estimated number of seats in parliament for the Freedom Party rose to 25. If we add this up with the predicted two seats for Verdonk's TON we may conclude that in 2009 public support in the Netherlands for anti-multiculturalist and anti-immigrant ideologies is just as strong as at the culmination point of the Fortuyn-revolt in May 2002.

Epilogue: populism turned mainstream?

Since May 2002, established political parties have gone a long way to meet the followers of Fortuyn in their discontent about multicultural society and the growing number of Muslim citizens (currently estimated at 850,000). How to explain this radical shift, which transformed the Netherlands from what seemed like a paragon of toleration and openness to a xenophobic and inward-looking country? Some scholars answer this question by going along with the new realist perspective. It is for instance argued that initially the Dutch were very willing to tolerate different ways of life even if they rejected them. What triggered the backlash was the more demanding multiculturalist requirement to positively recognize these cultural practices (Sniderman and Hagendoorn, 2007). Ian Buruma, on the other hand, considers the shift to be the result of a conservative backlash against the liberal revolt of the sixties (Buruma 2006). Others adopt the vocabulary of pathology to understand the Dutch turmoil. The murders of Fortuyn and Van Gogh were social drama's that recalled unresolved and painful moments in Dutch history accumulating into a cultural trauma (Eyerman 2008). Or it is claimed that the Dutch suffer from 'social hypochondria'. Their obsessive talk about integration produces precisely that which it wishes to undo, namely a gap between 'autochthones' and 'allochthones', between those who are already a (integrated) part of the social body, and those who are constituted as its 'outside' (Schinkel 2008). Remarkably enough, each of these explanations focuses exclusively on internal factors, while ignoring the extent to which developments in the Netherlands run parallel to similar developments in other Western European countries.

While we may puzzle our heads over how it came about that new realism turned mainstream in such a short period, the more urgent question concerns the prospects for the future.

As the political parties on the right (VVD and PVV) and the left (SP) have more or less identified with the nationalistic rhetoric of new realism, it is the positioning of the centre parties, who now make up the Balkenende IV government, that matters most. Current developments give some reason for optimism. In so far as they are themselves inspired by a religious outlook, the two Christian parties CDA and CU are not averse to citizens identifying and organizing themselves on the basis of a common faith, and at least sympathetic to people who feel offended when their belief is attacked. But the direction that the social democrats will take seems to be most crucial. The Labour Party is the only political actor that has both the political ideals and a large enough constituency to develop a strong alternative voice. Anxious not to lose touch with its traditional constituency, the party is currently wrestling to find the right balance between its social democratic ideals and a patriotic call for the affirmation of Dutch language, culture and history. In this process, Paul Scheffer, the man who successfully warned against 'the multicultural drama' almost a decade earlier, plays a crucial role. When his long awaited book, *Het land van aankomst* (The country of arrival) came out, it was welcomed by the political and managerial elite as an impartial, knowledgeable and hopeful account of the thorny issues of immigration and integration (Scheffer 2007).

Ella Vogelaar, the social democratic Minister of Housing, Communities and Integration, was among those who warmly welcomed Scheffer's contribution. And yet, in November 2008, Vogelaar was removed from her ministerial post by the leadership of the Labour Party. Her policy aimed at improving the living conditions in the poorest neighborhoods, where many immigrants live, and transforming them from 'problem districts' into 'show districts'. It was not so much because this policy had failed – her ministry of twenty months had been too short for any serious evaluation – but her image in the media that cost Vogelaar her post. While the party-leadership wanted to polarize more on issues of integration, Vogelaar had consistently emphasized the need to create ties between old and new Dutch, and to publicly acknowledge positive developments within immigrant communities. Her style was considered too close to the old-fashioned brand of multiculturalism, which Scheffer argued should be left behind.

In his book, Scheffer argues for an unprejudiced perspective on the conflicts and frictions caused by recent immigration. Building cross-cultural bridges, he claims, is possible only if the feelings of loss and alienation suffered by both immigrants and native residents are taken seriously. But Scheffer's own treatment of the perspectives of immigrants and natives is remarkably asymmetrical. Immigrants are required to become knowledgeable about the language, culture and history of their new home country, Muslims should learn to deal with criticism, and the Fortuyn revolt should induce the Dutch political elite to some serious soul-searching. The followers of Fortuyn, the Dutch 'ordinary people', however, although admittedly inclined to conformity and informal pressure to assimilate, are not urged to change their outlook. The recurrent invocation of the distinction between 'us' and 'them' affirms the very difference the book wants to overcome, as its final words nicely illustrate:

> When we understand that a relaxed society requires a great deal of effort, we can wholeheartedly say to people who are coming from far and near: welcome.
>
> (Scheffer 2007: 440)

The leadership of the Labour Party embraced Scheffer's book as a rich resource from which to mine catchy slogans. The initial draft of a recent party memorandum on integration contained phrases from Scheffer such as:

> 'The stage of avoidance is definitely over now' and 'Immigration involves feelings of discomfort and loss for both migrants and natives.' Newcomers, their children and grandchildren were asked to 'make an unconditional choice for the Netherlands'. Their emancipation required 'abandoning where you come from'.
>
> (Partij van de Arbeid 2008)

These and many other populist elements in the text led to a storm of protest. Nearly 400 amendments were submitted, forcing the party-leadership to radically adjust their text. The redrafted version no longer speaks of 'allochthones', but refers to immigrants as 'new Dutch' (nieuwe Nederlanders), who no longer need to choose unconditionally for the Netherlands, but may keep their old nationality if they wish so. The memorandum now also points to the extreme-right as part of the problem and shows an awareness that there are also positive developments, such as the successful integration of many 'new Dutch'. While the initial text ended with the claim that 'This is our country. And we belong to this country' (again a phrase adopted from Paul Scheffer), the second was subtly but significantly altered: 'This is our country. And together we are this country' (Partij van de Arbeid 2009). The revised memorandum will be discussed in a general party assembly in March 2009. At the moment of writing, it looks as if the party-leadership will have to retract at least part of its new realist rhetoric.

If we take account of the developments at the level of policies, the backlash against multiculturalism does not seem to have hit as hard as the tough public rhetoric suggests. Regarding, for instance, asylum seekers and immigration, the policy lines have surely become harsher. But at some points, the much praised pragmatic Dutch approach seems to have survived. We already mentioned how at the grass roots level problems of domestic violence are combated with culture sensitive measures wrapped upf in culture blind terms. Another example is the issue of the Islamic headscarf. Despite much talk about entirely banning the all-covering burka, women in public offices, like teachers in state schools, are allowed to wear the headscarf without much further ado.

Although there is no way to predict the impact of the current financial crisis on the position of and attitude towards immigrants, these developments give us modest hope that the majority of the Dutch population is getting tired of the hysteria induced by the anti-Muslim rhetoric, and will return to their previous matter-of-fact-like and tolerant attitude regarding cultural and religious difference.

Notes

1 Sociologist Hilda Verwey-Jonker coined the term 'allochthone' to refer to residents of whom either one of their parents, or they themselves are not born in the Netherlands (Verwey-Jonker 1971). The categories of (western and non-western) 'allochthone' and 'autochthone', however contested in public debate, are still frequently used by researchers doing statistics, and policymakers.
2 For the original script, see Hirsi Ali 2006.
3 In the end, Verdonk had to return Hirsi Ali her Dutch passport.

References

Blok, S.A. (2004) *Bruggen bouwen*, Den Haag: Sdu.
Bolkestein, F. (1991a) 'Integratie van minderheden moet met lef worden aangepakt', *De Volkskrant*, 12 September.
——(1991b) 'Interview met D. Eppink,' *NRC Handelsblad*, 12 September.
——(1992) 'Wie de verontrusting negeert, voedt juist het ressentiment jegens minderheden dat hij wil bestrijden', *De Volkskrant*, 5 September.
Bolkestein, F., Penninx, R., Kruyt, A. and Couwenberg, S.W. (1992) 'Een discussie over racisme', *Het Capitool*. Ned 3, NOS television, 22 March.
Buruma, Ian (2006) *Murder in Amsterdam: The Death of Theo van Gogh and the Limits of Tolerance*, New York: The Penguin Press.
Caldwell, C. (2005) 'Daughter of the Enlightenment', *New York Times Sunday Magazine*, 3 April.
CBS Statline (2009) Centraal Bureau voor de Statistiek. Online. Available HTTP: http://statline.cbs.nl/StatWeb/publication (accessed 1 February 2009).
Emancipatie: Vanzelfsprekend, maar het gaat niet vanzelf (2005) Meerjarenbeleidsplan 2006–10. Den Haag: Ministerie van Onderwijs, Cultuur & Wetenschappen.
Eyerman, R. (2008) *The Assassination of Theo van Gogh: From Social Drama to Cultural Trauma*, Durham and London: Duke University Press.
Fermin, A. (1997) *Nederlandse politieke partijen over minderhedenbeleid 1977–95*, Amsterdam: Thesis Publishers.

Fortuyn, P. (2001a) *Droomkabinet: Hoe Nederland geregeerd moet worden*, Amsterdam: Van Gennep.

——(2001b) *De islamisering van onze cultuur: Nederlandse identiteit als fundament*, Rotterdam: Karakter/Speakers Academy.

——(2002) De *puinhopen van acht jaar paars*, Rotterdam: Karakter/Speakers Academy.

Het Fenomeen Fortuyn (2002) Amsterdam: De Volkskrant/Meulenhoff.

Hirsi Ali, A. (2002) *De zoontjesfabriek*, Amsterdam/Antwerpen: Augustus.

——(2006) *The Caged Virgin*, London: The Free Press.

——(2007) *Infidel*, New York: The Free Press.

Jong, S. de (2000) 'Hollandse taboes', *HP/De Tijd* 39, 29 September: 32–41.

Kansen pakken, kansen krijgen (1998). *Integratiebeleid 1999–2002*. Den Haag: BiZa.

Lijphart, A. (1975) *The Politics of Accommodation. Pluralism and Democracy in the Netherlands*, Berkeley: University of California Press.

Minderhedennota (1983) *Regeringsnota over het minderhedenbeleid*, Den Haag: Staatsuitgeverij.

Onderwijs, integratie en actief burgerschap (2003) Brief (TK 2003–4, 29 536, no. 1 and 2), Den Haag: Sdu.

Partij van de Arbeid (2008) Verdeeld verleden, gedeelde toekomst, PB-resolutie Integratie. Online. Available HTTP: http://www.pvda.nl/download.do/id/320250112/cd/true (acessed 10 February 2009)

——(2009) Bijlage: Verdeeld verleden, gedeelde toekomst, Resolutie Integratie. Online, Available HTTP: http://www.pvda.nl/download.do/id/320261416/cd/true (accessed 25 February 2009)

PaVEM (2005) *Zij doen mee! Participatie agenda 2010*, Den Haag: Sdu.

Pels, D. (2003) De *geest van Pim. Het gedachtegoed van een politiek dandy*, Amsterdam: Anthos/AMBO.

Prins, B. (2004) *Voorbij de onschuld. Het debat over de multiculturele samenleving* (2nd rev. edn), Amsterdam: Van Gennep.

Prins, B. and Saharso, S. (2008) 'In the spotlight: a blessing and a curse for immigrant women in the Netherlands', in A. Phillips and S. Saharso (eds), *The Rights of Women and the Crisis of Multiculturalism*. Special Issue *Ethnicities*, 8 (3): 365–84.

Regeringsreactie op'Bruggen bouwen' (2003) (TK 2003–4, 28 689, no. 17), Den Haag: Sdu.

Saharso, S. and Lettinga, D. (2008) 'Contentious citizenship: policies and debates on the veil in the Netherlands.' in S. Kilic, S. Saharso and B. Sauer (eds) *The Veil: Debating Citizenship, Gender and Religious Diversity*. Special Issue *Social Politics. International Studies in Gender, State and Society*, 16(4): 455–80.

Samen werken, samen leven (2007) Beleidsprogramma Kabinet Balkenende IV 2007–11, Den Haag: Ministerie van Algemene Zaken.

Scheffer, P. (2000) 'Het multiculturele drama', *NRC Handelsblad*, 29 January.

——(2007) *Het land van aankomst*, Amsterdam: De Bezige Bij.

Schinkel, W. (2008) *De gedroomde samenleving*, Kampen: Klement.

SCP (1996) *Rapportage Minderheden 1996*, Den Haag: VUGA.

Sniderman, P. and Hagendoorn, L. (2007) *When Ways of Life Collide: Multiculturalism and its Discontents in the Netherlands*, Princeton: Princeton University Press.

Spijkerboer, T. (2007) *Zeker weten. Inburgering en de fundamenten van het Nederlandse politieke bestel*, Den Haag: Sdu.

Verwey-Jonker, H. (ed.) (1971) *Allochtonen in Nederland. Beschouwingen over de Gerepatrieerden, Ambonezen, Surinamers, Antillianen, Buitenlandse werknemers, Chinezen, Vluchtelingen, Buitenlandse studenten in onze samenleving*, Den Haag: Staatsuitgeverij.

Visser, A. (2003) 'Politiek is schadelijk voor mijn ideaal', *Trouw*, 25 January.

Vuijsje, H. (1986) *Vermoorde onschuld. Etnisch verschil als Hollands taboe*, Amsterdam: Bert Bakker.

Zembla (2006) De heilige Ayaan, VARA television broadcast, 11 May.

Zorg dat je erbij hoort! (2007), Integratienota 2007–11. Den Haag: Ministerie VROM/WWI.

5 "We're not all multiculturalists yet"

France swings between hard integration and soft anti-discrimination[1]

Patrick Simon and Valérie Sala Pala

After being one of the archetypical "assimilationist" countries (Favell, 1998), France has recently seen rapid change in its framing of the incorporation of "migrants" and "ethnic and racial minorities." Not only have the concepts and theories used to describe the processes behind the "remaking of the French mainstream" dramatically changed,[2] but the categories of those targeted by these processes are also being reconsidered. Foreigners, immigrants, young people with an immigrant background, second-generation Muslims, and even "visible minorities": the grammar of integration has developed a new vocabulary. While the 1980s were a short period of a sort of multiculturalism, an initial backlash occurred at the end of the decade with the invention of the "French model of integration" (Lorcerie, 1994). Integration was no longer only a philosophy or a conceptual tool designed in social science,[3] but was anchored in policies and public discourse. The integrationist hegemony was then contested by a rising concern about discrimination (Fassin, 2002). The current framing may be described as a strange mix of old-school integration and new European-style anti-discrimination. Despite these shifts in political paradigms, French society has never considered itself to be a multicultural society.

The very notion of multiculturalism remains, in France, strongly associated with international experience, especially the British, Dutch, and US models, and negatively perceived as the opposite of the French republican "model of integration." Conceived as a political model relying on the recognition and positive representation of ethnic communities and their cultural differences, multiculturalism is above all pictured as what French society has never been and should not become (Amselle, 1996). The reason multiculturalism is a bugbear in the French debate is that it is seen as a threat to national identity and republican values. Multiculturalism in the French context sounds like culturalism. The fear of the "balkanization" of French society and the rise of "communitarianism,"[4] i.e. the danger of the political mobilization of ethnic, racial or sexual minorities, provides the background for discrediting claims for recognition and the denunciation of discrimination and racial domination. This specific context has to be understood as a long-lasting consequence of the spread and implementation of the integration paradigm (Wieviorka, 1996).

The obfuscation of the division of society along ethnic or racial lines—French colorblindness—draws on a long tradition of assimilation discourse and techniques, crystallized in the "French model of integration" (Schnapper, 1991). In 1989, a new body was established, the High Council for Integration (Haut Conseil à l'Intégration, HCI) whose purpose was to inform and give advice to the authorities on the integration of immigrants. The HCI quickly launched a pro-active integration policy and devised in 1991 the official doctrine of integration:

> Integration means encouraging the active participation in society as a whole of all the women and men who will be living long term in our country, by genuinely accepting that some of their specific characteristics, particularly cultural, will remain, but stressing similarities and convergence in the equality of their rights and duties, in order to ensure the cohesion of our social fabric ... It seeks the contribution of these differences to a common project and not, like assimilation, their abolition or conversely, like insertion, a guarantee that they will be perpetuated.[5]

While continuing the assimilationist tradition, the HCI struck a delicate balance between the rights and duties of "women and men who will be living long term in our country,"[6] the acceptance of the basic values of the Republic, and the necessary transformation of French society in order to "allow opportunities" for newcomers in their social life. This "integration model" sums up the long history of immigration in France and captures the essential principles of the French integration policy. First, integration is an individual process. The State will not recognize immigrants in structured communities because such institutionalization poses a threat to the unity of the nation. Second, admission as a citizen, i.e., becoming a French national, remains the pivot of the integration process. Maintenance of an open code of nationality[7] allows for a rather sizeable admission of foreigners according to various procedures and ensures an ongoing "mixing" of populations (Weil, 2005a). This is also a way of avoiding the emergence and perpetuation of "minorities" with specific legal statuses as a result of confusions between the notions of citizenship and nationality. Third, the concept of integration is linked to the principle of equality in that it tries to enforce the practice of equality in social life.

Yet, despite this wording, the integration doctrine often clashes with institutional arrangements, which do not reflect these general principles. The opposition to the recognition of any structured communities which would add an intermediate layer between the State and the citizens is often challenged at the local level. The line between "tolerating specific cultural features" and promoting multiculturalism seems quite slim.[8] French integration policies involve a permanent quest to strike an unlikely—and, according to many observers, unattainable—balance between an active form of tolerance of differences (including some concessions to the public expression of such differences) and the vigilant reassertion of a "principle of non-differentiation" (Garbaye, 2005).

However, some recent developments suggest that this traditional framing of the debate is being challenged. The issue of racial and ethnic discrimination has been put on the political and intellectual agenda. Recognition of France's 150-year history of immigration has only recently come about due to an awareness campaign on the part of social scientists and through the increasing demands for recognition made by immigrants and their descendants. The creation in July 2004 of the Cité Nationale d'Histoire de l'Immigration, the first national museum dedicated to immigration history, is one crucial milestone in this process of recognition. The controversies concerning "subaltern memories," mainly memories of slavery and colonization, are also part of the picture. Recognition vs. *laïcité*, integration vs. anti-discrimination, colorblindness vs. diversity management: public controversies and political conflicts are reshaping the pattern of French diversity.

This chapter will address the chaotic and short history of multiculturalism in France through the controversies and debates that have occurred during the last twenty years. The first part will briefly summarize the main evolutions of the French model of incorporation, from assimilation to anti-discrimination through "integration." The second part will address what we would call the "multicultural debates," i.e., the main public controversies that have involved definitions of national identity, *laïcité* or the "subaltern memories" (history of immigration, colonization or slavery).

From assimilation to anti-discrimination

At the beginning of the 1980s, France went through a brief, unexpected "multiculturalist" period. For the first time since 1936, a left-wing government was in power and society suddenly opened up. Among social changes that had long been suppressed and were now released was a renegotiation of the place of immigrants in society. The March for Equality, known as the "March of the Beurs" (back slang for Arabs), which took place at the end of 1983 and its repeat "Convergence 84" the following year publicized the aspirations of young people "of immigrant background" to equality and recognition (Bouamama, 1994). Following on from the cessation of low-skilled labor migration in 1974, this movement revealed the undeniable presence in society of an immigration that had until then been considered to be a temporary and marginal phenomenon. France discovered itself as an "immigration society," but this new awareness did not yet involve any radical change in the frameworks for representing society. A new hybrid urban culture was emerging in areas that had escaped the influence of the centralized model. In the "disadvantaged neighborhoods" where "immigrants" mainly lived, new identities were being formed and "traditions" re-invented: references, history, language, and social practices were being redefined outside the national order. No longer stuck in factories, migrant hostels and *cités de transit*,[9] "immigrants" were now investing all spheres of social life and leaving behind pre-established social roles. At school, in neighborhood relations, in voluntary associations, otherness was imposing its visibility and becoming one of the components of everyday life and public debate (Ireland, 1994; Silverman, 1992). As this otherness became more familiar, its perception as legitimate and worthy of some recognition within the republican model produced the first conflicts of customs and norms. The reason was that the French conception was still stuck with the aim of assimilation, namely the reduction of immigrants' cultural and social specificities and their adjustment to the norms and values of the host society (Sayad, 1999). A system based on the firm conviction of a non-negotiable superiority. This cultural superiority was not only a privilege of the established against the outsiders, or the natives against the newcomers, it has found its roots in the French universalism.

The window of opportunity of 1983–84 quickly closed again with the sudden political expansion of the Front National. The emergence of "immigration" in political debate was due less to the disorders caused by massive flows of migrants gradually changing the face of major French cities, than to the refusal to open up the national model and a stiffening of "national identity." This resistance by the model also laid the bases for a resurgence of divisions from the colonial period and the demand for the recognition of memories made painful by being denied too long (Blanchard *et al.*, 2005). Although these developments occupied distinct positions, they were linked by their refusal of the French conception of integration, as it was used as a weapon of normalization and the restoration of the boundaries between "them and us."

At the end of the 1980s, the invention and promotion of the "French model of integration" marked a softening of, but not a break with, the assimilationist framework of thought. Although "immigrants" were now stakeholders in constructing "life in common," they were still perceived as exogenous to society and the enjoyment of equality of rights was subordinated to the accomplishment of duties left deliberately vague. These duties crystallized the integration controversy—and still do—since what is required of "immigrants," and more generally of all those who were required to "integrate," is defined by the majority group as the characteristics of an ideal citizen. Of course, most of the "natives" would not be eligible for integration if they were asked to perform a test using such criteria. References to national identity are used to exclude newcomers from the benefits attached to the belonging to the "national community." Rather as in an exclusive club, true citizenship is granted according to a "pedigree" acquired by seniority of residence and the adoption of norms, values, and practices that are more matters of culture than of political citizenship. The demands made of "immigrants" are designed to defend the pre-eminence of norms and practices that are those of a silent but powerful majority that intends to impose its supremacy over the many varied legacies and customs it does not recognize as its own (Guénif-Souilamas, 2006). A fiercely defended heritage also provides a definite advantage in the competition for education, employment, or accommodation. This asset is embodied in the slogan of "national preference," used in various forms by political forces that comprise more than the far right. This preference is only national in name, since those who are excluded may be foreigners or French-born citizens or whatever, but are ascribed a real or alleged origin that confines them to subaltern rights. The rhetoric of the "failure to integrate" has mainly reinforced the irremediable inferiority of "immigrants." It has also extended the frontier to their children. A process of creation of ethnic minorities appears to be well underway with their identification as a "second generation" and the expansion of systemic and institutional discriminations (Mouvements, 1999; Simon, 2000; 2003).

Since the early 1990s, various official reports and a few announcements from top government institutions have given a voice to an emerging concern with discrimination.[10] By placing the "principle of equality" at the very heart of the "French model of integration," the Conseil d'Etat's 1996 report triggered a debate on the possible consequences of cultural diversity in the population and the necessary adaptation of public action to this reality (Conseil d'Etat, 1997). This, in turn, brought about the conviction that illegitimate, if not downright illegal, differences in the way foreigners and indeed French citizens from minority ethnic or "racial" backgrounds are treated as well as unequal access to rights, goods, and services were a direct offence to the Republic's most fundamental values and at the same time undermined, by their very existence, any efforts towards restoring social cohesion.

While the report by the Conseil d'Etat came as a doctrinal legitimization for the suppression of any discrimination, it was beyond its authority to actually describe the mechanisms underpinning the phenomenon or its consequences. However, the feeling was that it was necessary to go beyond assertions of principle because even though those were widely accepted among the population, discrimination was still raging. Although racist and xenophobic attitudes are morally condemned, the number of acts of discrimination has, if not surged, at least increased while there is a growing feeling in public opinion that discrimination has become worse. Similarly, a wide consensus exists in the condemnation of racist and xenophobic attitudes and of their expression through daily acts of discrimination.[11]

The transposition of the EU directives taken in 2000 was achieved with three laws passed in 2001 (the 16 November 2001 Anti-Discrimination Act), 2002 (the 17 January 2002 Social Modernisation Act), and the recent new Anti-Discrimination Act (the 27 May 2008 Adaptation to European Law Act[12]) that has been voted in parliament. A specific law in 2005 also established the High Authority for the Fight Against Discrimination and for Equality (Haute autorité de Lutte contre les Discriminations et pour l'Egalité, HALDE), an independent equality body which addresses all motives of discrimination.

The strategy put forward by HALDE has been criticized for being too focused on litigation in court and poorly oriented towards positive action.

One issue is the debate on "positive discrimination" (a French neologism for "affirmative action") which is conceived as a topical US influence. Against all evidence, "positive discrimination" is also perceived as a British trade mark. And yet positive discrimination is widely practiced locally in France and is even becoming the main strategy adopted in education. The highly selective *grande école* Sciences Po has implemented "ZEP agreements" offering special admission procedures to students from high schools located in a few disadvantaged neighborhoods (Zones d'Éducation Prioritaires), in order to give them access to its higher education programs. After facing strong opposition and law suits in the name of equality of treatment, this example has been successful and copied by several *grandes écoles* (Sabbagh, 2002). The project of transposing the 10 percent plan from Texas to France, as a way to offer a direct admission for the 5 percent best pupils from high school to selective tracks (*écoles préparatoires*) is under review at the Ministry of Education and is strongly supported by some social scientists.[13]

Such increased awareness is, however, hampered by internal contradictions in the anti-discrimination framework:

- The interpretation and enforcement of the principle of equality tend to erase differences and lead to a failure to identify the criteria which are being overlooked in deviating from the principle of equality. The French conception of "colorblindness" actually prevents the perception of unfair treatment.
- Knowledge of the inner mechanisms of discrimination is still piecemeal and awareness campaigns are still allusive and lack of concrete targets. The specific contradictions of the "French model" are still an obstacle to a real recognition of the systemic and institutional dimensions of discrimination.
- All the above reasons explain why any action plan to fight discrimination rarely meets its objective. All too often, well-meaning declarations are not followed by effective policies with real resources. When it comes to ethnic and racial discrimination, equality policies remain formal and fail to promote effective equality. (Bleich, 2003)

All these developments show an emerging recognition of what is now called "diversity" and "minorities" in French debates. The conversion of big corporations to the promotion of equal opportunities for so-called "visible minorities" has ended in a new "diversity buzz." The process has begun at the beginning of the new millennium with the signature of framework-agreements between big businesses or an entire branch of the economy, representatives of the State, workers unions and state agencies. Parallel to these soft anti-discrimination policies, a Diversity Charter—without any legal value—has been implemented in the private sector, under the impetus of a report released in 2004 by the Montaigne Institute, a right-wing think tank, and widely covered by the media (Bébéar, 2004; Sabeg and Méhaignerie, 2004).

The Charter is mainly addressing human resources processes and awareness raising issues in an attempt to disseminate diversity management in the French economic circles. In October 2004, 40 CEOs signed the Charter, today more than 1800 firms have signed it.[14]

Despite these trends of action taking and awareness raising, the persisting influence of the republican categories, values and tradition hindered the shift of paradigms from assimilation to a more pluralist conception of the modes of incorporation. French society still has difficulties in representing itself as ethnically differentiated. It has even more difficulties in accepting the fact that French society itself and its institutions, private or public (school, police, hospital, social housing), play a role in reproducing those ethnic differences. The idea that French society is genuinely "anti-racist" and that discrimination has to be understood as mainly related to individual behavior prevents any strategy to cope with structural discriminations.[15] Last but not least, the increasing recognition of ethnic discriminations has triggered a competition between framings: the traditional framework of "social inequalities" is opposed to "racial hierarchies" (Fassin and Fassin, 2006), as if forms of domination should be understood as mutually exclusive, and not conceived in a pluralistic dimension. From this point of view, effective anti-discrimination policies will not be implemented at a short term.

Multicultural debates

The different crisis the traditional French model of integration has been through have generated intense and often violent debates in the political arena, as well as in the academic field. Those public debates and policy developments reveal some essential characteristics of the resistance to the emerging multicultural society. Among the numerous potential issues that could have been analyzed in this section (such as the cartoon affair, the debate on positive discrimination, etc.), we have chosen to evoke four "multicultural debates": the debates on postcolonialism, the November 2005 urban riots and their perceptions, the debates on *laïcité* and the headscarf affair, and finally the controversy on the so-called "ethnic statistics."

Postcolonialism

Since 2005, a growing debate has developed about the legacy of colonialism, the increasing "colonial divisions" and the debt of the French State towards the population of its former colonies, in North Africa, sub-Saharan Africa, and the West Indies (Blanchard *et al.*, 2005). The 10 May 2001 Taubira–Delannon Act, labeling slavery and slave trade as a crime against humanity, marked a first step in this recognition and led to solemn commemorations of the final French abolition of slavery (10 May 1848). In that context, the passing of the 23 February 2005 Act[16] (Mekachera Act), recognizing the contribution of French repatriates from North Africa (*pieds noirs*), triggered a scandal, because of its Article 4 asking official history curricula to give "the place that it deserves" to "the positive role played by the French presence overseas, especially in North Africa." This article was finally withdrawn after a petition of historians and a large mobilization against this rehabilitation of the colonial past (Bertrand, 2006).

In the meantime, there has been an increasing mobilization of the "victims" to ask for recognition, respect, and action against discrimination, as shown by the creation of the movement "We are the indigenous of the Republic" (Les indigènes de la république, January 2005) and of the Representative Council of Black Associations (Conseil representatif des associations noires, CRAN), uniting some 60 associations for the defense of black people. Claims for recognition of the legacy of slavery and colonial times and their persistent consequences in so-called "post-colonial society" are connected with the denunciation of discriminations. The idea of being more active in elections and presenting "black" candidates is also developing, with the candidacy of Christiane Taubira (Guyana) in the 2002 presidential election, although the presence of ethnic minorities remains slight in both local councils (Geisser, 1997) and Parliament. Ethnic minorities are poorly represented in political parties, on the right as well as on the left. The emergence of "black mobilization" engendered controversies on the danger of a competition between communities and memories. More generally, there is a growing division within the anti-racist movement. On the one hand, the traditional organizations such as SOS Racisme act as republican gate-keepers, stigmatizing any recognition of ethnic or racial minorities as an "ethnicization" of French society (Boutih, 2001; Sopo, 2005). On the other hand, new anti-racist organizations such as the CRAN or the Indigènes de la Republique call for the recognition of ethnic discrimination and of their particular identities and memories (Khiari, 2005).

The debate has also had an academic dimension, raising the question of the value or necessity of introducing a "post-colonial perspective" into French social sciences (Amiraux and Simon, 2006). The recent publication, in French, of a companion to postcolonial studies (Lazarus, 2006) and of several special issues of journals (Contretemps, 2006; Labyrinthe, 2006; Multitudes, 2006; Mouvements, 2007) may be seen as a sign that emerging recognition of post-colonial studies is likely to be "imported" for the analysis of the French experience. This new field of research, although tardy when compared to the Indian, British, Dutch, and US experiences, is still a controversial one and the extent to which postcolonial theories may apply to understanding the contemporary French situation is under discussion. Main critics about the use— and abuse according to the critics—of the postcolonial paradigm to describe and analyze the situation of racial minorities are focusing on the inaccuracy of the idea of a continuum between colonial times and the contemporary France.[17] The theory of the continuity of the colonial domination, or at least its long lasting sequels on contemporary France, is described as an historical fallacy which lacks of evidence. Opposing a logic of scientific expertise and a political claim, the post-colonial debate is somehow confused and misleading.

Urban riots

The 27 of October 2005 began an unprecedented cycle of civil unrests in France, after the violent death of two teenagers chased by the police forces in Clichy sous Bois (east suburb of Paris). During nearly 22 days, burning cars and public buildings and large-scale fights with police forces have taken place in more than 250 cities in France, mainly in deprived neighborhoods. Although no explicit claims have been put forward by rioters, most of the media and politicians have pointed out a "crisis of identity" (President Jacques Chirac, 10 November 2005) and a consequence of ethnic and racial discrimination. But the riots have also been predominantly framed by politicians, intellectuals, and media as an ethnic or religious uprising, as the symbol of an emergent communitarianism requiring a strong republican reaction. The then interior minister Nicolas Sarkozy spoke of getting rid of the "scum" of the estates and cleaning them out with a Kärcher high-pressure hose. The philosopher Alain Finkelkraut in a interview with an Israeli newspaper Haaretz called the events an "ethno-religious revolt;"[18] Hélène Carrère d'Encausse, perpetual secretary of the French Academy, saw their main cause in the "polygamy" of African families. The UMP deputy Jacques Myard called for the creation of "disciplinary battalions" to curb these "young people, French against their will, of Arabo-African descent."[19] Contrary to the discourses that overwhelmingly portrayed the riots as a collective identity crisis, many studies by social scientists (Lagrange and Oberti, 2006; Mucchielli and Le Goaziou, 2006) showed that social inequalities, police harassment, and racism against young people and racial discrimination were the main parameters of this tragic event.[20] The targets of the burnings and damages were mostly public premises—such as schools, post-offices, libraries, sport centers—or buses. The symbolic opposition to the welfare state calls for an explanation: something has failed and trust has been lost.

The political answer to the November 2005 riots was devastating. The first step was to launch a security emergency, with a curfew in a list of suburbs under an Act dating back to the Algerian war. The second answer was given with a new law called "Equal opportunity Act."[21] Although it is the first time that a law has been entitled "equal opportunity" in France, almost none of the articles dealt with anti-discrimination issues. The first objective of the Act was in line with the "traditional" territorial policy, i.e., the *politique de la ville*. Hence the main provision of the law is the creation of a national agency for social cohesion and equal opportunities (Agence nationale pour la cohésion sociale et l'égalité des chances, ANCSEC). This public body will carry out special projects in favor of social cohesion and equality of opportunities in "deprived neighborhoods." The problem is that, by maintaining the traditional territorial approach of the *politique de la ville*, such schemes tend to act as if ethnic discrimination could be treated as a territorial issue and ignore its structural dimension. The second orientation of the law is the "new" framing in terms of anti-discrimination and equal opportunity: strengthening of the powers of the Anti-discrimination agency (Haute autorité de lutte contre les discriminations, HALDE), anonymous CVs in hiring for enterprises of more than 50 employees, legal recognition of audit testing as evidence in discrimination cases in courts. Even if this can be seen as a reinforcement of the legal resources for fighting discrimination, these new provisions are still in the framework of a formal anti-discrimination policy. They do not include anything resembling a pro-active policy, with positive actions and duties of non-discrimination imposed on public and private institutions.

Laïcité *and the "headscarf affairs"*

Debates on religious symbols at school have been going on in France for years. During the 1970s, the theme of Islam was not greatly politicized and claims mainly targeted the creation of places of worship (Amiraux, 2005). Politicization of Islam really began with the first "Muslim headscarf affair" in 1989, when the director of a secondary school in Creil (near Paris) took the decision to exclude three young girls because he considered that their Muslim headscarf undermined the principle of *laïcité*. The Minister of Education Lionel Jospin asked the Conseil d'Etat to express its opinion on the legality of this exclusion. On 27 November 1989, the Conseil d'Etat stated that "The wearing of the headscarf does not contradict the values of the secular and republican school." It thus stated a liberal conception of *laïcité*, considering that the 1905 law on the separation of the Churches and of the State (usually called "law on *laïcité*") above all protects freedom of conscience and freedom of expression. The pupils can thus make use of their freedom of conscience. Only proselytism and the disturbance of school activities can lead to an exclusion. School directors were thus invited to assess the situations on a case-by-case basis.

The controversy returned in September 1994 with a regulation from the Minister of Education, which stated that the Muslim headscarf was "a conspicuous sign in itself" ("un signe ostentatoire en soi"), which thus displayed a proselytizing attitude, unlike the cross or the kippah.[22] The "Bayrou circular," as it is usually called, invited public schools to include in their school rules a provision forbidding "conspicuous signs." But, asked again to give its opinion after the exclusion of eighteen pupils from a secondary school in Strasbourg in October 1994, the Conseil d'Etat confirmed, on 10 July 1995, that the headscarf was not "a conspicuous sign in itself." It concluded that there could be neither a general prohibition nor a systematic exclusion of girls wearing the Muslim headscarf. It stated again that no sign was to be considered as "conspicuous" by nature and, referring to the 1905 law, it stated that a religious sign could not be in itself contrary to *laïcité*. Hence it maintained the position that it had defended in 1989.

Ten years later, the period 2003–4 was marked by an intense debate on the issue of the headscarf, widely covered in the media (Lorcerie, 2005; Tévanian, 2005). The President of the Republic Jacques Chirac set up the "Commission to examine the implementation of the principle of *laïcité* in the Republic," known as the "Stasi Commission." Just as the Stasi Commission started its public hearings in September 2003, the opening of the school year was marked by intense media coverage of the story of Alma and Lila, two sisters who were excluded from their secondary school in Aubervilliers because they refused to take off their headscarves.[23] The context was very different from that in 1989 and 1994. It was marked by increasing debates around Islam and increasing amalgams between Islam, "communitarianism," and "fundamentalism." The representation of Islam as a threat to the Republic, the principle of *laïcité*, and national identity had grown up during the 1990s. The context was marked, at the international level, by the post-9/11 political and intellectual climate of growing hostility to Islam and, at the national level, by the rise of a law and order political discourse.

The Commission gave its conclusions on 11 December 2003. Its final report[24] promoted a radical stance, as it proposed the adoption of a law forbidding religious signs in public schools. More precisely, the Commission proposed prohibiting the wearing of the headscarf in public schools, considering that the headscarf in itself was a conspicuous religious sign. Therefore, the Commission's proposal made a clear distinction between the Muslim headscarf (and also the kippah, even if it triggered much less debate), which should be totally forbidden in public schools, and other religious signs, that should be allowed, except if they were too conspicuous. Although the issue of the Muslim headscarf at school focused political and media attention, the report of the Stasi Commission ended with a series of proposals combining a strange mixture of strict respect of *laïcité* and a soft multiculturalism: reinforcement of the fight against racism and anti-Semitism at school and the adoption of a "Charter of *laïcité*" in public services; the strict respect of school's obligations and attendance to all of the curriculum and the accommodation of food in public canteens; the integration of the history of slavery, colonization, decolonization, and immigration in history curricula and recognition of Yom Kippur and Eid al-Adha as holidays in all public schools.

The report of the Commission was then used to launch a legislative process. After a three-month impassioned debate, a law "regulating, in application of the principle of *laïcité*, the wearing of signs or clothes displaying a religious affiliation in public primary, secondary and high schools" was passed on 15 March 2004.[25] The law contains only one article: "In public primary, secondary and high schools, the wearing of signs or clothes through which the pupils conspicuously display a religious affiliation is forbidden. The school rules shall specify that the implementation of a disciplinary procedure is preceded by a dialogue with the pupil." An administrative instruction of 18 May 2004 specified its conditions of application. It was published on 22 May 2004.[26] It states that "the prohibited signs and clothes are those by which, whatever they may be called, a person is immediately identified by his or her religious beliefs, such as the Muslim headscarf, the kippah or a cross of manifestly excessive dimension." Hence it adopted the position promoted by the Stasi Commission.

Considerations of space preclude the rehearsal of the case made for or against this law. The impressive number of books published during and after the legislative process reveals the importance of the topic in both intellectual and political debates. Considering the multiculturalist agenda, there is a pre- and post-law world. The tolerance for negative representations of Islam progressed considerably after this debate, and conversely the tolerance of public expression of cultural difference declined (Deltombe, 2005). As John Bowen has observed in the conclusion of his thoughtful overview of the debate on the headscarves, "Muslims who demand the right to be visibly different defy older cultural notions of France, not the political and legal framework of the Republic" (Bowen, 2007: 249).

The controversy about "ethnic statistics"[27]

The increasing recognition of ethnic discriminations has triggered a large debate between social scientists, activists, and policy makers on how to measure discrimination and how to name its victims. Debates around the so-called "ethnicization" of statistics have been particularly lively for a decade, as the idea to introduce ethnic categories in official statistics, or even only in social statistics collected by researchers, is perceived as in total contradiction with the principle of undifferentiation.

The controversy came out a year before the census of 1999, when the French press stated rumors of a plan to introduce ethnic categories in the census questionnaire. Since the end of the nineteenth century, the census collects information on the place of birth and the citizenship of the population, but has never asked about "ethnicity," nor "race" or religion. This political choice has been challenged by the need to produce accurate and reliable data on ethnic and racial discrimination. Amid a blaze of press articles, the controversy pitted a number of researchers ready to denounce the idea as part of a drift toward radicalization against a few researchers who called for modifying the statistical system. The issue covered two different dimensions: 1) making the diversity of the French population visible through its statistical description; 2) understanding the logics of inequalities based on ethnic and racial stratification. Both of these logics are of course challenging the "French model of integration" (Simon and Stavo-Debauge, 2004).

When the controversy resumed in 2004, the issue of statistics no longer concerned only the sphere of social scientists; it had become a political issue. The desire to make discrimination more conspicuous created more pressing needs for statistical data. References to skin color or to "visible minorities" had become omnipresent. Two petitions published in daily journals within less than a month of each other advocated opposing positions. In the first one—"Engagement républicain contre les discriminations" (Republican commitment against discrimination)[28]—the signatories argued that it was possible to combat discrimination effectively by using currently available statistics and limiting oneself to audit testing. The dangers of ethno-racial categorization were put forward to justify the use of alternative methods presumed to be operational so as to avoid the creation of "ethnic statistics." Sponsors of the petition sought to defend the "Republican model," worried as they were about the risk of sliding into ethnic conflicts and drifting into affirmative action. As a reaction to this petition, a manifesto was then published in the daily *Le Monde*.[29] The signatories—including the present authors—did not propose adopting a predefined set of categories; rather, they called attention to the deficiencies of current statistics as a basis for pursuing an anti-discrimination policy. They argued that, given the systemic discrimination that occurs in France, as in any other multicultural and postcolonial society, the use of accurate statistics was an indispensable tool and that the alternative methods proposed by opponents met neither the needs of research nor those of political action.

Because the issues in this controversy have clearly gone beyond what is customary in academic and technical debate, the discussions have attracted a great deal of media coverage, which in turn has made them all the more violently polemical. Concepts or principles of analysis are not the only matters involved: the opponents of "ethnic statistics" have rather sought to intervene, in the name of science, against what they see as a political danger. Apart from the various arguments against "ethnic statistics," the main issue is that statistics would reveal divisions within the French "République une et indivisible." Even if the groups identified by statistics would be used to monitor equal access to goods and services and the effective equality of opportunities, the side effect would be to reify ethnic groups, or even "races," whereas the main strategy against racism was to delegitimize the idea of race itself.

Let us close this discussion of the case against statistics by looking at the terminological pitfalls that beset the French-speaking world. While the terms race, ethnic group, or ethnicity are commonly used in English-speaking countries, they are highly charged objects of criticism in France. That being the case, could we not use other signifiers instead of "ethnic" and "racial" that would still preserve the meaning that has been attributed to them? A detour through geography, "culture" or national origin, however, raises some delicate issues. The notion of "culture" is scarcely more consistent (or less controversial) than that of "ethnicity," since using it tends to attribute explanatory power to the most obvious "cultural" features (notably language and religion) at the expense of more political and social dimensions of ethnicity. As for geography, which postulates the primacy of a territorial relationship and sees migration as the founding event of ethnicity, its relevance—already debatable but plausible with respect to immigrants—is more than doubtful with respect to their descendants. For them ethnicity has less to do with a continuous tie to a territory or national origin than with an individual's socialization in the family and in the educational milieu (communalization, to borrow a concept from Weber). It is a matter more of history than of geography. Indeed, the debate about "ethnic statistics" is itself best understood in light of the very special relation the Republican model has to history. The difficulty in taking into account, much less overcoming, colonial history as well as the way immigration has been managed by the Republic remains at the core of the controversy over statistics—at its core, but never fully acknowledged.

Conclusion

Since the beginning of the new millennium, the hegemony of the integration paradigm is challenged by the growing concern for discrimination. Equal opportunity policies have been on the agenda in response to internal pressure (the crisis of the "French model of integration") and incentives from the EU Commission. One could have expected a replacement of the old paradigm by the new one, but the current situation looks like an unstable cohabitation. Political tensions and intellectual confusion are resulting from this strange combination of conflicting paradigms. Indeed, when the integration policy seeks for a reduction of cultural specificities and actively generates invisibility of minorities to produce social cohesion, anti-discrimination policy promotes diversity and relies on a recognition and identification of groups and minorities (Simon and Stavo-Debauge, 2004).

This contradiction can also be observed at the EU level with the develop-ment of an "integration agenda" parallel to the anti-discrimination strategy. The quest for a harmonized European integration policy is gaining in cred-ibility, step by step. The bombings in London and Madrid, and the murders of Pim Fortuyn and Theo van Gogh in the Netherlands have fostered the efforts to implement "common basic principles for immigrant integration." These "basic principles" have been adopted by the European council in November 2004 and defined integration as "a dynamic, two-way process of mutual accommodation by all immigrants and residents of Member States," which "implies the respect of the basic values of the European Union." These principles have incorporated the contradiction between the respect for diverse cultures and religion, anti-discrimination concern, but also promotion of "European values" and, through the notion of "basic knowledge of the host society's language and history," a perceptive of uniformization of cultures and belongings. This tension clearly echoes Christian Joppke's analysis of a potent anti-discrimination framework that rests on a form of "equal opportunity liberalism," when governments simultaneously promote a backlash in favor of civic integration policies for immigrants that imply a form of "disciplinary liberalism" (Joppke, 2007).

The pendulum seems to swing back again to the assimilationist side. In France, according to the new immigration Act,[30] proofs of integration—including proficiency in French language—have been required for delivering a resident permit. The creation of a "ministry of immigration, integration, national identity and co-development" is a clear signal. The hard right-wing law-and-order approach to immigration policy promoted by the minister and the government in general tends to clash with the anti-discrimination priorities. Yet, French society, like all multicultural societies, is faced with a process of ethno-racial stratification that contributes to the formation of a system of discrimination. Reversely, everyday racism and racial discrimination are re-activating ethno-racial labels that have been designed, for some of them, during the colonial times. France's integration model has not prepared the country to provide any answers, nor any frames to figure out these processes. On the contrary, this model has helped to shape the system of discrimination in two ways: 1) by repeating a pejorative reading of the expression of otherness in political and social life, which reinforces stereotypes and prejudices; and 2) by obfuscating ethnic and racial divisions. Indeed, and paradoxically, the founding myth of equality fosters a denial of inequalities based on ethnic or racial origin.

Notes

1 This chapter uses some of the material collected for the European project EMILIE "A European Approach to Multicultural Citizenship. Legal Political and Educational Challenges," funded by the European Commission RTD DG, Sixth Framework Programme, 2006–9. Website: http://www.eliamep.gr/eliamep/content/home/research/research_projects/emilie/en/

2 To echo the title of a recent appraisal of assimilation by Alba and Nee (2003).

3 Although Durkheim has never thought explicitly integration as an individual characteristic, and certainly not in relation with migrants or any ethnic minority.

4 *Communautarisme* is an idiosyncratic French concept which is virtually impossible to translate into English (like *laïcité*).

5 This is a revised and more precise version of the definition presented in the first HCI report (HCI, 1993, p. 8).

6 Note the circumlocution that obscures rather than clarifies any appropriate term.

7 The degree of "openness" of the code of nationality is a matter of dispute since the granting of nationality is partially a specific attribute of the State. Although there are few refusals, especially on grounds of "lack of assimilation," there is a reported increase in adjournments on grounds of job insecurity, which in turn has an aggravating effect on the economic instability of migrant populations. Adjournment criteria in cases of lack of professional employment were eased at the end of 1998, in order to better take into account all "insertion efforts made by applicants." Linguistic proficiency in French is becoming one of the main criteria not only in naturalization procedures, but also for issuing residence permits to new migrants.

8 The HCI tries to balance the acknowledgement of the legitimacy of the ties and solidarities between ethnic groups with the warning of the danger in cultivating "long lasting community gatherings" and even more so to any institutional recognition of them.

9 "*Cité de transit*" was the generic name for the low-cost social housing built to rehouse the inhabitants expelled from shanty towns during the Urban renewal programs (1969–75).

10 The 1996 public report by the Conseil d'Etat deals with the "principle of equality" and the report by the High Council for Integration for 1998 addresses the "struggle against discrimination" (HCI, 1998). The Minister of Employment and Solidarity, Martine Aubry, made this a central issue in an attempt to re-stimulate the integration policy (Council of Ministers of 21 October 1998) and the Minister of the Interior, Jean-Pierre Chevènement, announced on 25 January 1999 the creation of

the Department Commissions for Access to Citizenship (Commissions Départementales d'Accès à la Citoyenneté or CODAC). Mr Chevènement defined the objectives of the CODAC in a letter to préfets in the following way: "helping young people born of immigrant parents to find a job and a position in society, and to combat the discrimination that they are confronted with in the spheres of employment, housing and leisure." In February 1999, J.-M. Belorgey wrote a report on the institutional organization of the struggle against discrimination (Belorgey, 1999).

11 The last Eurobarometer on discrimination (Eurobarometer, 2008) testifies that French population is very sensitive to ethnic discrimination, since France ranked at the third place in EU27 (76 percent of respondents do consider that ethnic discrimination is widespread in the country). They are nevertheless among the most critical on the policies tackling with discrimination: 38 percent of French respondents consider that "enough effort is made in France to fight all forms of discrimination," where the average in EU27 is at 47 percent and the highest proportions has to found in Finland with 66 percent.

12 http://admi.net/jo/20080528/MTSX0769280L.html.

13 See the report of the French American Foundation for the program "Equality of opportunity in Education and Employment: French American perspectives" (Kholer and Sabbagh, 2008): http://www.frenchamerican.org/cms/programreports. See as well one of the prominent advocate for this plan in France (Weil, 2005b).

14 The charter can be read at: http://www.charte-diversite.com/.

15 The anti-racist organization "SOS racisme" offers a topical illustration of this framing. See the recent book of its president (Sopo, 2005).

16 Loi no. 2005–2158 du 23 février 2005 portant reconnaissance de la Nation et contribution nationale en faveur des Français rapatriés, J.O 46 du 24 février 2005. Cf. http://www.admi.net/jo/20050224/DEFX0300218L.html.

17 See Saada, 2006 or Bertrand, 2006 for an example of these argumentations.

18 Haaretz, 17 November 2005.

19 Libération, 29 November 2005.

20 For a review of the different writings about the riots, see Sala Pala, 2006.

21 Loi no. 2006–2396 du 31 mars 2006.

22 For a discussion of these early affairs, see Gaspard and Khosrokhavar, 1995.

23 "Lila et Alma ne retourneront plus au lycée Henri-Wallon", Le Monde, 12 October 2003; "Alma et Lila à découvert," Le Monde, 15 February 2004.

24 Commission de réflexion sur l'application du principe de laïcité dans la République (2003), Rapport au Président de la République, remis le 11 décembre 2003, Paris, Présidence de la République, p. 78 This report is on line on http://www.ladocumentationfrancaise.fr/rapports-publics/034000725/index.shtml.

25 Loi no. 2004–2228 du 15 mars 2004 encadrant, en application du principe de laïcité, le port de signes ou de tenues manifestant une appartenance religieuse dans les écoles, collèges et lycées publics. J.O no. 65 du 17 mars 2004 page 5190. Cf. http://www.legifrance.gouv.fr/WAspad/UnTexteDeJorf?numjo=MENX0400001L (20 March 2007).

26 Circulaire relative à la mise en oeuvre de la loi no. 2004–2228 du 15 mars 2004 encadrant, en application du principe de laïcité, le port de signes ou de tenues manifestant une appartenance religieuse dans les écoles, collèges et lycées publics (18.05.2004) (JORF no. 118, 22 May 2004 p. 9033). www.education.gouv.fr/bo/2004/21/MENG0401138C.htm (20 March 2007).

27 Parts of this sub-chapter are issued from (Simon, 2008) to which we refer for more details on the controversy.

28 *Libération*, 23 February 2007.

29 "Des statistiques contre les discriminations," *Le Monde*, 13 March 2007.

30 Loi no. 2007–1631 du 20 novembre 2007 relative à la maîtrise de l'immigration, à l'intégration et à l'asile.

References

Alba, R. and Nee, V. (2003) *Remaking the American Mainstream: Assimilation and contemporary immigration*, Cambridge, MA: Harvard University Press.

Amiraux, V. (2005) "Discrimination and claims for equal rights amongst Muslims in Europe", in J. Cesari and S. McLoughlin (eds) *European Muslims and the Secular State*, Aldershot: Ashgate, pp. 25–38.

Amiraux, V. and Simon, P. (2006) "There are no minorities here: Cultures of scholarship and public debates on immigration and integration in France", *International Journal of Comparative Sociology*, 47 (3–4): 191–215.

Amselle, J.-L. (1996) *Vers un multiculturalisme français: l'empire de la coutume*, Paris: Flammarion.

Bébéar, C. (2004) *Des entreprises aux couleurs de la France, Rapport au Premier Ministre*, Paris: La Documentation française.

Belorgey, J.-M. (1999) *"Lutter contre les discriminations", Rapport à Madame la ministre de l'emploi et de la solidarité*, Paris: La Documentation française.

Bertrand, R. (2006) *Mémoires d'empire. La controverse autour du "fait colonial"*, Paris: Ed. Du Croquant.

Blanchard, P., Bancel, N., and Lemaire, S. (ed.) (2005) *La fracture coloniale: la société française au prisme de l'héritage colonial*, Paris: La Découverte.

Bleich, E. (2003) *Race Politics in Britain and France: Ideas and Policymaking since the 1960s*, Cambridge: Cambridge University Press.

Bouamama, S. (1994) *Dix ans de marche des Beurs. Chronique d'un mouvement avorté*, Paris: Desclée de Brouwer.

Boutih, M. (2001) *La France aux Français? Chiche!*, Paris: Editions Mille et une nuits.

Bowen, J. (2007) *Why the French Don't Like Headscarves: Islam, the State, and Public Space*, Princeton: Princeton University Press.

Conseil d'Etat (1997) *Rapport public 1996 du Conseil d'Etat—Sur le principe d'égalité*, Paris: La Documentation Française, Notes et Documents no. 48.

Contretemps (2006) *Postcolonialisme et immigration*, no. 16.

Deltombe, T. (2005) *L'Islam imaginaire. La construction médiatique de l'islamophobie en France, 1975–2005*, Paris: La Découverte.

Eurobarometer (2008) Discrimination in the European Union: Perceptions, experiences and attitudes, Special Eurobarometer 296, DG Employment, Social Affairs and Equal Opportunities, July.

Fassin, D. (2002) "L'invention française de la discrimination", *Revue française de science politique*, 52 (4): 403–23.

Fassin, D. and Fassin, E. (ed.) (2006) *De la question sociale à la question raciale? Représenter la société française*, Paris: La Découverte.

Favell, A. (1998) *Philosophies of Integration: Immigration and the idea of citizenship in France and Britain*, London: Palgrave Macmillan.

Garbaye, R. (2005) *Getting into Local Power: The politics of ethnic minorities in British and French cities*, Oxford: Blackwell.

Gaspard, F. and Khosrokhavar, F. (1995) *Le foulard et la République*, Paris: La Découverte.

Geisser, V. (1997) *L'ethnicité républicaine. Les élites d'origine maghrébine dans le système politique français*, Paris: PFNSP.

Guénif-Souilamas, N. (ed.) (2006) *La République mise à nu par son immigration*, Paris: La Fabrique.

Haut Conseil à l'intégration (1993) *L'intégration à la française*, Paris: UGE 10/18.

——(1998) *Lutte contre les discriminations: faire respecter le principe d'égalité, Rapport au premier ministre*, Paris: La Documentation Française.

Joppke, C. (2007) "Tranformation of Immigrant Integration. Civic Integration and Antidiscrimination in the Netherlands, France and Germany", *World Politics*, 59(2): 243–73.

Ireland, P. (1994) *The Policy Challenge of Ethnic Diversity: Immigrant Politics in France and Switzerland*, Cambridge, MA: Harvard University Press.

Khiari, S. (2005) *Pour une politique de la racaille. Immigrés, indigènes et jeunes de banlieue*, Paris: Textuel.

Kholer, I. and Sabbagh, D. (2008) *Promouvoir l'égalité des chances dans l'enseignement supérieur sélectif: l'expérience américaine des percentage plan et sa pertinence dans le contexte français*, French American Foundation. Online. Available http: http://www.frenchamerican.org/cms/programreports

Labyrinthe (2006) *Faut-il être postcolonial?* 24.

Lagrange, H. and Oberti, M. (ed.) (2006) *Emeutes urbaines et protestations. Une singularité française*, Paris: Presses de Sciences Po.

Lazarus, N. (ed.) (2006) *Penser le postcolonial. Une introduction critique (The Cambridge companion to postcolonial literacy studies)*, Paris: Editions Amsterdam.

Lorcerie, F. (1994) "Les sciences sociales au service de l'identité nationale", in D.-C. Martin (dir.) *Cartes d'identité. Comment dit-on "nous" en politique?* Paris: Presses de la FNSP.

Lorcerie, F. (ed.) (2005) *La politisation du voile. L'affaire en France, en Europe et dans le monde arabe*, Paris: L'Harmattan.

Mouvements (1999) *Le modèle français de discrimination: Un nouveau défi pour l'antiracisme*, 4.

——(2007) *Qui a peur du postcolonial? Déni et controverses*, 51.

Mucchielli, L. and Le Goaziou, V. (ed.) (2006) *Quand les banlieues brûlent ... Retour sur les émeutes de novembre 2005*, Paris: La Découverte.

Multitudes (2006), *Postcolonial et politique de l'histoire*, 26, October.

Saada, E. (2006) "Un racisme de l'expansion. Les discriminations raciales au regard des situations colonials", in D. Fassin. and E. Fassin (ed.) *De la question sociale à la question raciale?* Paris: La Découverte, pp. 55–71.

Sabbagh, D. (2002) "Affirmative action at sciences Po", *French Politics, Culture, and Society*, 20 (3): 52–64.

Sabeg, Y., Méhaignerie, L. (2004) *Les oubliés de l'égalité des chances*, Paris: Hachette Littératures.

Sala Pala, V. (2006) "Novembre 2005: sous les émeutes urbaines, la politique", *French Politics, Culture and Society*, 24 (3): 111–29.

Sayad, A. (1999) *La double absence: des illusions de l'émigré aux souffrances de l'immigré*, Paris: Seuil.

Schnapper, D. (1991) *La France de l'intégration. Sociologie de la nation en 1990*, Paris: Gallimard.

Silverman, M. (1992) *Deconstructing the Nation: Immigration, Racism and Citizenship in Modern France*, London: Routledge.

Simon, P. (2000) "Les jeunes de l'immigration se cachent pour vieillir. Représentations sociales et catégories de l'action publique", *VEI Enjeux*, 121: 23–38.

——(2003) "France and the Unknown Second Generation", *International Migration Review*, 37(4): 1091–1119.

——(2008) "The choice of ignorance: the debate on ethnic and racial statistics in France", *French Politics, Culture & Society*, 26–1: 7–31.

Simon, P and Stavo-Debauge, J. (2004) "Les politiques anti-discrimination et les statistiques: paramètres d'une incoherence", *Sociétés Contemporaines*, 53: 57–84.

Sopo, D. (2005), *SOS Antiracisme*, Paris: Denoël.

Tévanian, P. (2005), *Le voile médiatique. Un faux débat: "l'affaire du foulard islamique"*, Paris: Raisons d'agir.

Weil, P. (2005a) *Qu'est-ce qu'un Français? Histoire de la nationalité française depuis la révolution*, Paris: Gallimard.

——(2005b) *La république et sa diversité: immigration, intégration, discriminations*, Paris: Seuil.

Wieviorka, M. (ed.) (1996) *Une société fragmentée? Le multiculturalisme en débat*, Paris: La Découverte.

6   Denmark versus multiculturalism[1]

Ulf Hedetoft

Introduction

As the infamous cartoon case has demonstrated, Denmark and multiculturalism are strange bedfellows. Indeed, in a very real sense 'Danish multiculturalism' is an oxymoronic notion. Over the last decade, leading Danish politicians, from all agenda-setting parties, not just the present government, have repeatedly stressed that Denmark is not and does not intend to be a multicultural society; positive discrimination is never contemplated as a solution to integration problems; descriptive representation of ethnic minorities in political life is rejected; and cultural diversity more broadly is officially frowned on as an alien, 'un-Danish' notion (Hedetoft 2006a; Hervik 2006; see also note 25).

Unsurprisingly, all this is not a reflection of a nation state which has successfully stemmed ethnic diversity, kept globalization at bay, and halted migration at the Danish borders. Rather it articulates the principled view that an increasingly (though reluctantly) multi-*ethnic* society does not have to become politically multi*cultural*, but can insist on (and impose on immigrants and descendants) its cultural and historical identity in the face of global challenges. In that sense, Danish integration policies are necessarily assimilationist, though the word itself is usually eschewed. And though they may appear both contradictory and irrational, they have their own historical logic. This is a logic, however, that is currently under siege and is leading not just to more stridently cultural nationalism, shriller Islamophobia, and nostalgic notions of Denmark for the Danes (Trads 2002), but also to an ongoing, but somewhat covert, re-articulation of integration policies and discourses in order to take account of diversity and cope with unprecedented consequences of globalization. In this sense, Denmark is currently a country characterized by closet, street-level diversity practices, though the closet is only opened temporarily, and multicultural initiatives are introduced as makeshift measures by officials working on integration projects in municipalities, in residential neighbourhoods, or in the corporate world, where diversity management enjoys increased popularity.

The main part of this essay will try to unravel the whys and wherefores of these processes. The last part broadens the vision to contemplate the interesting comparative case of Denmark's Scandinavian sibling, Sweden, where, unlike Denmark, multiculturalism has been official integration policy for over 30 years. The point is both to demonstrate that in spite of similar historical paths toward modernity and similar political and social structures, small welfare-states based on culturally homogeneous histories do not necessarily spawn assimilationist integration policies. But it is also to expose the current normative problems of multiculturalism in Sweden (as well as a host of other countries) in the context of the problems ethnic assimilationism is encountering in Denmark. The conclusion is that we are seeing new configurations emerge between diversity and monoculturalism in both countries, and that it is reasonable to interpret these developments as a reflection of increasing convergence between two formerly very different models for handling diversity.

A politics of ethnic consensus

A central passage in a leading article[2] in the Danish daily *Jyllands-Posten*, appearing on 17 June 2003, argued that 'this is all about what makes a modern society function. And to that end, not all cultures are equally good.'[3] The occasion was a Government White Paper on integration, titled *The Government's Visions and Strategies for Better Integration* (June, 2003, henceforth GWP).[4] The passage is as revealing as the White Paper itself. 'Integration' of immigrants and their descendants is now debated and resolved in terms of 'culture' as the pivotal benchmark, not just in the sense of culture as a relative notion, but an absolute and axiomatic yardstick of 'core values' (*'fundamentale grundværdier'*),[5] which newcomers must be measured by and before which 'their own' culture must yield. In this political and discursive context, multiculturalism not only does not belong, but is a notion that must be decisively rejected.

In addition, the concept of culture conjured up here is not the 'thin' concept of cultural relativism or a multi-layered notion of culture (see, e.g., Suárez-Orozco 2002), but a thick, condensed, and politicized bundle of non-contestable values, behavioural practices, and universal orientations imagined to guarantee the functionality of 'a modern society'. Such explicit demands for cultural transformation represent a novel consensual discourse in Denmark – currently wrapped in the tinsel foil of a much-needed '*kultur-kamp*' ('cultural battle'), which is not only directed at coping with the external menace of immigration, but is simultaneously targeted at the enemy within, the Old Guard of 'cultural radicals', their putative defence of 'soft values', their ill-concealed admiration for leftist values, and their wrong-headed Europeanism and cosmopolitanism.

What is new, however, is not the assimilationist discourse itself, but, first, its near-total political hegemony (it has entirely superseded former discourses of humanitarianism, tolerance, and compassion); second, the nexus between 'culture', 'cohesion', and 'social functionality' that underlies both discourses and policies in the integration domain in an ever more intimate fashion; and, third, the way in which it has nevertheless, on its own terms and within a new kind of logic, started to assimilate what I have here chosen to term 'pluri-cultural discourses' ('we must leave room for diversity and learn to benefit from it', as the GWP *Resumé* has it).[6] Before delving further into this new type of ethnic policy regime in Denmark, it is relevant to diagnose a few other representative events in light of the transformative process of immigration/integration discourse and politics over the past decade.

The present Liberal–Conservative government came to office in November 2001, ousting the old Social Democratic/Radical (i.e. social-liberal) Party coalition after a general election largely fought on the issue of immigration. The then opposition parties, including the Danish People's Party (DPP), which now provides parliamentary backing for the government, accused the governing coalition of inconsequential, ambivalent, and far too lenient poli-cies and practices in the domain of asylum-seekers and refugees (integration, family reunification, residence permits and citizenship, and much more), ulti-mately prevailing in an election fought – in a post-9/11 atmosphere domi-nated by widespread Islamophobia – on a rather populist agenda promising stricter controls (fewer immigrants, more severe conditions for residence, reunification, and naturalization) and tougher policies such as increased demands on those who make it into the country or are already in Denmark. The general tone of the debate was acrimonious, bordering on vengeful, immigration being projected as the most imminent and most serious threat to the history, culture, identity, and homogeneity of 'little Denmark'.

The governing coalition, somewhat to its surprise, found itself on the defensive, in spite of having pushed through an array of proposals, policies, and practices over the previous five to six years which all contributed toward a tighter Danish immigration and integration regime.[7] While the opposition, astutely capitalizing on a debating climate pervaded by diffuse fears, moral panics, and unspecified enemy images, created expectations that not only could they put a virtual stop to any further inflows of undesirable aliens, but would also be able to reinstate Denmark to its imagined former status as a peaceful, stable, ethnically homogeneous, and politically sovereign welfare state – in other words to roll back or at least counterbalance the adverse effects of globalization and Europeanization. The opposition, thus, success-fully projected itself as the authentic and legitimate spokespersons for the people against their elites, who had let them down and allowed their true identity to be compromised.

In an important sense, therefore, the present government owes its life to the question of immigration and depends for its continued popular backing lar-gely on restrictive policies and successes in this field. However, the picture has recently become somewhat muddied by the need to import foreign labour into an economy where labour shortages are an urgent problem.

Consequently, one of the government's first initiatives was to create a new and separate ministry for these matters (*The Ministry for Refugees, Immi-grants, and Integration*), which had previously been handled by the Ministry of the Interior. Second, the tone set in the election campaign was continued by not just a barrage of tougher policy proposals, but, equally importantly, by a matching no-nonsense discourse of responsible behaviour, demands, values, obligations, and self-reliance – a heavily ideologized, value-ridden discourse mixing particularistic demands for national acculturation and expressions of gratitude for being allowed to live in the country, with a *laissez-faire*, self-help message of market-oriented individualism: 'prove that you can fend for yourselves', in the process relieving the state of financial burdens.

Accordingly, the prime minister, Anders Fogh Rasmussen, in his New Year's Speech to the Danish people, aired 1 January 2003, emphasized that 'Danish society rests on certain fundamental values which must be accepted by people wanting to live here', that these values are currently being 'challenged', and that Danes differ from many immigrants in having a freedom-loving and rights-respecting culture which will not allow gender discrimination, the politicization of religion, or genital mutilation. The toleration of such practices hitherto was characterized as 'gullible' (*tossegode*) attitudes: 'we have not dared to say out loud that certain things are better than others. But that is what we have to do now', as the prime minister put it, continuing to assert – in defence of the well-behaved immigrants – that he would not permit 'those who fled the darkness of the Mullahs to experience that … medieval forces find fertile soil in Danish society' (text of the speech can be seen in *Politiken*, 2 January 2003).

This discourse and the policy initiatives that have continuously flowed from the new ministry, first under the leadership of Bertel Haarder, later Rikke Hvilshøj, and now Birthe Rønn Hornbech – particularly the 24-year age threshold for transnational marriages allegedly intended to curb family reunification[8] – inspired a leading article in another national Danish daily, *Politiken* (18 January 2002), to characterize the new government's policies as focussed on 'ethnic purity' and on 'protecting the Danish tribe' (Gundelach 2002; Mellon 1992), which supposedly 'cannot abide being mixed with other inhabitants of the globe'. Hence, Denmark is to be 'protected against immigration', a project which in the view of the columnist is as depressing as it is illusory. 'Denmark for the Danes' may have been the state of affairs in the past, but is supposedly impossible in the present and future of globalization.

The counter-argument commonly heard is twofold: One is pragmatically functional – effective integration cannot be had without severe limitations on immigration.[9] However, on the background of the programmatic culturalism of the prime minister's speech (and a host of similar discourses), the functional argument comes across as unconvincing pragmatism packaging a real motive of protecting the Danish *ethnie* and the benefits of its cultural cohesiveness. The functionality lies here – not in any necessary limitation/integration nexus and the sophisticated statistical 'numbers game' that routinely accompanies it[10] – but in the political, institutional, and social realities of the Danish welfare state, which are thoroughly geared to and rooted in what Benedict Anderson (1983/1991) has termed the 'horizontal comradeship' of this political community and the tacit cultural normativities that underpin and partly constitute it.

This essentialist undergirding of the functional position also appears as an independent argument in its own right. Ideological spokespersons for the preservation of historical Danishness (especially – but far from exclusively – belonging to or sympathizing with the DPP) hardly ever justify their attack on immigration in functional, but preferably in existential, often apocalyptic terms. In April 2002, for instance, a central representative of the DPP, MP and vicar in the Church of Denmark, Søren Krarup, during the First Reading in Parliament of a proposal for the 'naturalization' of a number of named foreign citizens, argued that 'Danes are increasingly becoming foreigners in their own country ... Parliament is permitting the slow extermination of the Danish people.' He continued by predicting that 'our descendants' will 'curse' those politicians who are responsible for the increasing 'alienation of Danes in Denmark'. By admitting immigrants, Parliamentarians allegedly fail to 'take care of Denmark' and to 'safeguard the future of the Danes'. On this reading, the consensual compact of homogeneous Danishness is in danger of breaking down, due to politicians' betrayal of the national cause. The external menace – globalization as represented by hordes of cultural aliens – has entered into an unholy alliance with 'our own' elites, people elected to defend our interests and our collective historical destiny. It is this collusion, whether intended or not, which is supposedly putting the very future of Danishness in jeopardy.[11]

It is noteworthy that these statements are made by a political actor who sees himself and his party as the authentic representatives of Danish values, and who is much closer to the government and central processes than the politicians he fulminates against. This fact reveals such nationalist indignation as far removed from the powerless rantings of marginalized and 'alienated' groups. Rather, Krarup and his associates are on the rampage, settling the score with old political opponents of the 'cultural-radical' kind, constructing enemy imagery and moral panics for the revitalization of Danish nationalism in an ethno-religious mode blending nostalgia and fundamentalism,[12] and simultaneously making inroads on traditional social-democratic welfare territory. For despite the existentialism of Krarup's concerns for the survival of the special Danish species, the welfare state is very pragmatically at the heart of DPP policies when it comes to showing the way forward and identifying adequate political instruments. Immigration is projected as a threat both to historical Danishness and to the civic solidarity of all citizens, which the welfare state encapsulates (Brochmann and Hagelund 2005; Geddes 2003; Swank 2002). Welfare is all for the good and good for all, as long as this 'all' only involves authentic Danes who truly belong. In this way, welfare policies and the welfare state become focally linked to the Danish migration and asylum regime in a way that precludes multiculturalism. Simultaneously the strident rhetoric of ethnic consensualists draws its sap from a multi-ethnic context that can no longer be ignored.

Small states, homogeneity, and immigration

In *Small States in World Markets* (1985), Peter Katzenstein focused on the 'democratic corporatism' of small European states, emphasizing their vulnerability to change, dependence on world markets, open economies, and the resultant mechanisms deployed to avoid or deflect dysfunctional internal consequences: social partnership, centralized and concentrated system of interest groups, solution of conflicts through political bargaining and compromise. International pressures become funnelled through different domestic structures attempting to compensate for external fluctuations. The welfare systems of small states like the Nordic countries are thus set in the context of handling such external pressures springing from globalization. Global processes meet different domestic structures and capacities for absorption of change and 'shock'. Smallness is linked to cultural and historical homogeneity and provides the conceptual framework for explaining the robustness and relative success of many smaller nation states in a turbulent international environment (Campbell *et al.* 2006; see also Cohen and Clarkson 2004).

There are, however, important differences between the state of globalization in the early 1980s and now. Global processes have picked up speed, the differentiation between weak and strong states has been aggravated, the systems competition of the Cold War is gone, and the cultural diversity of national societies has increased due to migratory processes (Bauman 1998; Baylis and Smith 1997; Hedetoft 2003a; Hirst and Thompson 1996). In this context, and given that a compromise culture across interest groups and social groups has been a facilitator of national success and a cushion against external shocks, the current defence of Danish identity in the face of immigration can be seen as rooted in perceived effects of sovereignty erosion, rooted in the challenge that immigration from third countries poses to the politico-cultural framework which has historically ensured flexibility, adaptability, and consensualism. In other words: the combination of 'smallness', 'homogeneity', and 'success' – via flexible pragmatism externally and domestic socio-political consensus and trust internally (see also Campbell *et al.* 2006; Katzenstein 2000) – is an important parameter of Denmark's historical adaptation to changing international contexts and constraints, and has transformed itself into pride in the homogeneity of Danish culture, the consensualism of politics, and the normative value basis of political and social institutions (thus setting limits to institutional flexibility).[13]

This imposes on 'national culture' a heavy burden of *political* signification (Hedetoft 1998 and 2003b), particularly since the fusion of politics and culture is always greatest in homogeneous polities and becomes foregrounded in situations of perceived crisis. This will tend to increase the pressure on political actors to 'right-people the state', was Brendan O'Leary and his associates have called this process (2001).[14] Or in other words to ensure the maintenance of the cultural, linguistic, and political homogeneity, which more or less consciously, more or less rationally is linked with welfare, well-being, and (in the Danish case) relative success, because 'culture' and 'identity' have come to be defined and substantiated in these terms.

We are here dealing with real effects of a perceived threat: immigration may not be – indeed, is not – a material and quantitative menace in terms of, for instance, the real costs of integration.[15] The risk factor rather derives from the fact that it is perceived to put the 'political participation among equals' and 'consensual trust' model in jeopardy. Globalization manifests itself domestically as a kind of politicized ethnic diversity that is difficult to reconcile with the monocultural model, and hence sparks off both political responses, e.g. variations of populist politics, and popular reactions like increased mistrust of foreigners and stereotyping of immigrants.

The process involves a dual osmosis. On the one hand, the transformation of previous macro-strategies applied by the Danish state for coping with smallness and vulnerability into policies and political discourses about refugees and immigrants at the level of state and elites. And on the other, the transformation of these strategies into popular constructions of Danish identity as reliant on political consensus and cultural homogeneity in the context of welfare-state arrangements – leading in turn to widespread sceptical attitudes to and discourses about refugees, immigrants, and 'foreign cultures'. These attitudes and discourses have now cut themselves loose from their historical and political foundation and live an autonomous moral, cultural, and ideological existence according to their own immanent 'logic', i.e. the ethnic presumptions of Danish particularism. They will hence tend to deny their structural basis and historical origins, and routinely cast themselves in forms of national primordialism.

The implication of this argument is that political responses to and popular perceptions of the 'immigrant threat' contain more than sheer irrationality and prejudice. Rather they are structurally embedded, socio-psychological reactions to an 'external shock'. They may not constitute the most appropriate response, but are nevertheless explicable within a framework of culturally path-dependent thinking in a small-state context, based on solutions which have hitherto served the country well. This is not to say that other possibilities or priorities are not possible or imaginable (the fact that the model worked in the past does not mean that it will in future too), nor does it make dominant discourses couching arguments in terms of 'existential survival' and 'ethnic absolutism' more normatively acceptable.

By looking at dominant political discourses about Danish values and culture, there can be little doubt that 'immigration', as a kind of master signifier, has over the last decade come to be perceived as a significant external shock. The interesting question is therefore how the small statehood of Denmark is currently trying to come to terms with new conditions for the success-culture nexus: by blindly clinging to the old model, by tinkering with it, or by looking for an alternative trajectory involving a novel separation between, on the one hand, domestic welfare and consensual politics, and on the other, economic openness and pragmatic foreign-policy adaptation?[16]

Responses and solutions

As earlier parts of this chapter have demonstrated, Denmark's main strategy for dealing with immigration is still no doubt based on the assimilationism that fits seamlessly into the monocultural welfare model. On the other hand, official discourses have increasingly become adept at framing the question in terms of 'equal treatment' and at integrating elements of 'diversity talk' and 'diversity management' into programmatic statements: 'it's not that we don't accept differences ... ',[17] as the already cited Government White Paper from the summer of 2003 pointedly puts it. This approach has lately been exacerbated by the need to attract immigrant labourers into Denmark.

Thus, official documents[18] as well as legislation and social integration practices demonstrate that the way the government envisages the adaptation of the Danish welfare model to the 'immigrant challenge' – the fact that 'our basic perceptions are being put to the test' (ibid., p. 11) – goes by way of deploying a universalist human-rights discourse in the defence of Danish particularism, on the one hand, and assimilationist requirements based on the consensualism and orderliness of the Danish ethnic community on the other. This allows for the incorporation of diversity, freedom, and equality into the strategic vision, but also for the transgression of the private/public divide wherever necessary. Otherness is acceptable and diversity can be tolerated – but only in depoliticized forms or in pragmatically advantageous (economically lucrative) contexts. Otherwise 'consistent' state interventionism, into, for instance, family values, patterns, and practices, is apparently needed. Hence, whereas the divide existing in the 1980s and early 1990s between humanitarianism and nationalism has been superseded by a new-found consensus on the need for consistency between discourses and policies (Hedetoft 2003c, 2006a), this new mainstream consensus has opened the door to more complex patterns of interaction and division. First, political discourses and top-down initiatives of 'quid-pro-quo' toughness have been introduced in order both to enforce self-reliance on as many newcomers as possible and to discourage third-country refugees and asylum-seekers from selecting Denmark as their receiving country. Second, and due to a lack of manpower in key economic areas, increased emphasis has been put on the need for attracting desirable (mainly skilled) economic immigrants and utilizing cultural diversity for optimizing global marketing and corporate revenues. And third, the quasi-illicit practice of diversity policies and the adoption of multicultural instruments to further 'integration' at lower (local, regional, municipal, neighbourhood) levels have been emphasized. This has resulted in more social and cultural diversity, greater degrees of popular acceptance of 'foreign mores', and – due to the perceived gap between government discourse and useful integration practices on the ground – to greater ambivalence surrounding official policies than these policies themselves would have led one to believe.

The peculiarity of this modernized Danish integration policy regime can be summarized as different combinations of three apparently divergent policy approaches.

Assimilation. This approach draws on culturalist and universalist/western human rights discourse and legitimates the transgression of the public/private divide, wherever this may be either functional or morally called for. It reflects the incontrovertible 'claims of culture' (Benhabib 2002) in Denmark, the importance of maintaining 'Danish homogeneity'. Politically this position is most vehemently championed by the Danish People's Party, but has by now been very widely accepted across the political spectrum, and most emphatically by the government coalition between Liberals and Conservatives.

Integration. The second approach employs 'equal footing' and 'equal access' discourses, both as a set of demands on ethnic minorities and as a reason for calls on employers to behave in a non-discriminatory manner. This discourse respects the public/private divide, being liberal, republican, and legalist in a mode resembling French republicanism and *laïcité*. It also involves market-oriented self-help and self-reliance measures – but places surprisingly little emphasis on equality of political participation in the civic domain ('*medborgerskab*' – 'co-citizenship'), otherwise a solid pillar of support for the post-war welfare state in Denmark. The traditional spokespersons for this approach hail from influential sections of the Social Democrats, the Social Liberal Party, and recently the Socialist People's Party too.

Pluriculturality. The third approach relies on diversity (management) discourses, reflecting the factual existence of ethnic diversity and a plural world as well as the newfound need for economic immigration. This approach is thus solidly couched within a pragmatic-instrumental modality. Previously it was no doubt partly to be seen as lip service paid to pervasive claims from groups critical of the government policy line to allow for multicultural policies and respect international conventions, but demographic problems and labour-market needs have lent new urgency and sincerity to pluricultural discourses. This stance has traditionally been championed by political actors from the left of the political centre, notably the Unity List and the Socialist People's Party (as well as a minority in the Social Democratic Party). However, because of the corporate instrumentality of diversity management strategies (Lauring and Jonasson 2004), the openness dictated by economic needs, and partly the lessons learned from the cartoon crisis – it has now come to be widely accepted.

The order of the three is far from random. The priority ranking within the – by now near-hegemonic – discourse of the Danish ethnic regime is that in which they are listed, as befits a programme intended to modernize a consensual polity and maintain or restore both political trust and social cohesion.[19] In this way, the model comes across as a strange marriage of interest-based pragmatism and identity-based nationalism. The result is one where assimilationism often poses as diversity management and where 'integrationist' policies and discourses are positioned in the middle as a seemingly neutral mediator.[20]

This hybrid model for coping with immigration and ethnic minorities is intended as the answer to the practical puzzle of how to retain the traditional advantages – domestically and internationally – of the consensual welfare state and its compromise culture whilst at the same time coping with the multicultural challenge. It is thus both a reaffirmation of the axiomatic given that not all cultures are 'equally good' at making 'a modern society function' (cf. the previous statement from *Jyllands-Posten*) and an utterance to the effect that diversity, thus understood, may, under certain conditions, be compatible with the Danish model of ethnic consensus and 'deep' cultural cohesion. It implies that the functional benefits as well as the identity components of Danish homogeneity can be salvaged in the face of the risks involved in global migration flows, and that it is possible to control borders effectively. Finally, it implies that 'foreigners', assuming that their numbers are not 'excessive' and that they come with the right skills and primarily from the European cultural sphere, can be turned to national advantage.

The price, according to this discourse, is on the one hand the shedding of misconceived humanitarianism toward people who for the most part are not seen to be 'real refugees', and on the other leaving immigrants, more than previously, at the mercy of the market and their own capacity for self-preservation. The consequence is the attempt to manage migration by setting up two opposite migration regimes concurrently, regimes intended to operate independently of each other and based on contradictory logics. One regime is based on control, exclusion, and cultural purification. This is the nationalist regime directed at refugees and family dependents. Another regime aims at inviting foreigners to fill vacancies in an economy, which until recently was booming and where the unemployment rate still stands at record-low levels. This much more instrumental approach is operationally based on the existing job-card scheme, a recently introduced green-card system, and EU regulations concerning labour mobility. It is hence targeted mainly at citizens from the culturally and geographically 'near abroad' of, for example, Germany, Latvia, Poland, and Sweden. Whether or not the maintenance of this dual migration structure is a doable and manageable undertaking, only time can tell – but the signs are that the attempt to avoid mutual 'contamination' between them is facing grave challenges and the openness characterizing the regime of pragmatism is already affecting the regime of nationalist stricture.

Homogeneity vs multiculturalism: a Danish/Swedish comparison[21]

In a global age it is particularly appropriate to emphasize that nation states are different, not only with regard to size, economic strength, natural resources, and geo-political position, but also concerning history, form of state and government, institutions, demographics, and national identity. Nation states have grown into modernity in different ways and have developed diverse political, administrative, and institutional cultures in the course of history. In addition, the constitution of national consciousness and auto-perceptions has taken place on the background of different images of alterity and through nationally specific interactions between political and social mechanisms of inclusion and exclusion.

For the same reason, the ways nation states talk about, legislate for, and cope with ethnic and historical minorities differ from one another in significant ways, in spite of the indubitable fact that in all these cases we are dealing with the same universal object, *the* nation state, and that in many ways it makes sense to deal with its forms of manifestation analogously, as a reflection and outgrowth of the same form of political and ideological organization. Nevertheless, national migration and integration regimes (Favell 2001; Koopmans and Statham 2000; Spencer 2003) – specific, institutionalized configurations of closure and openness, cynicism and idealism, political and economic interests – vary on important dimensions. These variations, in turn, are intimately linked with differences of frames for national identity perception and different models for active citizenship.

These reflections also apply to nation states which normally appear to be very similar, because they structurally represent the same type of social formation, comparable interactions between state and citizens, and analogous political and cultural histories. An obvious example is Sweden and Denmark – both of them Scandinavian welfare states, both homogeneous 'people's homes' ('*folkshem*', as a Swedish term has it) with well-developed democratic structures, both old monarchies, both small states with a pronounced sense of social equality and just distribution, and both nurturing a perception of the other party as Scandinavian kith and kin, with whom one feels culturally and socially connected.

In spite of these similarities, the migration and integration regimes of the two countries are in many ways divergent, their interpretation of integration and ethnicity is different, and their public debates about these subjects and about the way they are dealt with in the other country are frequently at loggerheads. Danish homogeneity faces Swedish multiculturalism; a closed, exclusionary regime encounters one that is open and inclusive; assimilation contrasts with official recognition of difference; ideas that frame 'them' as the problem confront ideas framing the national society as a barrier to integration; welfare is variously projected as a hindrance to or a path toward integration; 'they' are seen as victims of or responsible for their own destiny; institutional rigidity faces flexible adaptation of institutions to new groups; and demands for single, exclusive citizenship stand in opposition to possibilities for multiple citizenship. In this light, the two countries are worlds apart; Danish discourses of national self-sufficiency seem to collide with a Swedish regime carried by international moralism and accountability, which in Denmark is pejoratively cast as 'political correctness' preventing a free debate and open acknowledgement of what and how huge the 'real problems' are.

If nothing else, these are the prevalent ideal types, substantiated by seemingly ever more divergent developments and mutual stereotypes over the past five or ten years. They reflect an incontestable fact regarding public discourses and government policies in the integration domain. They are less expressive of the practical implementation of policies at the regional and local levels; and they match even less specific, measurable effects of integration in decisive societal areas like the settlement patterns of ethnic minorities (where 'ghettoization' is still widespread in both countries), gender-specific labour-market integration, participation in social networks and civic institutions, or political representation – although on most of these counts, Sweden does have a slight edge.

That said, debates in both countries have changed somewhat recently and now less readily live up to stereotypical perceptions – in Sweden, immigrants now more frequently become framed as a source of social problems, no doubt under the influence of the Danish politicization of immigrants and integration, whereas in Denmark, critical parts of the Danish debate have been inspired by perceptions of Swedish tolerance and diversity practices. And it is no doubt true that there are 'no votes in xenophobia in Sweden', as Fredrik Reinfeldt, the new conservative Prime Minister (from the party called *Moderaterna*), has put it,[22] but public debates on these issues have become more polarized and objections that used to be taboo can now be articulated. Another significant indicator is that although 2006 was proclaimed as the official 'Year of Multiculturalism' (*'mångkulturår'*) in Sweden, government reports – like *The Blue and Yellow Glass House* (*Det blågula glashuset*)[23] – are less concerned with depicting and managing a multicultural polity than with combating 'structural discrimination'. This is a change which (together with the existence of the Swedish Ombudsman for ethnic discrimination) in subtle ways refers to a much less rosy reality than what has so far been painted with traditional brushstrokes – and a reality which uncannily resembles Denmark. Conversely, well hidden behind a wall of assimilationism in Denmark and somewhat perversely spurred on by the negative experience of the cartoon affair, we find a dawning realization that global challenges require more 'diversity management' in corporate Denmark, more openness toward and recognition of ethnic minorities, and a more flexible migration regime. These changes, as described above, can now be defined pragmatically as being in the undisputed economic and demographic interest of a small nation in search of continued economic growth and successful adaptation to globalization.[24] Even the Danish People's Party has recently revealed small chinks in the armour of national romanticism and welfare chauvinism on these counts.

Sweden has evolved from the paternalistic multiculturalism of the welfare state, through anti-discriminatory strategies, into an incipient acrimonious debate, where exclusionary strategies and integration demands firmly embedded in the values of the host country can now also be articulated, but are still in opposition to the dominant consensus. Denmark has moved from conditional tolerance in the 1970s and 1980s, through demands on newcomers for acculturation and financial self-sustenance, into a polarized debate, where exclusionary strategies and demands for integration on the conditions of the host country assume ever greater domination. However, there is now also a growing interest in the negative effects of institutional discrimination, a greater openness toward a proactive immigration policy, and an incipient moral rejection of the marginalizing consequences of monocultural power.

Common to both nation states is, apart from comparable political systems, the external context, the global challenge, and the image of the Islamic risk factor. However, there are limits to the extent and depth of the convergence between the immigration and integration regimes of the two countries.

First, the discursive relations of power are differently configured. Multiculturalism is still official politics in Sweden and should be compared to the official Danish model of ethnic homogeneity. The implication is that the direct Danish correlation between political rhetoric and practical policies ('consistency' is here the official codename) does not exist in Sweden, where the gap between the two is still both apparent and tangible.

Second, the two welfare models (once generally referred to as 'the Nordic model') are constructed on the basis of two different pathways toward consensus and social success. The Swedish one is corporatist, basing itself on centralized institutions, political co-optation, and top-down security for social and cultural interest groups. The Danish is based on decentralized networks, acceptance of freely concluded labour-market contracts, and an elastic and malleable 'flexicurity' model. In cultural terms, the Swedish model is geared to attempts to engender consensus, whereas cultural and identitarian monoculturalism is the implicit precondition for the functionality of the Danish.

Third, also in Denmark and Sweden it is true that *institutions matter* and tend to create their own path dependencies – handed-down patterns of thought, assessment, and social practices – even in the management of ethnic and immigrant issues. It is no coincidence, for instance, and not without social consequences, that Sweden has fostered the idea to create an ombudsman to deal with cases of ethnic discrimination, while Denmark has not (the idea has been rejected on several occasions); that Denmark has a law for the creation of government-sponsored civic (including ethnic and religious) associations; or that the Swedish Foreign Minister, Laila Freivalds, in March 2006, was compelled to resign due to ambiguous handling of a ramification of the cartoon affair in Sweden, while her Danish opposite number has stayed put and can rely on even stronger popular backing after the affair.

In sum, while it may be true that there is a greater degree of convergence between the two countries now, it is probably more precise to say that specific relations between divergence and convergence have undergone a number of significant changes, where some are related to an increasingly globalized migration context, others to internal changes in social structures and national heterotypes, and yet others to shifts in political accent, climates of debate, and discursive environments. The Freivalds case just mentioned is emblematic: although her *faux pas* was due to a multiculturalist knee-jerk reaction to stop the dissemination of the Mohammed cartoons in Sweden and thus prevent the tainting of Sweden's international image, the reason this act – which might well have gone unnoticed or even been publicly supported in the past – now ended in public disgrace was the very same principle that allegedly created the uproar in Denmark in the first place: the right of free speech and to publicly disdain ethnic minorities, particularly Muslims (Brix *et al.* 2003; Hervik 2006; Hedetoft 2006b).

Conclusion

The Danish model of integration mixes ethnic and civic-republican virtues (as well as attendant demands on the 'new Danes') on the assumption that the integration process can only accept difference and deviation from the traditionally practised notion of equality to a limited extent and on pragmatic-instrumental predications. This makes the model strongly path-dependent, meaning that the ideal of homogeneity is still adhered to despite a new and unprecedented globalization context, because it has previously proven its worth as a successful template for international adaptation, and because Danish decision-makers apparently have great difficulties in departing from well-tried and established practices.[25] Therefore it is still an open question if the process of increasing politicization of the ethnic field in Denmark should be regarded a 'surfeit problem' for a well-functioning welfare state, which is left with basically just this one really hard crunch to resolve, or, which is more likely, if we are witnessing a more thoroughgoing and universal challenge to small states in a global age, whose survival and prosperity vitally depend on the degree to which previous strategies will prove adaptable or dysfunctional. One way or the other, and regardless of the fact that in many ways the Danish case is probably unique, developments more generally, in the rest of the west, especially Europe, indicate that it is reasonable to regard Denmark as representative of comparable processes in other small and medium-size nation states (Campbell et al 2006).

The Swedish dimension can be viewed as representative of the inverse problem, i.e. the current crisis of multiculturalism (socially, politically, and normatively) at the intersection between the transformative process of national identity and transnational forms of belonging. Political identities find themselves in a process of transmutation because societies are becoming more multi-ethnic, whilst multiculturalism is increasingly experienced and debated as an impossible, unrealistic, even conservative model of resolution – recently in Sweden too. 'The nation', in politically communitarian forms, is striking back by tightening the net of demands around immigrants and descendants, often in populist forms, and making access to national spaces more and more difficult, even highly risky. Concurrently the values carrying and legitimizing these stringent policies become more clearly universalized – it becomes ever harder to tell apart the specific national features of states, which nevertheless project themselves as highly particularistic. This is happening simultaneously as national sovereignty and the differences between welfare regimes are severely challenged by global pressures. Further, in the transnational spaces a decoupling of nation and state is taking place: national forms of consciousness, communication, and belonging are 'stretched out', while the state itself tends to remain as the form in which civic-political belonging is organized. Finally, these new – regressive, conservationist, or expanding – forms of nationalism are complemented by others, which are properly cosmopolitan, the preserve mainly of global elites (Hedetoft 2004).

The entire field is thus in a process of thoroughgoing reformulation, partly due to globalization, partly to other kinds of political or economic transformation. Tendencies toward a re-nationalization of borders and belonging are no doubt real, but framing conditions are different from the heyday of nationalism, since an intimate and functional linkage between nation and state can no longer be taken for granted. In this way demands based on national cultural legacies and myths are radicalized at the same time as border-transgressing tendencies are becoming more pronounced. This dual process – symbolically articulated through the tension between single and multiple citizenship – is threatening to relegate mono-ethnic nationalism to the status of a modern anachronism, at a time when there is as yet no satisfactory and exhaustive alternative to the identity of the nation state in sight (religiosity being a possible exception). In this respect, multiculturalism as we know it won't do – it is too politically contradictory, too culturally essentialist, and, on the subjective level, too unable to combine ethnic and civic dimensions of allegiance and belonging in a stable yet forward-looking way.

Notes

1 This essay draws in part on my more in-depth analysis in Hedetoft 2006a.
2 *Kulturens vægt* [The importance of culture] by Ralf Pittelkow.
3 'Sagen drejer sig derimod om, hvad der skal til for at få et moderne samfund til at fungere. Og til det formål er alle kulturer ikke lige gode.'
4 *Regeringens vision og strategier for bedre integration.*
5 Government White Paper, *Resumé*, p. 3.
6 *Resumé*, p. 7. I use the term 'pluricultural' rather than 'multicultural' in order to avoid the multiple political and ideological connotations of the latter notion.
7 Particularly the Integration Act of 1999.
8 The law specifies that marriages between ethnic youth settled in Denmark and foreign residents can only take place if both parties have reached 24 years of age. It has had a number of unintended consequences involving 'genuine' Danes, for which reason the law is now under revision so that it may only affect naturalized Danes or people with permanent resident status from non-western countries.
9 This is of course a commonplace argument for justifying restrictive immigration policies in most western nation-states, and is not specific to Denmark, although its application is contextually specific.
10 Immigration and asylum policies over the last six years have to a large extent pivoted around statistical projections for the alarming proportional increase of ethnic minorities over the next three or four decades in light of the differential birth-rate between Danes and immigrants and on the assumption that the inflow characterizing the 1990s might constitute a continuing trend.
11 The translation of Krarup's views into English is mine. For the entire debate, which lasted for the entire day, April 2, 2002, see http://www.folketinget.dk/samling/20012/salen.htm.
12 Krarup's particular variant of essentialist Danishness is based on an almost pietistic Lutheranism combined with explicit non-democratic and in a sense highly non-populist elitism drawing its inspiration from enlightened absolutism. The ground tenor is that Danishness cannot be debated or relativized – it constitutes the absolute, natural, and incontestable conditioning of the very existence of 'ethnic

Danes', whether they are aware of it or not. His nationalism is thus a form of religiously inspired ethnic primordialism.

13 A problem is how the key variables interact and what role they play in the aggregate configuration: smallness, cultural/historical homogeneity, political culture of compromise – and which is the most important in the Danish context? This cannot be investigated in this essay, but the assumption is that it is the combination of the three elements which is significant rather than each of the factors taken in isolation.

14 Meaning the political and ideological process of adapting territory, state, people, and culture to one another in the way that seems to be optimal at any given time.

15 In 1997, net public expenditure due to immigration was, by three ministries, estimated at DKK 10. 3 billion (after an estimated positive net effect of immigrants from the Nordic Countries, EU, North America, Switzerland, Australia, and New Zealand had been deducted) (Tænketanken [Government ThinkTank] 2002, p. 37). Other calculations and more recent figures estimate a net loss to GNP upward of DKK 23 billion as from 2005 (ibid., p. 10) – when an estimated loss of tax revenue (if immigrants' employment rate were the same as that of other Danes) is factored into the estimate. Methods employed by Lars Haagen Pedersen/DREAM, however, result in significantly lower net costs for the state (Haagen Pedersen 2002, p. 34). A balanced estimate indicates that current net costs, inclusive of expenditure toward the upkeep of asylum seekers (Danish Immigration Service 2002, p. 24), are currently in the DKK 15 billion range.

16 The concomitant question, which cannot be pursued further in this context, is also if and to what extent immigration is truly the crucial differentiating factor – seeing that the liberalization of the social democratic welfare regime is inherent in globalization and Europeanization processes more broadly rather than in just one of its (visible) manifestations, i.e. immigration?

17 '*Ikke fordi der ikke må være forskelle*'.

18 See also *En ny chance til alle – regeringens integrationsplan* [*A new chance for everybody – the government's integration plan*], The Ministry for Integration Affairs, Copenhagen, May 2005.

19 Lise Togeby (2003) situates the Danish integration regime 'more or less in the middle' between ethnic assimilation, republican monism, ethnic segregation, and pluralism, but with an inclination toward republicanism (p. 31). On my analysis, the assimilationist tendency is dominant, due to declining respect for the public/private divide, the virtual absence of State/Church separation, and the aggressive culturalist discourses that have characterized the Danish debate and Danish policies for the major part of the last decade.

20 When former Integration Minister Bertel Haarder was asked by a journalist, in 2002, to cite an example of a well-integrated minority group, he interestingly singled out the Chinese – a group well-known for its adherence to their own cultural norms, which they usually pursue within their own relatively isolated territorial and private spaces. On the other hand, they meet another important criterion of current integration policies in Denmark, i.e. economic self-reliance and labour-market entrepreneurship. In that sense, they embody the hybrid nature of the modernized integration regime, positioned between assimilation to economic norms, integration into the labour market (though only a very specific niche), and official acceptance of ethnic diversity, if and only if the two former conditions are fulfilled.

21 For a detailed investigation of the differences and similarities between Danish and Swedish immigration and integration policies, see Hedetoft *et al.* 2006.

22 See article by Kristina Olsson in *Politiken*, December 4, 2005.

23 *Statens Offentliga Utredningar* [Government Reports], Stockholm 2005, no. 56.

24 As is apparent from, for instance, the report of the Danish Welfare Commission, December 2005, and the recommendations of the Government's Globalization Council, March 2006.

25 Three recent processes illustrate these paradoxes and tensions.

One is the Danish government's decision to ban female Muslim judges from wearing headscarves on the job, on the ground that wearing them would impinge on the appearance of neutrality which the judicial system should maintain. The public debate in this respect – which had no specific issue and no popular grudge as its starting-point, but was a politically constructed problem looking for a 'pre-emptive' solution (symbolic politics, in other words) – also focused on the possibility of banning scarves and other religious symbols from all kinds of public office, but this was eventually rejected.

The second is a rare public debate in the late spring/early summer of 2008 – triggered by a schoolbook on contemporary Denmark referring to the country as a multicultural society. This was roundly criticized, notably and predictably (but not only) by representatives of the Danish People's Party, whereas a former Minister for Integration, now Minister for Education, initially defended the statement. As public criticism persisted, however, he eventually reneged on his initial position, claiming that he had been misrepresented. The message from on high now is that Denmark is not multicultural because it contains a majority culture that is stronger and more dominant than the rest. Consensus and normality have been (temporarily) restored. On the one hand, Danish society obviously is multicultural; on the other, this state of affairs still cannot receive official political recognition. However, the fact that a debate of this nature takes place at all testifies to the paradoxes of Danish integration policies at a time, when discourses of monoculturalism and cohesion vye heavily with the reality of the country's ever more pressing need to open its borders to significant numbers of labour migrants – a subject that can no longer be kept from the public agenda, but is profusely (and for most political decision-makers: uncomfortably) present on a daily basis.

The third is a still ongoing and still unresolved debate about the (in)commensurability between the strict Danish immigration regime and EU rules regarding the freedom of movement for EU citizens across internal borders between member states. Following a recent ruling by the EC Court of Justice, the strained relationship between the two policy areas (which has been a fact of life all along, but has been kept from the public eye) is becoming increasingly obvious. Since Denmark is a full member of the Single Market, EU law in all matters regarding the creation of an ever closer Union in these respects takes precedence over national law. Thus, in spite of the Danish opt-out as regards Justice and Home Affairs, the strict regime it has taken the present and previous governments years to put in place (notably the 24-year rule) is in danger of being subverted and at least partly neutralized by Denmark's commitments to the Single Market and the freedoms it entails for capital, commodities, services … and people. At the time of writing (August 2008), the issue is looking to develop not just into a major crunch for Danish migration and integration policies, but also into a potential threat to the government's viability.

References

Anderson, B. (1983/1991) *Imagined Communities*, London: Verso.

Bauman, Z. (1998) *Globalization: the Human Consequences*, Cambridge: Polity.

Baylis, J. and Smith, S. (eds) (1997) *The Globalization of World Politics*, Oxford: Oxford University Press.

Benhabib, S. (2002) *The Claims of Culture*, Princeton: Princeton University Press.

Brix, H.M., Hansen, T. and Hedegaard, L. (2003) *I krigens hus. Islams kolonisering af Vesten [In the House of War. Islam's colonization of the West]*, Aarhus: Hovedland.

Brochmann, G. and Hagelund, A. (2005) *Innvandringens velferdspolitiske konsekvenser [The consequences of immigration for welfare policies]*, Copenhagen: The Nordic Council of Ministers.

Campbell, J., Hall, J.A. and Pedersen P.K.(eds) (2006) *National Identity and the Varieties of Capitalism: the Danish Experience*, Montreal: McGill University Press.

Cohen, M.G. and Clarkson, S. (eds) (2004) *Governing under Stress. Middle Powers and the Challenge of Globalization*, London and New York: Zed Books.

Danish Immigration Service (2002) *Statistical Overview*, Copenhagen: The Danish Immigration Service.

Favell, A. (2001) *Philosophies of Integration*, 2nd edn, London: Palgrave.

Geddes, A. (2003) 'Migration and the Welfare State in Europe', in S. Spencer (ed.) *The Politics of Migration. Managing Opportunity, Conflict and Change*, special issue of *The Political Quarterly*, Oxford and Malden, Mass.: Blackwell.

Government White Paper [*GWP*] (2003) *Regeringens vision og strategier for bedre integration [The Government's Visions and Strategies for Better Integration]* (main report and *Resumé*), Copenhagen: The Danish Government, June.

Gundelach, P. (2002) *Det er dansk [It is Danish]*, Copenhagen: Hans Reitzel.

Haagen Pedersen, L. (2002) *Befolkningsudvikling, integration og økonomisk politik [Demographic developments, integration, and economic policies]*, Copenhagen: DREAM (Danish Rational Economic Agents Model).

Hedetoft, U. (1998) *Political Symbols, Symbolic Politics*, Aldershot: Ashgate.

——(2003a) *The Global Turn*, Aalborg: Aalborg University Press.

——(2003b) 'Culture-as-politics: Meanings and Applications of "Culture" in Political Studies', opening keynote address for the conference What's the Culture in Multiculturalism, Danish Network of Political Theory, Department of Political Science, Aarhus University.

——(2003c) 'Cultural Transformation': How Denmark Faces Immigration, Open Democracy. Online. Available HTTP: http://www.openDemocracy.net (October 30).

——(2003d) *Denmark's Cartoon Blowback*, open Democracy. Online. Available HTTP: http://www.openDemocracy.net (March 1).

——(2004) 'Discourses and Images of Belonging: Migrants between New Racism, Liberal Nationalism and Globalization', in F. Christiansen and U. Hedetoft (eds) *The Politics of Multiple Belonging*, Aldershot: Ashgate.

——(2006) 'More than Kin, and Less than Kind: The Danish Politics of Ethnic Consensus and the Pluricultural Challenge', in J. Campbell *et al.* (eds) *National Identity and the Varieties of Capitalism: the Danish Experience*, Montreal: McGill University Press.

Hedetoft, U., Petersson, B. and Sturfeldt, L. (2006) *Bortom stereotyperna. Invandrare och integration i Danmark och Sverige [Beyond stereotypes. Immigrants and integration in Denmark and Sweden]*, Gothenburg: Makadam.

Hervik, P. (2006) 'The Emergence of Neo-Nationalism in Denmark, 1992–2001', in A. Gingrich and M. Banks (eds) *Neo-Nationalism in Europe and Beyond,* Oxford: Berghahn.

Hirst, P. and Thompson, G. (1996) *Globalization in Question*, Cambridge: Cambridge University Press.

Katzenstein, P. (1985) *Small States in World Markets*, Ithaca and London: Cornell University Press.

——(2000) 'Confidence, Trust, international Relations, and Lessons from smaller Democracies', in S.J. Pharr and R.D Putnam (eds) *Disaffected Democracies: What's Troubling the Trilateral Countries?* Princeton: Princeton University Press.

Koopmans, R. and Statham, P. (eds) (2000) *Challenging Immigration and Ethnic Relations Politics*, Oxford: Oxford University Press.

Lauring, J. and Jonasson, C. (2004) 'Organisational Diversity and Knowledge Sharing', paper presented at the conference Ethnic Minorities, Integration and Marginalisation, The Graduate School for Integration, Production and Welfare, Copenhagen, February 26–27.

Mellon, J. (1992) *Og Gamle Danmark. ... [And Old Denmark ...]*, Gylling: Narayana Press.

O'Leary, B., Lustick, I.S. and Callaghy, T. (2001) *Right-sizing the State*, Oxford: Oxford University Press.

Spencer, S. (ed.) (2003) *The Politics of Migration*, Oxford (special issue of *The Political Quarterly*).

Statens Offentliga Utredningar [Government Papers], Stockholm 2005, no. 56.

Suárez-Orozco, M.M. (2002) 'Everything You Ever Wanted to Know about Assimilation but were Afraid to Ask', in R. Schweder, M. Minow and H. R. Marcus (eds) *Engaging Cultural Differences. The Multicultural Challenge in Liberal Democracies*, New York: Russell Sage Foundation.

Swank, D. (2002) 'Withering Welfare? Globalisation, Political Economic Institutions and Contemporary Welfare States', in L. Weiss (ed.) *States in the Global Economy: Bringing Institutions Back In*, Cambridge: Cambridge University Press.

Tænketanken [Government ThinkTank] (2002) *Indvandring, integration og samfundsøkonomi [Immigration, integration, and the national economy]*, Copenhagen: Ministry for Refugees, Immigrants and Integration.

Togeby, L. (2003) *Fra Fremmedarbejdere til Etniske Minoriteter [From Foreign Workers to Ethnic Minorities]*. Magtudredningen [the Danish Power and Democracy Project]: Aarhus University Press.

Trads, D. (2002) *Danskerne først. Historien om Dansk Folkeparti [Danes First. The History of the Danish People's Party]*, Copenhagen: Gyldendal.

7 Switzerland

A multicultural country without multicultural policies?

Gianni D'Amato

> In Italy for 30 years under the Borgias they had warfare, terror, murder, and bloodshed, but they produced Michelangelo, Leonardo da Vinci and the Renaissance. In Switzerland they had brotherly love – they had 500 years of democracy and peace, and what did that produce? The cuckoo clock.
>
> (Orson Welles, *The Third Man*, 1949)

Introduction

As a small country located at the crossroads of Northern and Southern Europe, Switzerland is widely known for its neutrality and peaceful attitudes, its ethnic and linguistic diversity – German, French, Italian, and Reto-Romansch[1] are all national languages – and a decentralized government that makes most laws at the canton (or state) level.[2] But the nice picture of being a country privileged by Kantian 'eternal peace' is as correct as the supposition to be called the inventor of the Bavarian Black Forest time-piece. There is a good reason why control and integration policies figure large in a federalist country that was challenged since its birth – in the aftermath of the successful liberal Revolution of 1848 – by centrifugal forces on the religious, regional, political, social, and ideological levels. Certain foreign scholars, puzzled by Switzerland's apparent enduring stability (and overlooking the history of violent and disruptive conflicts from the civil war of 1847 until the social unrest of the 1930s), detected the source of this solidity in the clever management of a multicultural country through its federal institutions (Schnapper 1997). Others see Switzerland as a 'paradigmatic case of political integration' as a result of the subsidiary structure of the Swiss state which supports both the strong municipal autonomy and the comparatively high participation rate of the constituency in the polity (Deutsch 1976). Other authors see the source of the country's stability in the successful creation of a strong national identity, which helped overcome the social distrust that arose during rapid industrialization, and which was based on the country's small size, and the idea that Switzerland was under permanent threat of strong neighbouring countries ('Überfremdung') (Kohler 1994; Tanner 1998).

Notwithstanding this fear of being demographically and culturally overrun by foreigners, Switzerland had one of the highest immigration rates on the continent during the twentieth century. According to the 2000 census, 22.4 per cent of the total population of 7.4 million is foreign born, and 20.5 per cent, or nearly 1.5 million, are foreigners (defined here as persons with a foreign nationality). In relative numbers this number is twice as high as that of foreigners in the US, and considerably higher than that of Canada, two classic countries of immigration. In contrast to its internal pluralistic character, however, Switzerland does not consider itself as a country of immigration – in fact, it has denied the existence of an immigrant policy at the federal level before the nineties (Mahnig and Wimmer 2003). Another paradox concerns the handling of the admission and integration issue in the political arena. While Switzerland used to be a destination for employment-seeking French, Germans, and Italians, in the latter half of the twentieth century it became home to Eastern European dissidents, Yugoslavian refugees, and asylum seekers from the Middle East, Asia, and Africa. Only since the 1960s, after decades of complete absence of the social hardships encountered in its neighbouring countries (high unemployment rates among migrants, ethnic and social segregation, social unrest), the immigration issue became a contentious topic in Switzerland, a topic that gained, at certain times, hegemony over the political agenda. Is Switzerland a multicultural country missing policies of diversity?

This inconsistent situation must be explained through a careful analysis of how immigration and integration policies evolved in Switzerland, and which role multicultural approaches played in this development. In the second section I will describe the process of immigration and integration during the twentieth century by way of a brief historical overview, and present some demographic data. In the third and fourth sections I will emphasize the importance of the various stakeholders who had their influence on the definition of migration policies as public intellectuals, but also practically at different state levels, devoting our attention to external factors, which may have had an effect on the creation of these policies. I will also show that the political opportunity structures in Switzerland – influenced by its federalism and a consensus-oriented political culture – had their impact on the formulation of immigration policies as well, just as much as various external challenges (foreign governments, the European Union). In the Conclusion I will discuss the different factors that may have influenced the outcome of Switzerland's particular immigration and integration policy.

Immigration and immigrant policies in historical perspective

Switzerland's reputation as an ideal place for exiles dates back to the sixteenth century, when the Huguenots of France were welcome as religious refugees and found their place in the cultural, political, and entrepreneurial elite of Switzerland. But the modern transformation of Switzerland into a country of immigration – as it is known today – took place during its accelerated industrial take-off in the second half of the nineteenth century (Holmes 1988; Romano 1996). In contrast to its rural image, the Swiss Confederation is a European forerunner in various branches of the modern mechanical and chemical industries and has had an enormous need to invest in knowledge and infrastructures. While many rural inhabitants were leaving the country to make their living as peasants in the New World, many German intellectuals fleeing from the failed liberal revolutions of 1848–49 found their place in the local universities. Furthermore, Italian craftsmen and workers were recruited at the end of the nineteenth and early twentieth century, mainly in the construction business and the railroad sector.

During the late-nineteenth and early-twentieth centuries, the size of the foreign population in Swiss cities increased: 41 per cent of people in Geneva, 28 per cent in Basel, and 29 per cent in Zurich were born outside Switzerland. Nationwide, the Germans outnumbered the Italians and French (Efionayi-Mäder *et al.* 2005). Moreover, the proportion of foreigners in the total population increased from 3 per cent in 1850 to 14.7 per cent at the eve of World War I, mostly from neighbouring countries. During the two world wars, however, the foreign population decreased significantly. By 1941, Switzerland's foreign population had dropped to 5.2 per cent (Arlettaz 1985).

In the liberal period preceding World War I, immigration was largely the responsibility of the cantons, whose laws had to conform to bilateral agreements signed between Switzerland and other European states. Like other agreements from this period concerning the free movement in Europe, the Swiss agreements were open towards immigrants because they needed to ensure that Swiss citizens could easily emigrate if they needed to find work. However, after first campaigning against the presence of aliens in Switzerland during World War I, a new article in the constitution appeared in 1925, giving the federal government the power to address immigration issues at the national level, providing the legal basis for the Federal Aliens Police (*Fremdenpolizei*) and the Law on Residence and Settlement of Foreigners, which came into force in 1931 (Garrido 1990). This law allowed the new Federal Aliens Police to implement the immigration policy at discretion, although at the time their aim was to maintain the national identity rather than to regulate migration. Essentially, the authorities were primarily concerned with the country's moral and economic interests and the degree of 'over-foreignization' in Switzerland (*Grad der Über-fremdung*) in their decisions. The nationwide political consensus in assuring what was described as 'cultural purity' in Switzerland prevented the drafting out of any consistent immigrant policy until very recently. Foreigners, in principle, had to leave the country and were not allowed to settle permanently.

Post-war labour migration

Shortly after World War II, the economic recovery of neighbouring countries stimulated the rapid growth of the Swiss economy. In the context of the post-war economic boom, Switzerland signed an agreement with the Italian government in 1948 in order to be able to recruit Italian guest workers. These workers were mainly employed in the construction sector but also in textile and machine factories. Since then, a steady flow of foreign workers immigrated to Switzerland. Their number increased from 285,000 in 1950 (6.1 per cent of the total population) to 585,000 (10.8 per cent) in 1960 and to 1,080,000 (17.2 per cent) in 1970. Predominantly Italian during the 1950s, their composition diversified in the 1960s: while over 50 per cent were still Italians in 1970, about 20 per cent, were natives of Germany, France, and Austria, 10 per cent were Spaniards, and 4 per cent were Yugoslavs, Portuguese, and Turks (Mahnig and Piguet 2003). Initially, they were entitled to stay for one year, though the contract could be prolonged, which frequently happened.

To ensure that the workers did not settle permanently and could be sent home, the residence period required for obtaining a permanent residence permit was increased from five to ten years, and restrictive conditions on family reunion were adopted. This policy was called the 'rotation model' because it meant that new workers could be brought in as others returned home. As the economic boom continued throughout the 1960s, the Swiss government's guest-worker system became less tightly controlled. As Switzerland faced increasing pressure from Italy to introduce more generous family reunification laws, the number of Italian workers willing to come to Switzerland decreased and other destinations, such as Germany, became more attractive after the signing of the Roman Treaty. Also, the internal economic boom in Italy started a wave of internal migration, particularly to destinations in Northern Italy. In response, the Swiss government started to replace its 'rotation' system with an 'integration-oriented' scheme that facilitated family reunification, made foreign workers more eligible for promotions, and attempted to end labour market segmentation (Niederberger 2004).

Following the oil crisis in 1973, many workers became unneeded and had to leave the country because they did not have adequate unemployment insurance. This allowed Switzerland to 'export' its unemployed guest workers without renewing their resident permits (Katzenstein 1987). The total percentage of the foreign population fell from 17.2 per cent in 1970 to 14.8 per cent in 1980. But as the economy recovered, new guest workers arrived not only from Italy, but also from Spain, Portugal, and Turkey. Their part of the population increased from 14.8 per cent (945,000 persons) in 1980 to 18.1 per cent (1,245,000 persons) in 1990 and to 22.4 per cent in 2000 (nearly 1.5 million people) (Mahnig and Piguet 2003).

By the time the worldwide recession of the early 1990s reached Switzerland, the unskilled and aging guest workers suffered high rates of unemployment and found it very difficult to find new jobs. This situation led to an unprecedented level of structural unemployment and social hardship that Switzerland had not experienced in previous decades. Switzerland's larger cities, which, according to the subsidiary logic of the Swiss federal system, had to cover the expenses of welfare, urged the federal government to act and support extended integration patterns towards immigrant workers (D'Amato and Gerber 2005). A new admission policy was supposed to combine the evolving needs of a new economy with those of migration control. These initial debates were strongly influenced by arguments that combined a weak concept of integration with the need of social control on migration. Within this framework, multiculturalism was finally only discussed in academic circles, unable to establish itself as a new paradigm. Only the refugees of the 1960s and 1970s from Eastern Europe and South-East Asia were encountered with tolerance and patience, coming close to what is disavowed today as multiculturalism, whereas labour migrants continued to be faced with the need to adapt themselves to the dominant cultural values, assimilate as far as they could or they had to choose to return home. Before we turn our attention to the discursive opportunities of the policy-making process, we want to address the dynamics of the debate concerning multiculturalism (in the beginning mostly an academic affair) and integration policies in Switzerland.

Debates on multicultural Switzerland

An academic dispute

In continental Europe, the reception of multiculturalism was strongly influenced by the US-conservative critique interpreting it as a sort of institutionalized and canonized form of segregation. More than this, in the continental understanding the concept of culture and its relation to states are linked to the formation of ethnicity. Such a connection leads immediately to a discussion of legitimate political rights for minorities and their possibilities to live an autonomous life. Switzerland, seen by foreign scholars often as a successful example of peaceful coexistence of different ethnic groups, seems to be a challenge to models of more exclusive ethno-cultural nation-states (Habermas 1992). As a confederation Switzerland is supposed to have all the necessary tools to equilibrate potential ethnic tensions within the country. This optimistic assumption misreads the fact that public talk on multiculturalism is only referring to the established minorities. For a majority of Swiss citizens, it is completely self-evident that labour migrants are not part of multicultural Switzerland. Therefore, for some scholars, Switzerland seems to be far away from having realized multicultural democracy (Tanner 1993). They are stressing the fact that Switzerland is more homogeneous than the usual talk on Swiss cultural diversity suggests. This homogeneity is given by the reality that people with different languages, religious beliefs, mentalities, and economic structures are living in one territory with a common history, side by side. For more conservative observers, the condition that makes cultural diversity possible in Switzerland is linked to the principle of territoriality (Linder 1998; Steinberg 1996). For them, there is no Swiss multiculturalism in a strict sense since each cultural group is living in their own territory, the cantons, preventing in this respect an overlapping of other groups or a spill-over of their cultural influence.

Even though the advocates of an integrative and migration-related multi-culturalism were completely aware of the fact that the term was not promising Utopian incentives for a 'better' society, by using the term, they were nevertheless expecting a more realist approach to what they considered a social and irreversible change of society through migration. They used the term in order to overcome inhibitions and blockades with regard to the self-understanding of Switzerland. Multiculturalism was seen as an intellectual and practical tool which permitted to reorient the capacities of state administrations and the general public at large to comprehend reality and be able to act adequately in a modern society (Steiner-Khamsi 1992).

But some critics admonished this intention and expressed their fear that recognizing a society to be multicultural would lead to dangerous forms of segregation and to ethno-national exclusion (Brumlik and Leggewie 1992). According to Hans-Joachim Hoffmann-Nowotny, a former leading Swiss migration researcher who died recently, one culture has to dominate a society. In this respect a multicultural society is a contradiction in terms. What is generally understood as multiculturalism are therefore different communities 'living apart together' within a state territory; they could also be called 'sub-cultures'. An active encouragement of these sub-cultures within a territory would compromise the persistence of a shared knowledge ('Wissensbe-stand') – as Hoffmann-Nowotny defines culture. More than this, a perseverance of structural differences with regard to the new immigrants would directly lead to segregation, one of the most dangerous harms in modern societies. Besides this structural distance between immigrants and the local population, highlighting the cultural distance as – according to Hoffmann-Nowotny – multiculturalists do, would also lead to an active creation of minorities, a re-evaluation of old identities and in some cases a risky over-lapping of class and ethnic conflicts. For Hoffmann-Nowotny, the Swiss success story is not due to different groups living together, but to the spatial segregation of cultural diversity that makes it necessary for all, even for Swiss internal migrants, to assimilate to the dominant culture within the territory of Cantons.

This picture of Switzerland, which dominated the academic debate of the 1990s, had its part in legitimating the new Swiss immigration policy. The problems that Hoffmann-Nowotny foresaw were in particular directed to 'new' immigrants coming from outside of Europe. Their 'cultural distance' seemed, as the author argued with reference to the UK, France, and the Netherlands, to be problematic and to lead to disintegrative impacts. This argument was in line with the general policies of the Swiss government, which wanted to reorient its strategy with regard to immigration. The challenge of the 1990s was the integration of Switzerland within a larger European frame-work, about which large parts of the population felt sceptical. In order to gain popular support and convince the people to accept immigration from Europe, a so-called model of 'three circles' was presented. This concept relied on the idea that it is not the number of immigrants that causes problems, but their 'cultural distance'. In order to convince their own population to accept more European immigration and therefore to gain some margins of man-oeuvring with regard to the EU, the Swiss government tried to argue that the heterogeneity in the population should be as small as possible. The government decided to restrict this development defining the areas from which migrants should come in the future, mapping different 'circles': with regard to the first circle, people from the European Union and the European Free Trade Association should be able to circulate freely into Switzerland. People from the 'second circle' consisting of the US, Canada, and Eastern European countries and people of the third circle (the rest of the world) could only get access to Switzerland in exceptional cases, i.e. when they possessed high and needed qualifications. With the 'three circles' proposal of the government, a compromise between the economic need for labour and the pressure of xeno-phobic parties, Hoffmann-Nowotny introduced his concept of 'cultural dis-tance' in the Swiss political landscape, a concept trying to prevent unwanted immigration from countries that were 'culturally different'.

Obviously, this perception was strongly criticized in the academic and political arena. Hoffmann-Nowotny's description of Swiss history and the Swiss success story was ahistoric and oriented to a functional understanding of society following the American School of Sociology. To depict Switzerland as cultural areas 'living apart together' showed little understanding of the negotiations in Swiss nation-building (symptomatic in all nations). Therefore, Switzerland can hardly be portrayed as a successful 'Apartheid state'. Many critics could not understand why the persistence of different knowledge reservoirs on one territory should be problematic. Are 'cultures', once they are established, always the same, never changing shape and direction? Hoffmann-Nowotny had, as Stephen Castles (1994) wrote, no sensory for the fact that each group and even each person can have a large spectrum of cul-tural practices, which can also compete or influence each other. Within the same population, there are also important differences between sex, class, origin, age, and styles. However, there are also shared values built on common experiences and rationalities that are independent from origins. More than this, modern societies are differentiated and cannot be forced to correspond to one singular 'cultural model'. A certain amount of difference and non-integration will always persist in modern societies. At the end of the nineties, the academic and political critique of the 'cultural distance' model took the Swiss government to a general policy reformulation, reducing the three circles to only two: Europe and the rest of the world.

Walter Kälin, a leading expert on International Law at the University of Berne, contended Hoffmann-Nowotny's position on the importance of 'cul-tural distance' arguing in favour of cultural diversity as a pillar of liberal nation-states (Kälin 2000). For Kälin, states founded on liberal constitutions and the rule of law are obliged to preserve their liberal identity. His analysis evaluates different cases of intercultural conflicts: starting from tensions between cultural liberties and the equity of rights, Kälin tries to find ways that help migrants to integrate interpreting how cultural conflicts (confrontations caused by cultural agents such as religion, language, or ethnic background) are perceived by the involved actors. The fundamental rights given by the constitution create the framework in which conflicts are to be regulated. Normatively spoken, these rights are defining the principles that help to regulate conflicts in modern societies. These principles are the following:

- A state based on rule of law has to treat each person equally independent from his/her ethnic, religious or other origin (principle of non-discrimination).
- A state has to accept cultural differences if the application of 'neutral' rules penalizes and devaluates members of a particular group.
- The state has the right to exempt people from certain duties if this helps to promote their integration into institutions without compromising their well-functioning.
- The state has to apply the rule whereas religious freedom, freedom of education of the parents, as much as marriage and family building, are also valid for minorities.
- Limits of tolerance are met when certain behaviours are forbidden by international private law (e.g. forced marriage), when adults are submitting themselves to practices that are harming their physical and psychical indemnity, or when the well-being of a child is in danger.
- The immigration country can impose the respect of its '*ordre public*' (e.g. the central values of its own judicial order) to all inhabitants. But a state has to keep in mind the effects of such an imposition. A certain reluctance is to be applied when already discriminated persons will be put in a more marginal position (e.g. children of polygamous marriages).

According to Kälin, these principles constitute the fundamental rules for coexistence in immigration societies. Often cultural rationalizations are taken into consideration in order to explain conflicts. But it is necessary to find an equilibrium between particular interests, the principle of equality and the respect of one's own pursuit of happiness. Principles based on the constitution and on international law should be able to enforce social cohesion without recurring to assimilation, which is in its own a tool that creates difference.

Jurisdiction took notice of these scholarly informed distinctions and the Federal Supreme Court pronounced in the 1990s a remarkable sentence in which the right of religious minorities to exempt their children from swimming lessons was admitted. As an immediate reaction, public opinion and central-right wing policy makers responded with strong hostility to an enlargement of cultural civil rights to immigrants. In a country in which the fear to be overrun by foreigners is deeply rooted in public discourse, a policy that allowed the recognition of differences was felt as a provocation and turned out to be a red rug to right-wing populist parties, inciting them to mobilize against liberal jurisdiction. Until today, a legitimate utilization of the term 'multiculturalism' can only refer, if ever used, to the linguistic diversity of the autochthonous Swiss population. To understand this restrictive use and the preference for the term 'integration', it is important to briefly recapitulate the policy process on migration since the early 1960s giving a tighter scrutiny to the main actors involved in this course.

The discourse on integration

A public policy dispute

When the Swiss government dropped its 'rotation policy' in the early 1960s, it recognized that the alternative could only be a policy of integration. The belief – both then and now – however, is that in the course of time integration occurs naturally through participation in the labour market and in schools, as well as in associations, labour unions, clubs, churches, neighbourhoods, and through other informal networks (Niederberger 2004). But they are expected to dissociate themselves from their former community: 'After several years of residence, [they] should ... no longer be reliant on the community of their fellow countrymen, but start to live as Swiss' (Swiss Department of Economy and Work, 1964).[3] Since the 1970s, the Confederation's main integration policy has been aiming to improve the legal status of immigrants, reuniting families more quickly, and granting immigrants a more secure status. In order to facilitate the integration of foreigners and to respond to the public's concerns about foreigners, the government established the Federal Commission for Foreigners (FCF) in 1970 in order to 'study the social problems of foreign workforces, ... and to address in particular questions regarding social care, the adaptation to our working and living conditions, assimilation and naturalization' (Swiss Federal Council, Protocols of 18 November 1970, quoted in Niederberger 2004: 81). This commission, which, since the seventies, promotes the coexistence of the foreign and native populations, brings together municipalities, communities, cantons, foreigners' organizations, employers and employees, and churches. The FCF cooperates with cantonal and communal authorities, immigrant services, and immigration actors, such as charities and economic associations. It also publishes opinions and recommendations regarding general issues on migration, and provides testimony for political debates regarding migration-related policy.

After the migratory confusion of the eighties – the sudden increase of asylum seekers, a first asylum law, the substitution of the Italian guest workers with workers from Yugoslavia and Portugal – the concept of integration won acceptance in the nineties, since the metaphor of assimilation did not seem to be adequate anymore, but multiculturalism could not gain ground. The concept of integration took shape in particular in the context of the political discussions of the nineties on the revaluation of urban areas. Cities tried to position themselves in an international competition over geographic locations and were confronted meanwhile with social difficulties that were identified as strictly related to migration. The debate on integration was connected since the second half of the nineties with urbanism and urban development; it took to the formulation of official integration guidelines in cities such as Berne, Zurich, and Basle. Integration was the new buzz word, a fresh and powerful idea ready to shape the Swiss policies on immigrants. Exempt from the fug of ordinary social policies, but also from the debts towards 'old-fashioned' humanitarian beliefs, integration became an unexpected creative element for designing future migration policies.

This process took several years. A first legislative proposal of the government, sustained by all major parties, anticipated the new paradigm, but was refused 1982 in a popular ballot, when the radical right-wing party 'National Action' mobilized successfully against an expansion of rights to foreigners (Niederberger 2004: 132). At the beginning of the 1990s a government report stated that in the future 'to a larger extent than before, measures should be taken to encourage integration at all levels of the polity' (Schweiz. Bundesrat 1991). The promotion of integration was included in the legislative planning 1995–99 as a new target, and in 1996, the FCF submitted a report delineating the outlines of an integration policy (Riedo 1996). It referred only briefly and sceptically to the term 'multiculturalism', stating that cultural rootedness may be helpful in finding a useful handling with alienating experiences (p. 6). The pluralization of the migrants' origin and the rising social problems may explain this suspicious passage: 'It must be prevented, that certain groups of people, such as Muslims, Turks and nationals from the former Yugoslavia are pushed into the role of problematic foreigners, thereby being even more discriminated against and isolated' (Niederberger 2004: 148).[4] Therefore, after the strong lobbying of the cities during the economic crisis of the 1990s, the Swiss alien policy adapted to the new reality, considering the integration of foreigners as a prerequisite for achieving a politically and socially sustainable immigration policy. There was no clear and binding definition on the term: integration was open to a liberal and conservative interpretation of future policies. Liberals understood integration as a means to encourage participation into mainstream society. Migrants were supposed to be willing to integrate, but some of them needed particular help or promotion (*Fördern*). This open interpretation of integration was contrasted by a conservative reading which emphasized the need of mandatory and coercive measures in order to fight abuses of the right of hospitality accorded by Swiss administration. This closed interpretation is demanding a specific set of behaviour to which immigrants have to comply (*Fordern*).

Seen first as a liberal achievement included in the guideline of the City of Basle (Ehret 1999), the 'new policy' of '*Fördern und Fordern*' was meant to prevent populist challengers from charging local governments of being too soft on migrants, but wanted also to rely on the potentials of newly arrived migrants. On the basis of the Declaration of Human Rights and the Swiss Constitution, migrants should not be regarded as members of groups, but as individuals able to take their responsibility. Approaches of this new policy were 'future-oriented', meritocratic, emancipatory, taking individual responsibilities serious, based on same rights and duties (Kessler 2005: 110).

Hence, 'integration' stands for the participation of foreigners in the economic, social, and cultural life. The Integration Article in the old Alien Law, passed in 1999, paved the way for a more proactive federal integration policy; it also strengthened the FCF's role. Since 2001, the government has spent between 10 and 12 million Swiss francs (€ 6 million to € 7 million) per year to support integration projects, including language and integration courses and training for integration leaders. Cantons and larger municipalities also have their own integration and intercultural cooperation committees and offices, which offer language and integration courses. In many communities, foreigners participate in school boards and, in some cases, the municipal government. With the support of consulates and the local education department, larger communities offer courses in immigrant children's native languages and cultures. While churches proved to be among the major institutions to promote the coexistence of the Swiss and the foreign population, other non-governmental organizations have become interested in the process as well. According to this new spirit, Switzerland for the first time recognized to be a country of immigration that should provide help to integrate immigrants.

Whereas at the end of the 1990s and the beginning of the new decade emphasis was put on '*Fördern*', on the positive encouragement to integrate, a prudent reading of official papers would have indicated that a coercive reading was always present. Indeed, '*Fördern und Fordern*' got a magic connotation that allowed each side to read integration as they wished:

> It is not the host society that is responsible for the integration of the migrants, but this is largely their own responsibility. Only someone who is ready to do so can count on the appropriate opportunities and expect help in improving one's personal situation. The promotion of integration remains always help to self-help.
>
> (Schweiz. Bundesamt für Migration 2006)[5]

But in 2003, the electoral gains of the Schweizerische Volkspartei (SVP: Swiss People's Party), a former peasants' party that mutated to a radical right-wing populist contender of the established political system both at the cantonal and in particular the federal level, dramatically changed the centre of gravity of the consensus on integration. Bringing the charismatic SVP-Chairman Christoph Blocher into service as the new Head of Justice, the legislation on migration and integration experienced a massive turn during the Parliamentary debate in 2005, underlining the expectations third country nationals have to fulfil if they want to stay in Switzerland.

As a final point, the new immigration law, a legislative project finalized by Christoph Blocher, which passed a popular ballot with a large majority of 68 per cent in 2006 (and came into operation 2008), foresees that immigrants have to fulfil certain criteria that should facilitate their integration. Permanent residents and their families are required to integrate on both the professional and social levels as soon as possible (Efionayi-Mäder *et al.* 2003). Those who fail can be deported home. But these considerations are only related to low-qualified third country nationals. This restrictive component corresponds in its content to the criterion of 'qualitatively high standard immigration'. The level of education and the professional qualifications are interpreted to improve the integration of foreigners and guarantee their vocational reintegration in the case of unemployment. Restrictions aim at avoiding the errors that were committed in the past, i.e. the granting of temporary work permits to low-qualified seasonal workers. Furthermore, it explicitly foresees that it is the immigrant's duty to make every effort necessary to facilitate his or her integration.

The new integration paradigm as it is enforced by this very recent '*Ausländergesetz*' is configured by two components: On the one hand integration is linked to the restriction of immigration, on the other hand it is relying on the understanding that EU/EFTA citizens are fully integratable whereas third country nationals are supposed to have deficits if they are not highly qualified personnel. These assumed deficits are located either in the culture, religion, or language of those migrants or in the alleged missing acceptance of their duties towards Swiss society, in particular the omitted respect of laws and constitutional rights.

The new approach, originally meant to discipline immigrants, can also be deducted by the dissolution of the FCF and its integration into the Federal Department of Police and Justice. The general tendency to dissociate public integration institutions from Departments of Social Affairs to the Police Department can also be observed in different cantons and may underline the assumption that integration has undergone a political ideologization and securitization, as it was the case before with the assimilation paradigm. Integration has won with its orientation to individual achievements a coercive character, and in most instances, any alternative understanding of the term has lost significance. Namely, it was not considered that integration could also be linked to the dismantling of obstacles, such as the discrimination in the labour and housing market, the non-recognition of foreign diploma, the codification of residence rights, and the barriers to real participation. These forms of promotion are by far not as cost-intensive as 'integration programmes', but they would correspond better to the concept of a liberal society that relies on incentives (Wicker 2009). The fact the new '*Ausländergesetz*' is putting third country nationals under general suspicion is not only wrong, but it relies on an ahistorical reading of its own immigration history if compared to the successful integration of former migrant groups. And it may be counterproductive if the message of distrust reaches the second- and third-generation youth. What still remains impressive, is the semantic shift of integration as a concept that included emancipation, to a term that now comprises coercion and repression.

Interests and orientations

As discussed in the previous section, integration (far more than multi-culturalism) has been the issue of public political contention in Switzerland. In this respect, different comparative studies have confirmed the perseverance of interests and orientations in the discourses on migration politics (Brubaker 1992; Hollifield 1992; Ireland 1994). In the case of Switzerland, it has been shown that politics of migration are shaped by three major ideal-typical arguments (see Mahnig 1996). Whilst these arguments are hardly ever expressed in their pure form, they set the argumentative frame of Swiss migration politics. The 'liberal position' argues that the free market represents the ideal regime of migration regulation. According to this position, migration has not to be prevented or restricted but handled in a similar fashion as the free trade of capital and goods. Any kind of state intervention is seen as economically highly ineffective, except if it is meant to reduce immigration control or to adapt immigration rates to business demands. The 'internationalist position', too, advocates a critical standpoint towards national immigration control, but for different reasons. The argument here is based on the proliferation of international human rights discourses which should globally standardize legal and social equality for individuals. From this view, migration policy is seen as an instrument of social compensation between rich and poor countries. Finally, the 'nationalist position' seeks to defend Swiss national interests against immigrants. These interests contain economic and labour market dimensions (e.g. protection of certain economic sectors, favouring local workforce), on the one hand, and are oriented towards the protection of national identity which seems constantly threatened, on the other hand.

It appears that at the beginning of the 1990s, a set of changes due to internal (comprehensive citizenship reform, prolonged economic crisis) and external factors (end of the Cold War, European integration process, changes of the naturalization laws all over Europe) forced the government and policy-makers to redirect their policy orientations from a 'nationalist-liberal' to a more 'liberal-internationalist position' (Jacobson 1996; Soysal 1994). Adjustments to the European Union, acceptance of dual citizenship, attempts to reform citizenship laws, and protection of cultural rights through the recently created Federal Commission against Racism are indications for this process of adjustment to the new political environment. This clear shift in matters of immigration, citizenship, and cultural rights represents also new challenges to actors that were always present on the Swiss political scene and opens for them a new space of contention: the right-wing populist parties, discussed further below.

The way in which interests and orientations on social cohesion are contended, and in particular the outcomes of such a debate, can only be understood if the Swiss institutional context of the policy-making process is considered. Three areas are relevant for the study of Switzerland: its federalism, and its consociational and direct democracy.

The institutional context of the policy-making process

Federalism

As mentioned before, it is primarily through the institutions of federalism that the country succeeded in accommodating its cultural and religious diversity. Switzerland is a confederation of 23 cantons, which have a large measure of autonomy as regards their policy on education, police, and taxes. According to this principle, the Swiss Parliament functions on two levels, the National Council (*Nationalrat*, which represents the people) and the State Council (*Ständerat*, which represents the cantons). New laws have to pass both chambers but can be immediately vetoed by a popular referendum with 50,000 signatures.

With regard to the admission and integration of migrants, federalism plays an important role in many domains, among others in the field of education, presented here as a paradigmatic case (as religious matters or the quest for political rights could also have been used for this purpose). In Switzerland the educational system is organized by the cantons, which want immigrants to adopt the dominant cantonal language and culture. During the 1970s cantonal education systems had difficulties in accommodating the different social (and cultural) situation and could not guarantee equal educational opportunities (Schuh 1987). Problems of school segregation still persist at the level of curricula, even if the federal education authorities (Schweizerische Erziehungsdirektorenkonferenz EDK) regularly publish recommendations for the better integration of immigrant children (Schweizerische Konferenz der kantonalen Erziehungsdirektoren 1972, 1976, 1982, 1985, 1991, 1993, 1995a, 1995b, 2003). Some cantons give more support to immigrant children and promote their integration in school, by, for example, giving more resources to local schools, introducing institutional changes such as team-teaching and an intercultural programme that favours the insertion of children with a migrant background (Truniger 2002b). But not all cantons implement these recommendations; in fact, several favour discriminatory practices. Contrasting cantonal responses roughly correspond to linguistic and also political cleavages. In German-speaking cantons one can generally observe a tendency to set up specific institutions for immigrant children, with the exception of the urban cantons that have the necessary tools to give support to their school bodies without enforcing segregation (Truniger 2002a), whereas in French and Italian-speaking areas of Switzerland the response has been to integrate all children in mainstream institutions.

Since Switzerland has a highly federalized institutional system, characterized by vertical segmentation and horizontal fragmentation, allowing both institutions and cantonal parties a high degree of organizational and political autonomy, special attention has to be given to the cantonal level. As seen in the case of voting, the cantons can use their autonomy to experiment with various approaches in migrant related political fields and try to influence the decision-making at federal level. Its body, the *'Ständerat'*, makes it necessary for federal authorities to secure the loyalty of the cantons and to make sure that strong cantonal political entrepreneurs do not quit the consensus. Therefore, if the perception of the cantons does change, the federal level has to adapt. But ever since recently, when the general mood became anti-immigrant, the example of the autonomous educational system makes it clear that cantons have enough space to manoeuvre and do not have to share a common approach to all fields related to migrants.

Consociatonal and direct democracy

Consociational and direct democracy, two characteristics of the Swiss political system, are responsible for the high politicization of migration issues in Switzerland and for the exclusion of migrants from political participation (Mahnig and Wimmer 2003). 'Consociational democracy' refers to the proportional representation of different minorities (linguistic, political, religious) in the federal institutions and the search for compromise between political forces that goes beyond the search for simple majorities (Linder 1998). All members of the government as well as the higher administration are chosen in proportion of their party affiliation ('magic formula') and their linguistic and regional origins. Swiss politics is characterized by a permanent process of compromise-building between these groups. The 'consultation procedure' is another important means to influence the political decision-making process. This procedure is the phase in the preparation of legislation when draft legal acts of the Confederation are evaluated by the cantons, parties, associations, and sometimes also by other interested circles throughout Switzerland, in order to ascertain the likelihood of their acceptance and implementation. The Federal Council then passes the main points of its proposal on to the Parliament. The Federal Council debates the draft legal act in the light of the outcomes of this consultation.

'Direct democracy' gives social groups some opportunities to participate directly in the political process through the already mentioned popular initiative and referendum. These are operative at the federal as well as on the local level. All laws voted in Parliament can be submitted to a referendum and therefore need the support of large alliances within the political elite (Neidhart 1970). In the domain of immigrant policy these two main characteristics of the political system provoke a high politicization of the migrant issue and the exclusion of immigrants from the political participation (Mahnig and Wimmer 2003). Because of the long decision-making process in a consociational democracy in which a compromise has to be negotiated, this system involved long periods of indecision with regard to immigration issues, since the interests in this political field are too divergent for the parties to come to an agreement easily. Furthermore, the instruments of direct democracy have forced the political elite to negotiate the concept of 'overforeignization' with populist challengers. Immigration policies that had permitted the various actors to come to an agreement to accommodate the economic needs of the country became one of the contested and controversial issues since the 1960s when radical right-wing populist parties started to gain public support in claiming that Switzerland was becoming 'over-foreignized' by the ever-increasing number of immigrants. Using the tools of direct democracy, these xenophobic movements succeeded in vetoing liberal government reforms and put their parties under pressure through the launching of eight popular initiatives and several referendums, asking to curb the presence of foreigners. Although none of these initiatives passed, they have consistently influenced the Swiss migration policy agenda and public opinion on immigration issues urging the Swiss government in adopting more restrictive admission policies (Niederberger 2004).

Very recently one political entrepreneur with a profiled anti-immigrant agenda has successfully entered the federal government by basically referring to a political campaign focused on the costs of immigration, control, security, and restriction: the right-wing populist Swiss Peoples Party (SVP), which had won the biggest share of the parliamentary votes in the 2003 and 2007 general elections. Since its main representative, Christoph Blocher, took responsibility in the national party and started to campaign against immigrants, Europe and the '*classe politique*' (to which he belonged), the SVP increased its electoral share from 11.9 per cent (1991) to 26.7 per cent (2003) and 28.9 per cent in the last election of 2007. Already the SVP's victory of 2003 upset the traditional consociational system which, since 1959, had distributed the seven seats in the Federal Council among the four leading political parties (Liberal-Radical Party, Social-Democratic Party, Christian-Democratic Party, and the SVP). Following the elections, the SVP forced the Parliament to accord them one more seat (at the cost of the Christian-Democratic Party) in the Federal Council and to elect Blocher as a member of government. Therefore, the historic leader of the SVP became Minister of Justice and Police in charge of migration and asylum questions. The strengthened position of the SVP in the government led it to approve several of Blocher's restrictive proposals on illegal migration, undocumented workers, asylum law abuses, and unsatisfactory international cooperation with regard to the readmission of rejected asylum seekers (D'Amato and Skenderovic 2008).

In the 2007 electoral campaign, once again immigrants were made responsible for social disorder, crime, youth violence, and welfare abuses. Worldwide attention attracted their posters accompanying the launch of the initiative to deport criminal immigrants, showing a white sheep throwing a black one out of country. The *New York Times* reported that the 'subliminal message of this campaign is that the influx of foreigners has somehow polluted Swiss society, straining the social welfare system and threatening the very identity of the country' (*New York Times*, October 8, 2007) Amazingly, the end of the campaign was – unusual for Switzerland – heavily focused on the figure of Christoph Blocher. The party wanted his position in the Federal Council to be strengthened through a larger share of the SVP in Parliament. The strategy worked and the party booked another incredible success at the election of October 21 with a share of nearly 30 per cent, displacing the Social Democrats and the Liberal-Radical Party to the second row. The SVP's strengthened presence in the Federal Council since 2003 put it into a win–win situation where the party can set the agenda for parliamentary debate and if they fail, they can launch a veto against any reform they oppose through a referendum. The tools of direct democracy enable them to highlight issues in ways that Parliament cannot contain. But even if this double game between government and opposition was appreciated by a large minority of the electorate, members of Parliament increasingly disapproved and opposed the dysfunctional role of Blocher who refused to be only one member among others of a consociational government. The fact that a cooptation and integration of Blocher into the federal government had failed took the Parliament to vote for Evelyn Widmer-Schlumpf, a moderate SVP representative, as new member of the Federal Council in December 2007. The parliament thereby demonstrated its disapprovement towards the populist, anti-Parliamentarian strategy and style of Blocher and his party.

Surprisingly, even if the electorate of the SVP has nearly tripled in the last 16 years, the share of those members opposing more opportunities for immigrants has not changed. Moreover, the leaders of the SVP have been able to mobilize that proportion of the population that since the 1960s voted for xenophobic issues at popular referenda but were electing other political parties (Skenderovic and D'Amato 2008).

The direct democratic possibilities of intervention offered by the political system make it quite likely that in the future the SVP will enforce its oppositional role using migration policy as a major issue, since controversial questions can never be contained to Parliament alone. Other European countries may be able to adopt policies 'behind closed doors' to extend political and social rights to migrants (Guiraudon 2000), but this is nearly impossible in Switzerland. However, even such a determined right-wing strategy may not always find popular support. An important point of reference is the defeat of the SVP at the voting of 1 June 2008. This voting on 'democratic naturalizations' was focused on their intention to abolish by a popular initiative the rule of law in the acquisition of Swiss citizenship, enforcing again the power of the municipalities to take even arbitrary decisions. Their final failure proved that even a strong and resolute party cannot always gain support, especially when their arguments hurt the sense of equal and just access to rights.

Concluding remarks

Is there any chance for multiculturalism in Switzerland, even for a renewed one? The answer is yes and no. The response is no if we consider the very recent developments in the Swiss political landscape. The rise of one of Europe's major right-wing populist parties, its relative majority in Parliament despite its switching between governmental responsibility and opposition (partly due also to their mobilization against a 'misleading multicultural policy', or in short: to any form of integrative programmes targeted towards immigrants) corresponds to the development of what can be called the rise of a new right-wing movement that is deeply anti-civil in its character. Their mobilization is due to their repugnance for any form of expanding cultural and citizenship rights to non-citizens. In general, the success of similar movements and parties all over Western Europe led to an enforcement and stabilization of ethno-centric attitudes, and contributed to the forming of a potential mindset that is influencing the cohesiveness of modern societies in a new way. The populist parties in all Europe share their opposition to multi-culturalist programmes, to human rights discourses and the unconditional rule of law. This is also the case in Switzerland. Strategically, they are convincing with conservative and utilitarian arguments, disseminating the opinion that certain incompatible social realities in the composition of our populations have to be acknowledged. They are accusing other parties to still believe in values like 'participation' or 'equal rights', in their eyes completely irrational attitudes with regard to an unbearable situation in the country. According to them, the way out of the multicultural 'mess' can only be indicated by 'true democrats' that pursue the interests of the 'true people'. Preferably, these policies follow conceptions of exclusive identity policies that should keep the autochthonous population free from any impositions of a migration society.

Indeed, the political and institutional structures of Switzerland, its consociational and direct democratic procedures favour the activation of neo-nationalist arguments and political initiatives. It will depend on the ability of 'multiculturalists' to counter these nationalist semantics with liberal concepts of a differentiated and plural society. This will be helped by the real practices of public institutions regarding immigrants. Schooling and formative curricula have already adopted long enduring measures that are labelled integrationist, even if they can be understood as multicultural in other contexts. In everyday practice the social and ethnic background of the public is taken into consideration, and used to amplify the investment in the careers of immigrants' children. Whether or not multiculturalists will be able to prove the success of their path is still an open question. Yet, the important challenge is to find adequate answers to the contemporary needs of the real world.

Notes

1 The cultural minority who speak different dialects of this romance language consists of around 50,000 people who live in the canton of Graubünden in the Eastern part of Switzerland.
2 Indeed, migration and integration policies are matters of cantonal sovereignty to a certain degree.
3 'Nach mehrjährigem Aufenthalt sollten [sie] ... nicht mehr auf die Gemeinschaft von Landsleuten angewiesen sein, sondern unter Schweizern und wie Schweizer zu leben beginnen' (Schweiz. Bundesamt für Wirtschaft und Arbeit 1964).

4 'Es muss verhindert werden, dass gewisse Gruppen von Menschen, wie etwa die Muslime, die Türken und die Angehörigen aus dem ehemaligen Jugoslawien in die Rolle von Problemausländern gedrängt, dabei noch mehr diskriminiert und isoliert werden.'

5 'Nicht die Aufnahmegesellschaft ist es letztlich, die den Migranten und die Migrantin integriert, sondern dies liegt weitgehend in deren eigener Verantwortung. Nur wer dazu bereit ist, soll auch mit entsprechender Chancengleichheit und Verbesserung der persönlichen Lebenssituation rechnen dürfen. Integrationsförderung bleibt somit stets Hilfe zur Selbsthilfe.'

References

Arlettaz, G. (1985) 'Démographie et identité nationale (1850–1914): la Suisse et "La question des étrangers"', *Etudes et sources*, 11: 83–174.

Bommes, M. (2003) 'The Shrinking Inclusive Capacity of the National Welfare State: International Migration and the Deregulation of Identity Formation', *Comparative Social Research*, 22: 43–67.

Brubaker, R. (1992) *Citizenship and Nationhood in France and Germany*, Cambridge, MA: Harvard University Press.

Brumlik, M. and Leggewie, C. (1992) 'Konturen der Einwanderungsgesellschaft. Nationale Identität, Multikulturalismus und Civil Society', in K.J. Bade (ed.) *Deutsche im Ausland – Fremde in Deutschland*, München: C.H. Beck, pp. 430–41.

Castles, S. (1994) 'La sociologie et la peur de "cultures incompatibles": commentaires sur le rapport Hoffmann-Nowotny', in M.-C. Caloz and M. Fontolliet Honoré (eds) *Europe: montrez patte blanche!: les nouvelles frontières du 'laboratoire Schengen'*, Genève: Centre Europe-Tiers Monde, pp. 370–84.

D'Amato, G. and Gerber, B. (eds) (2005) *Herausforderung Integration: städtische Migrationspolitik in der Schweiz und in Europa*, Zürich: Seismo.

D'Amato, G. and Skenderovic, D. (2008) 'Outsiders Becoming Power Players: Radical Right-Wing Populist Parties and Their Impact in Swiss Migration Policy', in M.A. Niggli (ed.) *Right-wing Extremism in Switzerland – An International Comparison*, Baden-Baden: Nomos.

Deutsch, K. W. (1976) *Die Schweiz als ein paradigmatischer Fall politischer Integration*, Bern: Haupt.

Efionayi-Mäder, D., Lavenex, S., Niederberger, M., Wanner, P. and Wichmann, N. (2003) 'Switzerland', in J. Niessen and Y. Schibel (eds) *EU and US Approaches to the Management of Immigration: Comparative Perspectives*, Brussels: Migration Policy Group, pp. 491–519.

Efionayi-Mäder, D., Niederberger, J. M. and Wanner, P. (2005) *Switzerland Faces Common European Challenges*. Online. Available HTTP: http://www.migrationinformation.org/Resources/switzerland.cfm.

Ehrenzeller, B. and Good, P.-L. (2003) *Rechtsgutachten zu Handen des Gemeinderates von Emmen betreffend das Einbürgerungsverfahren in der Gemeinde Emmen*, University of St Gallen.

Ehret, R. (1999) *Leitbild und Handlungskonzept des Regierungsrates zur Integrationspolitik des Kantons Basel-Stadt*, Basel: Polizei-und Militärdepartement des Kantons Basel-Stadt.

Garrido, A. (1990) 'Les années vingt et la première initiative xénophobe en Suisse', in H.U. Jost (ed.) *Racisme et xénophobies: colloque à l'Université de Lausanne, 24–25 novembre 1988*, Lausanne: Université de Lausanne, Section d'histoire, pp. 37–45.

Guiraudon, V. (2000) *Les politiques d'immigration en Europe: Allemagne, France, Pays-Bas*, Paris: L'Harmattan.

Habermas, J. (1992) *Faktizität und Geltung. Beiträge zur Diskurstheorie des Rechts und des demokratischen Rechtsstaats*, Frankfurt a. Main: Suhrkamp.

Hollifield, J. F. (1992) *Immigrants, Markets, and States the Political Economy of Postwar Europe*, Cambridge, MA: Harvard University Press.

Holmes, M. (1988) *Forgotten Migrants: Foreign Workers in Switzerland before World War I*, Rutherford: Fairleigh Dickinson University Press.

Ireland, P. R. (1994) *The Policy Challenge of Ethnic Diversity: Immigrant Politics in France and Switzerland*, Cambridge MA: Harvard University Press.

Jacobson, D. (1996) *Rights across Borders Immigration and the Decline of Citizenship*, Baltimore: Johns Hopkins University Press.

Kälin, W. (2000) *Grundrechte im Kulturkonflikt: Freiheit und Gleichheit in der Einwanderungsgesellschaft*, Zürich: NZZ Verlag.

Katzenstein, P. J. (1987) *Corporatism and Change Austria, Switzerland and the Politics of Industry*, Ithaca: Cornell University Press.

Kessler, T. (2005) 'Das Integrationsleitbild des Kantons Basel-Stadt', in G. D'Amato and B. Gerber (eds) *Herausforderung Integration. Städtische Migrationspolitik in der Schweiz und in Europa*, Zürich: Seismo, pp. 104–11.

Kohler, G. (1994) 'Demokratie, Integration, Gemeinschaft: Thesen im Vorfeld einer Einwanderungsgesetzdiskussion', in *Migration: und wo bleibt das Ethische?* Zürich: Schweizerischer Arbeitskreis für ethische Forschung, pp. 17–34.

Leuthold, R. and Aeberhard C. (2002) 'Der Fall Emmen', *Das Magazin*, 20: 18–31.

Linder, W. (1998) *Swiss Democracy: Possible Solutions to Conflict in Multicultural Societies*, Houndmills: Macmillan Press.

Mahnig, H. (1996) *Das migrationspolitische Feld der Schweiz: eine politikwissenschaftliche Analyse der Vernehmlassung zum Arbenzbericht*, Neuchâtel: Forum suisse pour l'étude des migrations.

Mahnig, H. and Piguet, E. (2003) 'La politique suisse d'immigration de 1948 à 1998: évolution et effets', in H.-R. Wicker, R. Fibbi and W. Haug (eds) *Les migrations et la Suisse: résultats du Programme national de recherche 'Migrations et relations interculturelles'*, Zurich: Seismo, pp. 63–103.

Mahnig, H. and Wimmer, A. (2003) 'Integration without Immigrant Policy: the Case of Switzerland', in F. Heckmann and D. Schnapper (eds) *The Integration of Immigrants in European Societies: National Differences and Trends of Convergence*, Stuttgart: Lucius & Lucius, pp. 135–64.

Neidhart, L. (1970) *Plebiszit und pluralitäre Demokratie. Eine Analyse der Funktion des schweizerischen Gesetzesreferendums*, Bern: Francke.

Niederberger, J. M. (2004) *Ausgrenzen, Assimilieren, Integrieren: die Entwicklung einer schweizerischen Integrationspolitik*, Zürich: Seismo.

Riedo, R. (1996) *Umrisse zu einem Integrationskonzept*, Bern: Eidgenössische Ausländerkommission.

Romano, G. (1996) 'Zeit der Krise – Krise der Zeit: Identität, Überfremdung und verschlüsselte Zeitstrukturen', in A. Ernst and E. Wigger (eds) *Die neue Schweiz? eine Gesellschaft zwischen Integration und Polarisierung (1910–1930)*, Zürich: Chronos, pp. 41–77.

Schnapper, D. (1997) 'Citoyenneté et reconnaissance des hommes et des cultures', in J. Hainard and R. Kaehr (eds) *Dire les autres: réflexions et pratiques ethnologiques: textes offerts à Pierre Centlivres*, Lausanne: Payot, p. 377 p.: ill.; 8.

Schuh, S. (1987) 'Luciano und die Höhle der Elefanten – Selektionsdruck im Spannungsfeld zwischen zwei Welten', in A. Gretler, A.-N. Perret-Clermont and Edo Poglia (eds) *Fremde Heimat: soziokulturelle und sprachliche Probleme von Fremdarbeiterkindern*, Cousset: Delval, pp. 223–39.

Schweiz. Bundesamt für Migration (2006) *Probleme der Integration von Ausländerinnen und Ausländern in der Schweiz: Bestandesaufnahme der Fakten, Ursachen, Risikogruppen, Massnahmen und des integrationspolitischen Handlungsbedarfs*, Bern-Wabern: Bundesamt für Migration.

Schweiz. Bundesamt für Wirtschaft und Arbeit (1964) *Das Problem der ausländischen Arbeitskräfte: Bericht der Studienkommission für das Problem der ausländischen Arbeitskräfte*, Bern: Eidgenössische Drucksachen-und Materialzentrale.

Schweiz. Bundesrat (1991) *Bericht des Bundesrates zur Ausländer-und Flüchtlingspolitik vom 15. Mai 1991*, Bern: Eidgenössische Drucksachen-und Materialzentrale.

Schweizerische Konferenz der kantonalen Erziehungsdirektoren (1972) *Grundsätze zur Schulung der Gastarbeiterkinder, vom 2. November 1972*, Bern: Schweizerische Konferenz der kantonalen Erziehungsdirektoren.

——(1976) *Grundsätze zur Schulung der Gastarbeiterkinder: Ergänzung vom 14. Mai 1976*, Bern: Schweizerische Konferenz der kantonalen Erziehungsdirektoren.

——(1982) *Ausländerkinder in unseren Schulen: nach wie vor ein Problem?* Genf: Sekretariat EDK.

——(1985) *Empfehlungen zur Schulung der fremdsprachigen Kinder, vom 24. Oktober 1985*, Bern: Schweizerische Konferenz der kantonalen Erziehungsdirektoren.

——(1991) *Empfehlungen zur Schulung der fremdsprachigen Kinder, vom 24./25. Oktober 1991*, Bern: Schweizerische Konferenz der kantonalen Erziehungsdirektoren.

——(1993) *Interkulturelle Pädagogik in der Schweiz: Sonderfall oder Schulalltag? Zusammenstellung der Tagungsbeiträge: EDK-Convegno, Emmetten, 1992*, Bern: EDK, Schweizerische Konferenz der kantonalen Erziehungsdirektoren.

——(1995a) *Empfehlungen und Beschlüsse*, Bern: Schweizerische Konferenz der kantonalen Erziehungsdirektoren (EDK).

——(1995b) *Erklärung zur Förderung des zweisprachigen Unterrichts in der Schweiz, vom 2. März 1995*, Bern: Schweizerische Konferenz der kantonalen Erziehungsdirektoren.

——(2003) *Aktionsplan 'PISA 2000' – Folgemassnahmen*, Bern: Schweizerische Konferenz der kantonalen Erziehungsdirektoren.

Skenderovic, D. and D'Amato, G. (2008) *Mit dem Fremden politisieren. Rechtspopulistische Parteien und Migrationspolitik in der Schweiz seit den 1960er Jahren*, Zürich: Chronos.

Soysal, Y. N. (1994) *Limits of Ccitizenship: Migrants and Postnational Membership in Europe*, Chicago: University of Chicago Press.

Steinberg, J. (1996) *Why Switzerland?* Cambridge: Cambridge University Press.

Steiner-Khamsi, G. (1992) *Multikulturelle Bildungspolitik in der Postmodern*, Opladen: Leske + Budrich.

Tanner, J. (1993) 'Multikulturelle Gesellschaft – eine Alternative zur "nationalen Identität"?', *Friconomy. Zeitschrift der Wirtschaftsstudenten der Universität Freiburg*, 2: 16–20.

——(1998) 'Nationalmythos, Überfremdungsängste und Minderheitenpolitik in der Schweiz', in S. Prodolliet (ed.) *Blickwechsel: die multikulturelle Schweiz an der Schwelle zum 21. Jahrhundert*, Luzern: Caritas-Verlag, pp. 83–94.

Truniger, M. (2002a) *Qualität in multikulturellen Schulen, QUIMS: Schlussbericht der Projektleitung über die zweite Phase (1999 bis 2001)*, Zürich: Erziehungsdirektion.

——(2002b) *Schulung der fremdprachigen Kinder und interkulturelle Pädagogik: Überprüfung der Umsetzung der Empfehlungen (Schuljahre 1999/2000 und 2000/01): Bericht zuhanden des Bildungsrats*, Zürich: Erziehungsdirektion.

Wicker, H.-R. (2009) 'Die neue schweizerische Integrationspolitik', in E. Piñero, I. Bopp and G. Kreis (eds) *Fördern und fordern im Fokus. Leerstellen des scheizerischen Integrationsdiskurses*, Zürich: Seismo.

8 Germany

Integration policy and pluralism in a self-conscious country of immigration

Karen Schönwälder

Introduction

Multiculturalism has become a derogatory term in present day Germany. Politicians tend to either omit it from their vocabulary or to emphasize their distance from 'multicultural dreams'. Few public figures still commit themselves to a policy of multiculturalism. The term is now almost exclusively used as a negative image of the past, as a synonym for the ills and illusions of a liberal left that allegedly caused many of the problems German society currently faces.

Of course, Germany has not abandoned an official policy or leading paradigm of multiculturalism. Such an official policy never existed – at least on the federal level. In Germany, attitudes to multiculturalism are important as part of a political and cognitive framework that determines future developments. This framework has, in the past few years, changed in important ways. While in the past commitment or opposition to multiculturalism divided those who welcomed or resisted Germany's transformation into an immigrant society, today these old trenches have largely disappeared, as the last major political force, the Christian Democrats have slowly moved towards an acceptance of immigration. In a statement typical of the stance taken by the Conservatives of Angela Merkel's government, the Christian Democratic Union (CDU) Minister for integration, Maria Böhmer (2005), said that while Germany was not a classic immigration country, Germans had to face the fact that, of Germany's inhabitants, 14 million had a migration background. While it was a government of Social Democrats and Green Party that pushed through the long-awaited reform of the citizenship law, Conservative politicians have taken steps towards the symbolic recognition of religious plurality and of the key importance of the integration of migrants: it was Interior Minister Schäuble who hosted the first official Islam Conference and Chancellor Merkel who played host to the first Integration Summit of the federal government in July 2006. Today, the old battles about whether Germany is a country of immigration seem settled, and the doors seem wide open towards constructive efforts to improve the position of immigrants and their descendants in German society. Germany's inhabitants now have to determine what kind of future this immigrant society envisages for itself and what space will be allowed for the development of immigrant cultures, languages and religions. But while the facts of past immigration and the resultant plurality of backgrounds and experiences in the German population are now accepted, this is not accompanied by a generally positive approach to cultural diversity and public representation of minorities as groups. Germany's life as a self-conscious country of immigration begins in a climate unfavourable to an active promotion of minority rights and identities.

In this chapter, I shall first analyse policy changes of the past decade in greater detail. I will then turn to reasons for the weakness of multicultural positions focussing on popular attitudes. The following section draws attention to the fact that, in spite of an official policy that has traditionally been hostile to immigration and that is still hostile to institutionalized plurality, elements of multicultural policies exist in Germany. I shall conclude by offering some thoughts on the prospects for the development of an explicit policy of pluralism and public recognition of minorities.

Political reorientations: Germany as self-conscious country of immigration and the challenge of integration

The policy reorientations of the past few years, marked by the new Citizenship Act (in force since 2000) and the Immigration Act (in force since 2005), can be seen as parts of an incremental, slow policy change spanning three different governments (Schönwälder 2004, 2006). The core substance of this change was to put an end to attempts to revise immigration processes resulting from past labour recruitment and instead to accept past immigration as a fact. Previous policy, beginning with the recruitment ban in 1973 and including financial incentives for migrants to return to their countries of origin, was guided, to a considerable extent, by the aim to counteract settlement processes of former guest workers and keep permanent immigration levels to a minimum. Around 1990 this policy was given up. Cautious changes to the citizenship law under Conservative Chancellor Helmut Kohl represented first steps towards an explicit official acceptance of the guest worker immigrants as German.[1] At the same time, new immigration was to be prevented by severe restrictions to the right to asylum, among other measures. The policy change was pushed further under the Social Democratic and Green Party Coalition (elected in 1998), which introduced a kind of *ius soli* citizenship principle and tried to open Germany's borders to new immigration.[2] The fact that the Conservative-led grand coalition formed in 2005 has continued this policy signals that the Conservatives have given up their no-immigration stance, at least in regard to past processes.[3] The old conflicts, however, continue in the form of struggles about stricter conditions for the acquisition of German citizenship. There is a danger that new restrictions and the symbolic effect of debates about which new citizens are deemed worthy or unwelcome may counteract the intention of increasing the naturalization rates of immigrants and hinder their full incorporation into German society.

As one aspect of the policy change, a political consensus has emerged over the past few years that major efforts must be made to improve the integration of permanent immigrants into German society. The government has declared integration a key political theme for the coming years and stressed the importance of this issue by elevating the Commissioner for Foreigners' Affairs to a *Staatsminister* in the Chancellory, who is responsible for migrant integration. Occasionally, the revision of Conservative policy is presented as mainly an adjustment to changing realities, thus obscuring the real extent of change. 'Immigration is no longer our problem', Interior Minister Schäuble claimed, 'our problem is integration' (2006a). According to this view, the times when all efforts were concentrated on fencing off a relentless stream of refugees and controlling the immigration of ethnic Germans are over.[4] Attention can now turn to the integration of permanent immigrants into society. Both Schäuble and Integration Minister Böhmer (2005) have announced a paradigm change from migration to integration policy. But what does 'integration' mean, how assimilationist is this concept and how much space does it allow for ethnic plurality?

It would be too simple to say that current integration concepts are aimed exclusively at cultural assimilation. Rather, integration is viewed in both socio-economic and cultural terms. The disastrous educational and labour market situation of individuals with a migration background[5] are much debated topics, and creating better opportunities to participate (*Teilhabechancen*) has been announced a political goal. But integration and equal opportunities are not promised to everyone: only some groups of immigrants are to be integrated, and the opportunities granted may not be equal. Furthermore, there is an emphasis on cultural and identificational assimilation, and themes like sanctions, pressure and selection are constantly reiterated.[6]

A government website explained what 'integration' meant by emphasizing that individuals who desire to stay in Germany permanently have to fulfil certain requirements, firstly to learn the German language. German society shall, on the other hand, grant permanent immigrants wide-ranging chances to participate in its societal, political and economic life, 'if possible' on an equal footing.[7] Group rights and legitimate claims to recognition do not feature in this concept. On the contrary, the claim that no society can tolerate 'an internal separatism based on cultural divisions' may be read as a rejection of multiculturalism.[8]

Typical features of current government statements on integration include an emphasis on mutual exchange and living together, on communication and command of the German language, as well as the demand that key constitutional values and German culture be accepted by the immigrants. Asked about his criteria for a successful integration process, the Interior Minister replied: 'Our values and principles have to be accepted and respected', and referred to women's rights, freedom of opinion and the renunciation of violence (Schäuble 2006b). Integration Minister Böhmer, explaining how immigrants could be firmly 'rooted' in German society, said: 'They have to speak our language, know our history, and accept our values and our law' (2005). The slogan of '*fordern und fördern*' (challenge and support), frequently used to describe the core principle of official (integration and general social) policy, legitimizes a focus on the individual who is offered help but is in turn constantly required to prove his or her willingness to co-operate and achieve the necessary preconditions for employment. It is frequently alleged, more or less explicitly, that it is mainly the immigrants who are to be blamed for deficits in interethnic contact, German-language competencies and educational achievements. Immigrants are criticized for allegedly retreating into secluded communities and for failing to make the necessary efforts to successfully integrate into German society. Multiculturalism is being derided as the concept that legitimized the alleged retreat into minority cultures and as a policy that remains indifferent towards non-integration as well as social and cultural segregation.[9]

Currently, Conservative politicians seem to be setting the tone of the integration debate. But any outline of the public debate should, of course, include other actors as well. The Social Democrats (SPD) never committed themselves unequivocally to a policy of ethnic pluralism. In 2006, an SPD policy paper approved by a leading body (*Präsidium*) was publicly presented as taking a position equally distant from right populism as from 'multicultural dreams' (SPD 2006a and b). 'Fair chances, clear rules' is their motto that replicates the '*fordern und fördern*' rhetoric of rights and obligations. Migrants are urged to make greater efforts to integrate and to express more clearly their support for the constitution. At the same time, programmatic texts often include statements emphasizing the value of cultural diversity. Thus, the SPD faction in the federal parliament has stressed that the 'different life worlds, values, traditions' of people from different countries of origin have contributed to shaping German society. Living together required mutual recognition of this cultural diversity (SPD-Bundestagsfraktion 2006).[10] It is often the documents and speeches addressed to a wider audience that focus on reminding the migrants of their obligations and delineating the limits of tolerance. Thus, Gerhard Schröder (2004), still Chancellor at the time, stated that 'The plurality of cultures in our societies is a fact that cannot be reversed' – only to continue by defining the limits of such plurality: 'But no culture may be allowed to remove itself from the fabric of society.' Altogether, the Social Democrats are more likely than the Conservatives to stress the values of diversity, but there is much overlap between their positions, and the Social Democrats sometimes appear more fearful of xenophobic voters than the Christian Democrats.

The Green Party, once the key representative of multiculturalism, nowadays prefers a more cautious approach. In the media, a new policy paper of the parliamentary faction was widely interpreted as a retreat from past positions. In fact, even though the term 'multicultural' appears only once in the 15-page paper, the Greens still emphasize the gains from immigration and the positive values of diversity (Bündnis 90/Die Grünen 2006). But attacks against discrimination and racism as well as demands for the active promotion of minority cultures, group representation, and so on, have clearly been moved to the background. Instead Green Party politicians now emphasize that more has to be asked of the immigrants themselves – thus falling into line with the mainstream at least in this respect.[11]

There are, however, still voices in the political debate that defend the values of diversity, sometimes explicitly under the heading of multiculturalism. The Social Democrats and the Green Party have attracted criticism for failing to clearly commit themselves to the values of a plural society (Tagesspiegel, 11 July 2006; contributions in 'Dossier Multikulturalismus'). The *Türkische Gemeinde in Deutschland*, an umbrella organization of German-Turkish groups, has recently published a policy paper that demands a 'transcultural policy' for a 'multicultural society' and contains many classic demands ranging from minority representation in school curricula and the media to the recognition of migrant groups as official representatives of parts of the population (tgd 2006). The Berlin Senate's Commissioner for Integration and Migration has publicly insisted that multiculturalism, properly defined, is a useful concept to describe the potentials that the diversity of German society contains for the future (Piening 2006). The Berlin government's integration concept propagates the promotion of diversity (Senat Berlin 2005).

Nevertheless, the dominating picture is one in which integration is strongly linked to obligations on the part of the migrants and adjustment to mainstream culture and values. The latter is not merely related to a wish for uniformity but also seen as a precondition to improved opportunities – and yet, adjustment is the demand of the time.

Public opinions on ethnic plurality

To what extent does the political debate reflect public opinion, and how strong is resistance against diversity policies among the German population? Public opinion is not enthusiastic, to say the least, as regards ethnic diversity. There are a number of surveys that contain information on attitudes towards cultural diversity. They do not, however, provide a detailed longer-term picture of the development of such attitudes, and only some of these surveys allow for sound international comparisons. Nevertheless, it is safe to say that there is strong support for the demand that immigrants should adjust to German ways and that Germans are on average more sceptical as regards the benefits of ethnic diversity than some (but not all) of their European neighbours.

As part of the regularly conducted ALLBUS-survey participants are asked whether they agree or disagree with the opinion that foreigners living in Germany should adjust their lifestyles a bit more to that of the Germans. This opinion has enjoyed majority support since 1980. Furthermore, between 1994 and 2002 support went up from around 50 to more than 70 per cent (even 46 per cent of Green Party voters agreed in 2002), and in 2006 it reached

79 per cent. This clearly indicates that demands for an adjustment of culture and lifestyles have recently become more popular. Support for other clearly discriminatory positions, however, went down over time (Datenreport 2004: 584–89; GESIS 2007).[12]

Eurobarometer Surveys show that resistance to multiculturalism is relatively high in Germany (it is higher in Greece and on a similar level in Belgium), but that a few years ago a majority of Germans held a generally positive opinion of diversity. In 1997, 55 per cent of Germans 'tended to agree' with the statement that 'It is a good thing for any society to be made up of people from different races, religions or cultures', and in 2000 53 per cent still held that opinion (SORA 2001: 55; in the UK 75 per cent and 67 per cent agreed; in the Netherlands 76 per cent and 74 per cent in 1997 and 2000, respectively).

It should be noted, however, that when asked more specifically, respondents everywhere in Europe tended to become more sceptical: In Germany, only 34 per cent in 1997 and 39 per cent in 2000 'tended to agree' with the statement that 'Germany's diversity in terms of race, religion or culture adds to its strengths' (SORA 2001: 55; in the UK 51 per cent and in the Netherlands 53 per cent tended to agree to the respective question). These different responses may indicate that people passively accept diversity ('It is a good thing ... '), whereas the assumption that it strengthens their society is perceived as a stronger statement and is therefore not as widely accepted.

With regard to ethnic plurality in the classroom, public opinion in Germany is closer to that in the UK and in the Netherlands. 53 per cent of Germans tend to agree with the statement 'Where schools make the necessary efforts, the education of all children can be enriched by the presence of children from minority groups'. This was the same percentage as in the UK, while in the Netherlands 62 per cent shared this opinion (SORA 2001: 44).

Unfortunately, the Eurobarometer results reported here are already a few years old, and results for 2003 are not yet available in full detail. Thus recent developments, including reactions to the terrorist attacks since 2001, are not reflected. Responses to questions asked in the context of a major regular election survey indicate that public opinion may have changed significantly. For summer 2001 (July, i.e. before 11 September) the responses show a level of support for cultural plurality similar to that shown by the Eurobarometer: When asked whether they agreed that foreigners represented 'a cultural enrichment', 54 per cent of Germans agreed. By 2006, however, support for this opinion was down to 38 per cent (May 2004: 43 per cent). Mirroring this shift, a majority of respondents in 2006 perceived foreigners as a threat: When asked whether they saw foreigners living in Germany as representing a 'threat of foreignization' ('*eine Gefahr der Überfremdung*'), 54 per cent responded affirmatively. Five years earlier, when a majority had supported pluralism, only one third of respondents had felt threatened (2004: 48 per cent, surveys of the *Forschungsgruppe Wahlen*; see *Süddeutsche Zeitung* 2004; 2006).

Given that a significant share of immigrants in Germany are Muslims, it is particularly worrying that in 2006 only 36 per cent of Germans said they had a very or somewhat favourable opinion of Muslims (The Pew Global Attitudes Project 2006: 10). In France and Britain, more that 60 per cent registered favourable opinions – in spite of Islamist terrorism and urban riots. As many as 70 per cent of those questioned in Germany believe that there is a conflict between being a devout Muslim and living in a modern society – while among German Muslims themselves, 57 per cent do not see such a conflict (Pew 2006: 23). Respect for the cultural achievements of Muslim societies has declined steeply: in 2005 almost half of Germans rejected the statement that 'Islam has produced an admirable culture'; this is up from 37 per cent in 2003 (Leibold *et al.* 2006: 4).

Hostile opinions among the population explain, to some extent, why politicians tread cautiously when positioning themselves with regard to rights and responsibilities of immigrants. Assimilationist demands are popular, and many Germans have turned against ethnic pluralism in the past few years. And yet, it should not be overlooked that a majority of Germans held positive opinions of ethnic diversity only a couple of years ago. There is no insurmountable opposition to a policy that recognizes and promotes distinct identities.[13] This is further underlined by the observation that, in spite of the widespread rejection of 'multiculturalism', some policies that can be regarded as typical for such an approach do exist in Germany. In the following section, I will give a few examples of such policies and then try to explain this apparently contradictory picture.

Multicultural policies without multiculturalism?

If we apply a definition suggested by Keith Banting and Will Kymlicka, fully developed multiculturalism policies hardly exist in Germany. According to their definition multiculturalism policies are policies that 'go beyond the protection of the basic civil and political rights guaranteed to all individuals in a liberal-democratic state, to also extend some level of public recognition and support for ethnocultural minorities to maintain and express their distinct identities and practices' (Banting and Kymlicka 2006: 1). In Germany, wide-ranging official policies linked to an explicit programme of recognizing and promoting ethnic plurality do not exist. However, there are clear elements of policies often linked to multiculturalism (Banting *et al.* 2006: 56–57).[14]

Several cities with a high percentage of foreigners among their inhabitants, such as Stuttgart[15] and Frankfurt on Main,[16] have committed themselves to multicultural or intercultural[17] policies. According to Dieter Filsinger (2000: 232), an intercultural turn occurred in the mid-1990s when foreigner policy was replaced with integration strategies that included an adjustment of mainstream institutions to the reality of immigration rather than providing specific counselling services for foreigners. There are no indications that these policies are currently subjected to major revision. It seems more typical that concessions are being made to predominating trends without necessarily changing the substance of what is being done. Thus, in a 2002 policy paper, Stuttgart distanced itself from a [theoretical] form of multiculturalism that favours coexistence without interaction, and instead subscribes to an 'intercultural approach' characterized by multiple exchange, encounters and dialogue. The city still emphasizes its positive attitude to diversity and a plurality of lifestyles, which are perceived as a resource for the city's development, and its commitment to participation and fighting exclusion.

Several cities have built up offices responsible for migrant integration, intercultural activities, conflict mediation and sometimes problems of discrimination. The most prominent example is Frankfurt's Office for Multicultural Affairs (*Amt für Multikulturelle Angelegenheiten, AMKA*). The AMKA was established in 1989 with the deliberate aim of coordinating the work of all administrative bodies in relation to issues of cultural pluralism. Through the composition of its staff, it was simultaneously meant to act as a body that would give immigrants a voice within the local administration. It was considered an innovative institutional response to the multiethnic structure of the city's population. One of AMKA's main tasks has been to convince local government bodies of an agenda of anti-discrimination. Its altogether persuasive approach involves mediation, conflict resolution, counselling services, campaigns for tolerance, support for migrant organizations, the promotion of cultural activities, and measures to increase the labour market participation of immigrants (Amt für Multikulturelle Angelegenheiten 1990; Leggewie 1993: 46–60; Radtke 2003: 63–66).

Detailed research on local policies is scarce. It seems there is often no clear agenda or policy statement, and the content and purpose of such policies remain vague. Typically, policies include measures intended to support the process of German-language acquisition, to improve the educational performance of children from immigrant backgrounds, the introduction of intercultural elements in school curricula, and the development of community-based institutions and projects devoted to promoting contacts and exchange between native Germans and immigrants. More recently, attempts to adapt the structure of the local administration to a changed socio-cultural environment ('intercultural opening of institutions') have been at the centre of local policies (Filsinger 2002: 16–19; see also Ireland 2004: 60–115). Cities have also developed sets of measures to welcome new residents, ranging from brochures to introduction courses.

In a federal state, the regional states (*Länder*) play a major part in many policy areas that are relevant to the incorporation of immigrants into society and society's attitudes to ethnic diversity. Education, for instance, is the responsibility of *Länder* authorities. In fact, a number of school curricula contain elements of multicultural, or rather intercultural education. In 1996, the *Kultusministerkonferenz* (the body of regional ministers for culture and education) passed recommendations on intercultural education in German schools. As Krüger-Potratz (2004) argues, this was a response to internationalization, European integration, as well as increasing cultural plurality in Germany. Aims include the promotion of tolerance and humanitarian principles, knowledge about and respect for other cultures, and the ability to deal peacefully with possible interethnic, religious and cultural conflicts. Regional authorities are encouraged to make sure that in school education no society or culture is marginalized or denigrated and that non-German students are offered opportunities for positive identification.

Mother-tongue education does exist – although there is considerable regional variation and these programmes are not necessarily part of multicultural policies.[18] The teaching of immigrants' mother tongues was not introduced as a minority right but in order to enable guest worker children to reintegrate in their countries of origin. The fact that it continues to exist after this policy has been abandoned demonstrates the persistence of once-established structures as well as the continuing demand for such classes, but it is probably also due to the support of 'multiculturalist' officials and teachers. Language classes are usually not integrated with regular education, and attendance is voluntary (Gogolin *et al.* 2001). Immigrant languages play, at best, a marginal role in state education. But even in now CDU-governed North Rhine-Westphalia, the Education Act still prescribes that schools respect and promote the ethnic, cultural and linguistic identities (mother tongue) of non-native speakers among the students. In spite of such provisions, there is a clear trend towards an emphasis on German language teaching. Under the pressures of a politically unfavourable climate and budgetary restrictions, mother tongue education is under attack, and there are clear indications that resources will be diverted towards German-language education (Gogolin 2005).

In many cities and on the regional level, there are bodies to consult with ethnic communities – or rather foreign citizens.[19] In the regional state of North Rhine-Westphalia in 2004, 97 such local bodies existed, elected by, on average, 13 per cent of the electorate. They are organized in an umbrella organization (*Landesarbeitsgemeinschaft der kommunalen Migrantenvertretungen Nordrhein-Westfalen, LAGA NRW*; see www.laga-nrw.de). This body receives subsidies from the regional government. The [previous] government of North Rhine-Westphalia described the 'strengthening of the foreigners' ability to represent themselves' as an issue of great importance (NRW 2000: 29). In Berlin, a new body consisting of representatives from immigrant communities was formed in 2003, but it is too early to assess its impact. To some extent, the new bodies represent the search for alternatives to the older Foreigners' Advisory Councils (*Ausländerbeiräte*). Assessments of these councils are more or less devastating, due to a variety of factors including their limited popularity among foreign citizens and their extremely limited rights (Hoffmann 2002).

Ethnic group organizations or activities, occasionally and on a very limited scale, receive funding from the federal, regional and local authorities. North Rhine Westphalia, as one of the first regional states, in 1997 began to financially support migrant organisations and a limited number of projects by ethnic group organizations (NRW 2000: 32; Rütten 1998: 26–27). Berlin did the same even earlier. Other states and some local authorities also provide funding for such initiatives. To give just one example, the federal government's Commissioner for Culture and the Media subsidizes a couple of institutions, for example an Afghan refugee centre and a Vietnamese cultural centre, under the heading of 'promotion of the independent cultural life of ethnic minorities in Germany' (Bundesregierung 2005: 219). A national, comprehensive overview of funding for ethnic group organizations does not exist. Neither do we have evaluations of the effects of such support on ethnic group organisation or consciousness. However, in spite of the probably very limited financial and political support, the fact that official funding for ethnic minority activities is provided demonstrates that there is some room for manoeuvre for a promotion of diversity, and that policies are not consequently assimilationist. Even the recently elected Christian Democratic government of North Rhine-Westphalia states in its 'Action Plan for Integration' (*Aktionsplan Integration*) that the government pursues a policy of equal opportunities and respect for cultural and religious differences – thus repeating the exact phrase of its Social Democratic predecessors (NRW 2004: 121; NRW 2006: 14). The government even intends to quantitatively and qualitatively extend its support for the 'promotion of the cultural practice of immigrants'. Furthermore, there are indications that, within integration strategies, migrant organizations are being discovered as useful actors. In the plural structures of the German welfare state, these organizations may increasingly play a role as agencies whose specific competence and access to co-ethnics enables them to implement integration strategies more effectively than other institutions.

As regards other measures listed by Banting and Kymlicka as typical elements of multiculturalism policies, representation of ethnic groups in the media does occur, insofar as some of the bodies controlling public broadcasting stations include representatives from the foreign population, such as the *Rundfunkrat* (Broadcasting Council) of the *Westdeutscher Rundfunk* (West German Broadcasting Service). However, journalists with a migration background are still underrepresented, and media reporting is subject to widespread criticism for its inadequate reporting on immigration issues (Geißler and Pöttker 2005).

Overall, some interventions often regarded as typical of multiculturalism policies do exist in Germany, in spite of a past political framework marked by the dominance of anti-immigration policies. There are several reasons why these interventions might continue to exist in a framework hostile to multiculturalism: General norms to which any liberal democracy subscribes (respect for individual rights, religious freedom, freedom to practise one's own language and culture) can form the basis for some of the measures mentioned. (However, the example of a Dutch city that banned the public use of languages other than Dutch shows that one may doubt how firmly such rights are indeed anchored in a liberal framework.) Tolerance of other cultures and peaceful coexistence are nowadays common ideals in education. Furthermore, the German constitution guarantees a fairly strong protection of religious freedom (Lepsius 2006) – although the building of mosques is often a conflict-laden issue at the local level, and the two major Christian Churches enjoy a privileged position with the state. In contrast to France, headscarves have not been banned for Islamic students – although, in several regional states, teachers are not allowed to wear them.

Some measures that can be seen as serving 'multicultural' intentions have arisen from intentions other than promoting the identities and group representation of current immigrant groups and may survive for such reasons. Thus the promotion of minority cultures has a long tradition in Germany and goes back to pre-war national minorities policy. With regard to 'national', in particular ethnic German minorities, there is a long-established and wide-ranging consensus that they should enjoy certain collective rights and that their cultural activities be supported. Although sharp dividing lines have been drawn between immigrant and national minorities, the former occasionally profit from positive attitudes to the preservation of a group's cultural heritage and integrity.[20]

Further, as the examples listed above demonstrate, due to the federal structure of the German state, there is considerable room for different strategies on the regional and local level, which allows for the implementation of even explicitly 'multicultural' programmes (like in Frankfurt on Main).

Such room for manoeuvre also exists because attacks on multiculturalism are, to a certain extent, rhetorical and not necessarily accompanied by a consequent move to abolish any pluralist intervention. Indeed, Christian Democratic attacks on multiculturalism may mainly be directed at their own supporters. By creating an imaginary picture of a multicultural past, they can present their own policies as innovative and distract from the fact that, rather than breaking with a multicultural past, they have revised their own policy. Recently, some scholars have argued that the analysis of migration policy has been hindered by a one-sided concentration on public presentations of political intentions, while real policies have been neglected. Christian Joppke and Ewa Morawska, for instance, have argued that differences between states with regard to their commitment or rejection of multiculturalism were over-emphasized, and that in stressing them, academics 'have become captive of political surface rhetoric' (2003: 7). Indeed, the political discourse and actual policies should both be analysed and not *per se* assumed to be identical.

And yet, while it is hardly questionable that, despite the absence of a multicultural programme, some policy interventions do exist in Germany that also form characteristic parts of multicultural policies, this does not amount to an undeclared 'de facto' multiculturalism.[21] Several of the measures listed above exist only on a minor scale. Education may be intercultural in ministerial declarations and in some curricula, but it is doubtful whether it is in the majority of classrooms. Ethnic pluralism is so far hardly represented in the staff of schools and universities or in the upper levels of companies and public institutions. In parliaments, immigrants are still rare. Affirmative action for disadvantaged immigrant groups is non-existent. Moreover, the under-representation of individuals with a migration background in higher positions is rarely even considered a deficit of German institutions. However, following European Union legislation, an anti-discrimination law was finally passed in summer 2006. But so far, the law and the office responsible for its implementation appear weak.

Last but not least, individual local and regional measures lack the support of a declared official policy on the federal level. Political declarations do make a difference and should not be dismissed as mere rhetoric. Public com-mitments to diversity, for instance, can help legitimize the demand for greater minority representation in higher positions.[22] By co-operating with minority organizations, the government can help raise their public image. High-level celebrations of the values of diversity and the contributions of immigrants may influence public opinion and further convince immigrants that they are welcomed and regarded as an integral part of German society. Immigrants may thus feel encouraged to play an active part in Germany's future. A society that generally sees itself as being shaped by immigration and as gaining from its plurality will be less likely to have an 'us' versus 'them' mentality, in which immigrants are expected to adjust to a given entity. Such a country is in a better position to undertake the project of shaping society as a joint endeavour of long-term residents and immigrants.

Concluding remarks

Is it at all conceivable that a German government will, in the foreseeable future, turn to an explicit public policy of recognizing and promoting diver-sity? Currently, strong objections exist in the German population as well as among Germany's political élites against multicultural projects. Multi-culturalism, never popular with mainstream politicians, has lost its hege-monial position in the left-liberal spectrum. Here, commitments to multiculturalism mainly served as a symbolic counterweight to nationalism and ethnic conceptions of the German people. As more or less everyone now accepts that Germany's population has importantly been shaped by immi-gration, the campaign has lost its major driving moment. Additionally, the growing criticism of multiculturalist policies in other European states has a strong impact, and ethnic diversity is now often seen as detrimental to social cohesion and to improved life chances of immigrants. Creating more equal educational and labour-market opportunities seems far more important than ethnic diversity, and improved opportunities are often not regarded as being positively interlinked with public recognition of diversity.

It is unlikely that this situation will change in the foreseeable future. How-ever, popular attitudes are not static and can be influenced by public debates. For example, less than ten years ago, religious and cultural plurality were viewed by the majority as positive things for German society – even in the absence of an official campaign supporting an image of Germany as a country characterized by ethnic diversity. Furthermore, majority attitudes do not necessarily dictate people's behaviour – thus the number of interethnic marriages keeps growing in Germany.[23] The issue of equal, or at least improved, opportunities for immigrants in German society is on the agenda, and new energy has been mobilized in the local communities, and in welfare and interest organizations, and so on, for initiatives aiming to contribute to this objective. Germany's federal state and corporate welfare state structures provide space for a variety of political interventions. Furthermore, the immigrant population itself may become more vocal and influential in the future, as the share of those holding German citizenship and voting rights increases. Immigrants do not necessarily advocate multicultural policies, but a new multicultural lobby could potentially arise from their ranks. Given the share of immigrants in German society and particularly among its youth, we should expect more pressure for increased representation in political office and in the higher ranks of firms and administrations as well as for more public recognition of the experiences and contributions of immigrants. Such pressure is the most likely source of any move towards a more active policy of diversity.

Notes

1　Reforms in 1990 and in 1993 simplified naturalization for young immigrants aged 16–23 and for those who had spent 15 years or more in Germany.

2　A government-appointed commission suggested that a points system be introduced. After lengthy debates, no parliamentary majority could be found for this suggestion.

3　However, German authorities actively strive to reverse settlement processes of refugees, whose residence rights are frequently revoked and return to an allegedly safe home country is demanded.

4　In fact, at 96,000 in 2005, net immigration remained significant.

5　This is now the official term that has, at least in official discourse, largely replaced the reference to foreign citizenship expressed by the term '*Ausländer*'. Definitions of a relevant migration background vary. In the most recent sample census, the federal statistical office included those with a foreign citizenship, naturalized citizens and ethnic German immigrants (*Spätaussiedler*) as well as those with at least one parent to whom these criteria applied. This was true for 15.3 million people. German statistics do not use an ethnicity concept comparable to that of the British census.

6　The Interior Minister has indicated that those who do not fulfil their integration obligations and parents who do not accept their children living like Germans are misplaced in Germany (Schäuble 2006b).

7　On the government website www.zuwanderung.de 'integration' is explained as follows: '*Zuwanderern soll eine umfassende, möglichst gleichberechtigte Teilhabe in allen gesellschaftlichen Bereichen ermöglicht werden. Zuwanderer haben die Pflicht, die deutsche Sprache zu erlernen sowie die Verfassung und die Gesetze zu kennen, zu respektieren und zu befolgen.*' ('Immigrants shall be granted comprehensive and, if possible, equal participation in all spheres of society. Immigrants are obliged to learn the German language and to know, respect and obey the constitution and the law.' Translation K.S.)

8 In January 2007 the text on the website had become shorter and no longer included this statement. It used to state: 'Einen inneren Separatismus, der auf kulturellen Trennungen beruht, hält eine Gesellschaft nicht aus' (www.zuwanderung.de, 29 June 2006).

9 Already the previous Social Democratic Interior Minister Schily spoke of a 'Multikulti-Seligkeit' ('a multiculti cloud cuckoo land') (*Die Welt* 2004). The new Integration Minister has proclaimed that the times of complacency and indifference are over (Böhmer 2006).

10 Concrete measures listed include the representation of diversity in the media, bilingual and intercultural education, and the integration of migrant organizations in local networks. Similarly, in 2001, the SPD's parliamentary faction in the federal parliament stressed the need to ensure representation of minority cultures in public life and to recognize cultural differences.

11 See, for example, a statement by Katrin Göring-Eckart (2006), a member of parliament and former spokesperson for the faction, who believes that the main task is to shape democracy according to the principle that diversity will be its future and holds promise. At the same time, she finds it right and necessary to demand that migrants be prepared to integrate and learn German.

12 People were asked whether they agreed with the opinion that foreigners should be prohibited from engaging in any political activity or that they should be sent home when jobs became scarce. Both views were opposed by majorities of those questioned.

13 In a survey conducted by Munich's city authorities, people were asked about issues the city should spend more or less money on. A surprisingly large share (almost 50 per cent of respondents) thought that more money should be spent on the 'integration of foreign co-citizens,' and only about 10 per cent wanted to see expenditure reduced (the rest thought it should stay the same) (Landeshauptstadt München 2002: 102). Surely 'integration' is not identical with multiculturalism policies, but at least these figures indicate that there may be considerable support for some measures from which immigrants stand to benefit.

14 In the following section I have used passages from Kraus and Schönwälder 2006.

15 Stuttgart is a city in southwest Germany with 591,000 inhabitants, 22 per cent of whom hold a non-German passport (2004). Estimates put the immigrant population – consisting of foreign citizens, the naturalized and Ethnic Germans – at 34 per cent (Lindemann 2005).

16 Of the German cities with more than half a million inhabitants, Frankfurt has the highest share of foreigners among its population (25 per cent).

17 'Intercultural' sometimes refers mainly to a recognition of cultural/ethnic plurality. Institutions are meant to serve all groups of the population, and separate provisions are rejected.

18 In the 1960s and 1970s mother tongue education was part of a policy which envisaged the return of the migrant children to the countries of origin. Since the early 1980s, this objective is no longer pursued (see Reich 2000: 114). For a regional example see Migrationsreport Hessen 2002 (p. 161): in Hessen, mother-tongue education is, since 2000, voluntary and participation has dropped by about 10 per cent. Still, of the pupils from seven large nationalities concerned, 54 per cent attended the language classes.

19 In some regional states, naturalized German citizens as well as foreign citizens are eligible to vote and to be elected.

20 But it is widely off the mark to describe Germany as a country 'where the predominant orientation is toward recognition and institutionalization of distinct religious/ethnic minorities' (Portes and De Wind 2004: 843, referring to Kastoryano).

21 Joppke and Morawska (2003) have argued that 'There is certainly a widespread de facto multiculturalism in liberal states' which does not significantly differ from the officially declared version of such policy.
22 The federal government has now launched a campaign '*Vielfalt als Chance*' ('Diversity as an Opportunity') that aims to increase the recognition of the potential represented by immigrants and to encourage employers to promote ethnic diversity among their employees.
23 In 2000, 16 per cent of all marriages recorded in Germany were between a German citizen and a partner with foreign citizenship. In 1960 the respective figure was 4 per cent.

References

Amt für multikulturelle Angelegenheiten (1990) *Ein Jahr multikulturelle Arbeit*, Bericht [Report. One year of multicultural work], Frankfurt.
Banting, K. and Kymlicka, W. (2006) 'Introduction: Multiculturalism and the welfare state: setting the context', in K. Banting and W. Kymlicka (eds) *Multiculturalism and the Welfare State: Recognition and Redistribution in Contemporary Democracies*, Oxford: Oxford University Press, pp. 1–45.
Banting, K., Johnston, R., Kymlicka, W. and Soroka, S. (2006) 'Do multiculturalism policies erode the welfare state? An empirical analysis', in K. Banting and W. Kymlicka (eds) *Multiculturalism and the Welfare State. Recognition and Redistribution in Contemporary Democracies*, Oxford: Oxford University Press, pp. 49–91.
Böhmer, M. (2005) Interview, *Die Welt*, 1 December.
——(2006) Speech in the federal parliament (Bundestag) on 5 April, extract, www.bundesregierung.de.
Bundesregierung (2005) *Integrationsaktivitäten des Bundes*. Bestandsaufnahme im Rahmen der Interministeriellen Arbeitsgruppe Integration, www.bamf.de.
Bündnis 90/Die Grünen-Bundestagsfraktion (2006), *Perspektive Staatsbürgerin und Staatsbürger. Für einen gesellschaftlichen Integrationsvertrag*, 30 May.
Datenreport 2004 (2004) *Zahlen und Fakten über die Bundesrepublik Deutschland*, ed. by the Statistisches Bundesamt in cooperation with the Wissenschaftszentrum Berlin für Sozialforschung and the Zentrum für Umfragen, Methoden und Analysen, Mannheim, Bonn: Bundeszentrale für politische Bildung.
Dossier 'Multikulturalismus', www.migration-boell.de.
Filsinger, D. (2002) 'Die Entwicklung der kommunalen Integrationspolitik und Integrationspraxis der neunziger Jahre' [The development of local integration policies and practice in the 1990s], *iza*, 24/2: 13–20.
——(2000) *Kommunale Integration ausländischer Kinder und Jugendlicher. Kommentierte Bibliographie*, München: Deutsches Jugendinstitut.
Geißler, R. and Pöttker, H. (eds) (2005) *Massenmedien und die Integration ethnischer Minderheiten in Deutschland. Problemaufriss, Forschungsstand, Bibliographie*, Bielefeld, transcript Verlag.
GESIS (2007) 'Langfristige Trends: Akzeptanz von Ausländern steigt, die Forderung nach mehr Anpassung auch'. Press release, 9 October.
Gogolin, I. (2005) 'Bilingual Education – the German Experience and Debate' in Arbeitsstelle Interkulturelle Konflikte und gesellschaftliche Integration (ed.) The Effectiveness of Bilingual School Programs for Immigrant Children, Berlin: Social Science Research Center, pp. 133–43.

Gogolin, I., Neumann, U. and Reuter, L. (eds) (2001) *Schulbildung für Kinder aus Minderheiten in Deutschland 1989–1999* [School education for minority children in Germany, 1989–99], Münster: Waxmann.

Göring-Eckart, K. (2006) Thüringische Landeszeitung, 4 May.

Hoffmann, L. (2002) 'Ausländerbeiräte in der Krise' [Foreigners' advisory councils in crisis], *Zeitschrift für Ausländerrecht und Ausländerpolitik*, 21/2: 63–70.

Ireland, P. (2004) *Becoming Europe. Immigration, Integration, and the Welfare State*, Pittsburgh: University of Pittsburgh Press.

Joppke, C. and Morawska, E. (2003) 'Integrating immigrants in liberal nation-states: policies and practices', in C. Joppke and E. Morawska (eds) *Toward Assimilation and Citizenship: Immigrants in Liberal Nation-States*, London: Palgrave/Macmillan, pp. 1–36.

Kraus, P. and Schönwälder, K. (2006) 'Multiculturalism in Germany: rhetoric, scattered experiments and future chances', in K. Banting and W. Kymlicka (eds) *Multiculturalism and the Welfare State: Recognition and Redistribution in Contemporary Democracies*, Oxford: Oxford University Press, pp. 202–21.

Krüger-Potratz, M. (2004) 'Migration als Herausforderung für Bildungspolitik' [Migration as a challenge for education policy], in R. Leiprecht (ed.) *Schule in der pluriformen Einwanderungsgesellschaft*, Königstein/Taunus: Wochenschauverlag.

Kultusministerkonferenz (1996) *Empfehlung der Kultusministerkonferenz 'Interkulturelle Bildung und Erziehung in der Schule'*, Beschluss vom 25.10.1996, www.buendnis-toleranz.de ['Intercultural education in schools' – Resolution of the Standing Conference of the Ministers of Education and Cultural Affairs of 25 October].

Landeshauptstadt München (2002) *Münchner Bürgerbefragung 2000; Soziale Entwicklung und Lebenssituation der Münchner Bürgerinnen und Bürger* [Munich citizens survey; Social development and life situation of Munich's citizens], München. www.muenchen.de/Rathaus/plan/Stadtentwicklung/grundlagen

Leggewie, C. (1993) *Multi Kulti. Spielregeln für die Vielvölkerrepublik* [*Multi Kulti. Rules for the multinational republic*], 3rd edn, Berlin: Rotbuch Verlag.

Leibold, J., Kühnel, S. and Heitmeyer, W. (2006) 'Abschottung von Muslimen durch generalisierte Islamkritik?', *Aus Politik und Zeitgeschichte*, 1–2: 3–10.

Lepsius, O. (2006) 'Die Religionsfreiheit als Minderheitenrecht in Deutschland, Frankreich und den USA', *Leviathan*, 34 (3): 321–49.

Lindemann, U. (2005) 'Stuttgarter Einwohner mit Zuwanderungshintergrund', in *Statistik und Informationsmanagement (Stadt Stuttgart)*, vol. 64, no.2, pp 30–40.

Migrationsreport Hessen 2002 (2002). *Bevölkerung, Ausbildung und Arbeitsmarkt*, Forschungs-und Entwicklungsgesellschaft Hessen, FEH-Report Nr. 637, Wiesbaden.

NRW (2000) Ministerium für Arbeit und Soziales, Qualifikation und Technologie des Landes Nordrhein-Westfalen, *Zuwanderung und Integration in NRW [Immigration and Integration in NRW]*. Bericht der Interministeriellen Arbeitsgruppe 'Zuwanderung' der Landesregierung, Düsseldorf.

——Ministerium für Generationen, Familie, Frauen und Integration des Landes Nordrhein-Westfalen, *Nordrhein-Westfalen: Land der neuen Integrationschancen. Aktionsplan Integration [Northrhine Westfalia: state of new integration opportunities. Action plan integration]*, Düsseldorf 27 June.

——Ministerium für Gesundheit, Soziales, Frauen und Familie des Landes Nordrhein-Westfalen, *Zuwanderung und Integration in Nordrhein-Westfalen [Immigration and Integration in Northrhine Westfalia]*. 3. Bericht der Landesregierung, Düsseldorf.

Pew Global Attitudes Project (2006) *Europe's Muslims More Moderate. The Great Divide: How Westerners and Muslims View Each Other*, 13-Nation Pew Global Attitudes Survey, Washington.

Piening, G. (2006) 'Interview', *Dossier Multikulturalismus*, www.migration-boell.de/web/integration/47_762.asp.

Portes, A. and De Wind, J. (2004) 'A Cross-Atlantic Dialogue. The Progress of Research and Theory in the Study of International Migration', *International Migration Review*, 38 (3): 828–51.

Radtke, F.-O. (2003) 'Multiculturalism in Germany: Local Management of Immigrants' Social Inclusion', *International Journal on Multicultural Societies*, 5 (1): 55–76.

Reich, H. H. (2000) 'Die Gegner des Herkunftssprachen-Unterrichts und ihre Argumente' [The opponents of mothertongue-teaching and their arguments], *Deutsch lernen*, 2, pp 112–26.

Rütten, A. (1998) 'Integrationspolitik der Landesregierung Nordrhein-Westfalen' [The integration policy of the state government of North Rhine-Westphalia], in Forschungsinstitut der Friedrich-Ebert-Stiftung, Abt. Arbeit und Sozialpolitik (ed.) [Electronic edn] *Ghettos oder ethnische Kolonie? Entwicklungschancen von Stadtteilen mit hohem Zuwandereranteil*, (Gesprächskreis Arbeit und Soziales; 85, Bonn), pp. 15–28.

Schäuble, W. (2006a) 'Unser Problem ist die Integration', Spiegel-Gespräch, *Der Spiegel*, 21: 36–38.

——(2006b), Interview, *Berliner Zeitung*, 6 April.

——(2006c), TV-Interview in 'Berlin direkt', 9 April, transcript on www.bmi.bund.de.

Schönwälder, K. (1996) 'Minderheitenschutz: Anerkennung kultureller Pluralität oder Ausdruck "völkischen Denkens"?' in F. Deppe, G. Fülberth and R. Rilling (eds), *Antifaschismus*, Heilbronn: Distel, pp. 453–67.

——(2004) 'Kleine Schritte, verpasste Gelegenheiten, neue Konflikte. Zuwanderungsgesetz und Migrationspolitik' [Small steps, missed opportunities, new conflicts. Immigration law and migration policy], *Blätter für deutsche und internationale Politik*, 49(10): 1205–14.

——(2006) 'Politikwandel in der (bundes-)deutschen Migrationspolitik', in U. Davy and A. Weber (eds), *Paradigmenwechsel in Einwanderungsfragen? Überlegungen zum neuen Zuwanderungsgesetz*, Baden-Baden: Nomos, pp. 8–22.

Schröder, G. (2004) 'Rede von Bundeskanzler Schröder zur Preisverleihung für Verständigung und Toleranz an Johannes Rau', 20 November, http://archiv.bundesregierung.de

Senat Berlin (2005) *Vielfalt fördern – Zusammenhalt stärken. Integrationspolitik für Berlin* [Encouraging Diversity – Strengthening Cohesion. An integration policy for Berlin]. Das am 23.8.2005 vom Senat beschlossene Integrationskonzept für Berlin. Berliner Beiträge zu Integration und Migration, Berlin.

SORA (2001) *Attitudes towards Minority Groups in the European Union*. A special analysis of the Eurobarometer 2000 survey on behalf of the European Monitoring Centre on Racism and Xenophobia, Vienna.

SPD (2006a) *Leitlinien zur Integrationspolitik [Guidelines on integration policy]*. Beschluss des Präsidiums der Sozialdemokratischen Partei Deutschlands vom 10.7.2006.

——(2006b) *Vogt: Integration braucht 'faire Chancen' und 'klare Regeln'*, press release of 11 July.

SPD-Bundestagsfraktion (2001) Querschnittsarbeitsgruppe Integration und Zuwanderung, *Die neue Politik der Zuwanderung: Steuerung, Integration, innerer Friede. Die Eckpunkte der SPD-Bundestagsfraktion* [The new policy of immigration: control, integration, internal peace. The key points of the parliamentary faction of the SPD] (Berlin).

——(2006) *Integrationspolitik: Positionen der SPD-Bundestagsfraktion* [Integration policy: views of the SPD Bundestag faction] (as of 14 July 2006).

Stuttgart (2002) *Ein Bündnis für Integration. Grundlagen einer Integrationspolitik in der Landeshauptstadt Stuttgart*, Stuttgart, September.

Süddeutsche Zeitung, 29–31 May 2004; 29 April 2006.

Tagesspiegel (2006), 11 July.

tgd (Türkische Gemeinde in Deutschland) (2006) *Gleichstellungs-und Partizipationspolitik statt Ausländerpolitik*, Vorlage beim Integrationsgipfel der Bundesregierung am 14.7.2006, Berlin.

Welt, Die (2004) 'Schily warnt vor "Multi-Kulti-Seligkeit" ', 18 November.

9 Dynamics of diversity in Spain

Old questions, new challenges

Ricard Zapata-Barrero

Some years ago, Spain's immigration situation was usually presented in light of the fact that Spain was being transformed from an emigration country to an immigration country. Today, immigration is a consolidated demographic reality. In the Spanish case, however, immigration is not a specific type of diversity separate from other types of diversity (linguistic, religious, national), but rather an example of multiple diversities (see also Kymlicka, this volume). In this chapter I will demonstrate how immigration to Spain has provoked discussions about already existing diversities, such as religious and national diversity, that were placed aside during the democratic transition of the 1970s.

There are two relevant normative questions that exist today within the context of discussions about the 'backlash against multiculturalism'. The first question is how to manage this new process of diversity alongside the different dynamics already existing in Spain: the processes of recognition of religious and national diversity. The second question takes up the link between existent policies, political discourses and conflicts related to the diversity on the one hand, and public opinion on the other. That is, emphasis is placed on the importance of not just the relation between diversity and political responses,[1] but also the much more complex relation between diversity and societal responses. With respect to this point, there exist deficiencies in current debates concerning immigration that the case of Spain brings to light and invites us to consider. Understanding the Spanish context may help contribute to extending the meaning of what Vertovec calls 'super-diversity', pointing to the necessity of considering multi-dimensional conditions and processes affecting not only immigrants, as Vertovec highlights, but also debates surrounding other diversities, such as religious and national diversity, that are activated by the presence of immigrants (Vertovec 2007).

In the first part of this chapter, I address the question of how immigration is affecting the way Spain is managing religious and national minorities, as well as how different dynamics of diversity are becoming more complex in practice, and more ambiguous and problem-focused in public discourse and in the political arena. In the second part, I analyse the context of the Spanish immigration debate. I will thereby place particular emphasis on the interconnection between policies, political discourse, social conflicts, and public opinion related to immigration, highlighting the link between 'what the government does' and 'what the citizens believe'. It is this link that is at the basis of what I will call the 'governance hypothesis', which is formulated as follows: the negative attitude of citizens is not so much directed at immigration, rather at the government (and politics) and its (in)capacity to govern issues related to multiculturalism and to respond to citizens' expectations. This governance hypothesis will allow us to understand the ambivalence found when we compare border and cultural accommodation issues in Spain.

Conditions of diversity in Spain: religious and national pluralism

If indeed there exists a historical dimension of diversity inherent to the very identity of Spain, during these last few years this diversity, understood as multinationalism, is witnessing the addition of another type of diversity which results from immigration. Theoretically, we will argue that immigration is not so much a component of diversity as it is a vehicle through which existing diversities are brought to the fore. That is, the arrival of immigrants, with their different religions, languages, and cultures is also reactivating other debates that remain unresolved since the period of democratic transition, such as those related to the management of religion, linguistic pluralism, and cultural pluralism. The question of how to manage the conditions of diversity, in this respect, takes on a mirror effect regarding how Spain conceives of itself as a diverse society. In the next section, I take up two emerging debates: the debate about religious pluralism in a state that perceives itself as non-confessional, and the link between immigration and multinationalism, especially challenging from the normative point of view of Catalonia.[2]

The management of religious pluralism: old answers to new questions

From the perspective of the state and society, the so-called new minority religion of Islam in Spain needs to be conceptualized within the context of the historical experience of the country. The presence of Muslims in Spain for more than eight centuries makes the reactions to Islam different from other European countries. The fact that most conflicts of multiculturalism in Spain are related to the Muslim community can be understood when considering that Spanish identity has been constructed, in part, based on a traditionally negative perception of the Muslim in general, and the Moroccan in particular, considered in pejorative terms as 'the Moor' (*el moro*) (Zapata-Barerro 2006: 143).

The collective construction of the negative stereotype of the 'Moor' started with the Christian victory over the Muslims in 1492, following eight centuries of Muslim presence in the peninsula, after which the Spanish monarchs (Queen Isabel and King Ferdinand) expelled Muslims, Jews, and Roma from the country. The Muslim presence ended completely in 1609 with the expulsion of the *moriscos* (Muslims who converted to Christianity and stayed in Spain after the *Reconquista*) (Zapata-Barrero 2006). Martín Corrales (2002) illustrates how representations of the Moor in the propaganda of the *Reconquista* devalued the Islamic religion and created stereotypes of Moors as being impure, treasonous, false, cruel, cowardly, and so on. The negative image of the Moor in other phases of Spanish history, such as the occupation of Morocco (which became a Protectorate in 1912) after the African War and the participation of Moorish troops on the pro-Franco side in the Civil War, has further contributed to the production of *Maurophobia* (fear of the Moors). In opposition to the Moor, Spanish identity has been built on the idea of *Hispanidad*, a political discourse of exclusion based on the idea of a community of people linked together by linguistic and religious criteria. *Hispanidad* is a political term that was created to encompass the entire Spanish area of influence, designating a linguistic (Spanish) and religious (Catholic) community and creating a sense of belonging, excluding non-Spanish speakers, atheists, Masons, Jews, and Muslims (García Morente 1938). The Franco regime (1940–75) reconstructed this term as a symbol of homogeneity and unity in order to create a sentiment of loyalty and patriotism (González Antón 1997: 613).

After the transition to democracy, the Spanish state changed from being a confessional (Catholic) state to a non-confessional state. The basic difference between this model and that of laicism is that a non-confessional state does not guarantee religious equality. Article 16 of the 1978 constitution provides for religious freedom and the freedom of worship by individuals and groups, and guarantees that 'no faith shall have the character of a state religion'.[3] The constitution thereby establishes Spain as a secular state, but also obliges the state to maintain relations with religious communities. In 1992, a cooperation agreement was signed between the Spanish state and the Islamic Commission of Spain (*Comisión Islámica de España*), initiating institutional recognition of Islam as a minority religion in Spain. This agreement grants the Muslim population of Spain several privileges[4] and is regarded as the most extensive legal framework for the recognition of Islam in the European Union (EU).[5]

Let me now highlight the key issues related to diversity management. Regarding the issue of the Catholic Church's legal power, it should be noted that while Jews and Protestants have been granted similar benefits as Muslims, the Catholic Church enjoys a number of additional privileges. These benefits derive from four accords signed with the Holy See in 1979. They cover economic, educational, military, and judicial matters. The growth of minority religions like Islam has contested these privileges. The most important issue within this context is the finance the Catholic Church receives through voluntary tax contributions and, until recently, through direct payments. In 2004, leaders of the Protestant, Muslim, and Jewish communities sought to claim treatment comparable to that enjoyed by the Catholic Church by requesting the government to revise the national income tax forms to allow taxpayers the option to donate a percentage of their taxes to non-Catholic entities (US Department of State, Spain 2006). Although these negotiations ended without an agreement, a legislative change in September

2006 ended direct payment, but increased the voluntary contribution to the Catholic Church from 0.52 to 0.7 per cent. For voluntary contributions two options are available to taxpayers: the Catholic Church and social work (Zapata-Barrero 2006).

A second key question of the debate relates to the efforts by Muslim leaders to persuade the government to provide for public religious education. In 2004, legislation was approved that provides for funding for teachers of courses in Catholic, Islamic, Protestant/Christian, and Judaic studies in public school when at least ten students request them. As these courses are not mandatory, those students who do not elect them are obliged to take an alternative course covering general social, cultural, and religious themes. In 2004, the government also set aside funds to pay for twenty Muslim teachers to teach courses on Islam to public school students. Along with the teaching of minority confessions, there are also religious schools for Catholic, Protestant, Muslim, and Jewish students (US Department of State, Spain 2006). But the main education challenges stem from the high concentration of immigrant students in certain public schools, the existence of racist admission practices, and the lack of religious education other than Catholicism. Although the 1992 agreement between the state and the Islamic Commission of Spain guarantees the right of Islamic education to Muslim students in both public and private schools, in practice many schools do not provide this opportunity and local governments do not give much priority to Islamic education (SOS Racismo 2003: 193).

A final key issue is the right to places of worship. The Spanish law (Ley Orgánica de Libertad Religiosa, article 2.2) recognizes the right of confessions and religious communities to establish places of worship for all persons, nationals and foreigners (see also article 3 of Ley 4/2000). In accordance with the Agreement of 1992, mosques and other recognized religious spaces are inviolable and profit from a favourable fiscal arrangement. The only requirements for Islamic communities wishing to open 'oratorios' and/or build mosques is the consent from the *Islamic Commission of Spain* and the commitment to dedicate the places of worship to prayer and religious education alone (Jefatura de Estado 1992). Local governments are obligated to provide land for the opening of places of worship, but in practice this law is often ignored by local municipalities.

Summing up, despite the 1992 agreement that guarantees religious pluralism by law (Jefatura de Estado 1992), the Muslim community lacks the infrastructure that would lead to a normal religious life. Religious demands have resulted in several conflictive situations between Muslims and non-Muslims, public administrations, and the private sector. The building of mosques is probably the most important religious demand. The protests of neighbours and resistance of local governments show a major source of social conflict.

The debate concerning religious pluralism is still in its initial stages. The way Spanish authorities answer the 'Islam question' is intimately linked to the way Spain will solve the question of religious pluralism more generally.

The management of linguistic diversity in a multinational state: the case of Catalonia

Linking immigration and the multinational state is a political requirement for the differentiated questions that immigration raises in the context of a nation without a state, as in the case of the Autonomous Region of Catalonia. Immigration and multinationalism are two dynamics whose relation should be articulated politically. The form in which this link is managed is an important issue in Spain, given that it reactivates and focuses a debate already present. The demands for accommodation by immigrants with respect to conceptions of national, non-state identity may have effects on demands for self-governance (Zapata-Barrero ed. 2009). For example, how are immigrants perceived within the process of national, non-state identity construction? How should the accommodation of immigrants be considered within the context of national identities articulated at sub-state levels?

Catalonia, in its search for reasons that legitimate its demand for self-governance of matters of immigration, is not focusing solely on claims related to responsibilities of political and legislative management, but is also opening up a debate about the identity particular to Catalonia. The framework of current discussion, in which a National Pact for Immigration (PNI)[6] is being projected, is serving precisely as a context for the introduction of identitarian themes into the political debate of Catalonia and of Spain. A debate that relates immigration, self-governance, and identity is fundamental. The major minority nations (for example, Quebec and Flanders) link their nationalist politics directly with the politics of immigration (Zapata-Barrero 2009).

Until now, there has been a focus on demands of competency to be able to control the flows of immigrants, with the implicit argument that the majority of immigrants who enter Spain settle in Catalonia (Catalonia is the Autonomous Community with the greatest number of immigrants in Spain, reaching a million in 2008 of a total population of seven million). Other demands are more related to recognition, like the fact that immigrants must affirm their loyalty to the king in order to receive Spanish nationality and are required to speak the Spanish language, while, by contrast, other languages are not insisted upon in order to adapt to bilingual territories, or simply in order to acquire nationality. What would happen if a Moroccan that speaks only Galician/Basque/Catalan refused to speak Spanish at work?

When the debate is established in terms of national (non-state) identity, certain normative questions arise. The national identitarian discourse may provoke an ethnicization of the nationalist project itself, as has occurred in Flanders, with unforeseen consequences.[7] Within this context, it might be useful to re-focus the discourse, articulating a language of accommodation of the new diversity (immigrants) alongside the diversity that already exists (multinationalism). These two processes need not necessarily clash when they coincide in the same territorial space, but rather ought to fuse together. This means that it is legitimate to request or provide instruments to assure that immigrants who want to settle in Catalonia also speak Catalan. This is, in fact, the philosophy that is motivating the debate about a National Pact for Immigration (PNI), where a 'common public culture' is delimited based on the Catalan language, among other features.

But in this case as well, we ought to recognize that people speak the language of their workplace. The motivations that people of immigrant origins may have to speak Catalan will be directly proportional to two factors: their intention to settle permanently in Catalonia, and the necessity of utilizing the Catalan language for work and for ascending professional and social hierarchies. In this case, it is also important to be careful not to utilize the regional language as an ultimate measuring stick of integration: an immigrant may very well say, 'I speak Spanish (Catalan/Basque/Galician), but I do not feel integrated'. The actual debate regarding the law of incorporation, centred fundamentally on the link between the reception of newly arrived immigrants, social opportunity and the Catalan language, pretends precisely to deal with this question.[8]

The example of linguistic diversity in a multinational state demonstrates that state immigration policy worsens the situation of minority nations in that it does not provide minority nations with either the tools or the resources for the nation itself to manage this process that affects its very development as a cultural community. We are thus facing an issue intimately bound up with the politics of self-government, that is, those politics that have as their ultimate basis of legitimacy the management of a given minority cultural community. What is dealt with here is an examination of this age-old issue, but in societies where there exists a double-belonging: that of the state's majority political community and that of the community expressed by the minority nation.

In the following section, I will turn to the public discourse on diversity in Spain. First, I will contextualize immigration relating to diversity in Spain. Second, I will identify the categories that characterize most negative opinions in Spain, following a contextual focus and taking the 2005 CIS (Centro de Investigaciones Sociológicas) surveys as the main source. Finally, I shall conclude by way of summarizing the main findings into one that defends the *governance hypothesis*.

Contextualizing immigration-related diversity in Spain

Spain has a relatively short history of immigration. In twenty years it has been transformed from a country of emigration to one of the main immigrant receiving countries of the European Union. Although Spain still ranks relatively low in terms of numbers of immigrants compared to some other European countries (between 6.1 per cent and 9.3 per cent of the population on 1 January 2006),[9] the foreign population has more than doubled in five years. Economic and historical connections with North Africa and South America have been the main trigger of immigration flows.

In the year 2000 political parties started to include immigration in their electoral campaigns (Zapata-Barrero 2003) and immigration became institutionalized after several legislative changes. In the aftermath of 9/11, immigration became increasingly linked to security, resulting in the enhancement of border control, increased focus on combating irregular immigration flows and a restriction of immigration law. Fluctuations in Spanish immigration law over the last six years demonstrate that a political discourse on immigration is still in construction. Overall, the development of immigration policy has mainly been (and to a large extend still is) focused on controlling immigration flows (prevention), while lacking in effective policies for the social integration of immigrants. The pressure of undocumented immigration at Europe's outer border has dominated the social and political debate on immigration. There is an increasing awareness that these irregular immigration flows are not merely a Spanish but also a European problem. Spain is pressing the European Union (EU) to take responsibility for its borders (Zapata-Barrero and de Witte 2007).

In spite of this crisis of 'border control', there are also tensions related to cultural diversity resulting from immigration. Spain has a diverse immigrant population, the largest groups coming from Latin America (35 per cent), Africa (23 per cent), the EU (22 per cent) and non-EU European countries (12 per cent). As mentioned earlier in this chapter, conflicts of migration-related diversity in Spain have mainly arisen from the cultural and religious demands of those immigrants that are most 'visible' within the Spanish society: Muslims.

Indeed, there is an informal acceptance by public authorities and society in general that two categories of immigrants exist: those 'visible' and those 'non-visible'. Potential conflict is related to the former. The three dimensions by which visibility becomes explicit are skin colour, language, and religion. Used as criteria for policy orientations, much of this entails what can be labelled as the return of *Hispanidad* (Christians) (Zapata-Barrero 2006).

The first social conflict with social and political consequences occurred in 2000, when riots against Moroccan immigrant workers took place in El Ejido, an agricultural town (*ciudad-cortijo*) in south-eastern Spain. Riots started with street occupations and the burning of pictures denoting Moroccan presence. Soon the situation escalated into what was also described as a 'Moor hunt' (Zapata-Barrero 2003). Some Moroccan workers opted to strike against the racist attacks and to claim improvements in working and living conditions. After reaching an agreement on labour conditions (but not on regularization), the immigrants went back to work (Zapata-Barrero 2003). A similar conflict was witnessed four years later in Elche, a long-time shoe-making town in the coastal province of Alicante, where Spanish workers set fire to two Chinese shoe warehouses in an (unauthorized) demonstration with nearly 500 people against Chinese shoemakers. The demonstrators protested against the presence of Asian businessmen because Spaniards felt their age-old social customs, employment norms, and labour relations threatened by the new competitors, which resulted in racism as an effect (see also Cachón-Rodríguez 2005).

Both El Ejido (2000) and Elche (2004) reflect the racist sentiments in Spanish society and highlight the precarious working and living conditions of immigrants. After the September 11 terrorist attacks in the United States in 2001 and the March 2004 bombings in Madrid, an upsurge in hostility against Muslims has been reported in Spanish society (see for example European Monitoring Centre on Racism and Xenophobia, 2001 and 2006; and International Helsinki Federation for Human Rights, 2005). In this way social conflicts have been centred around the Muslim immigrant community. This has also been reflected in political discourse (Zapata-Barrero and Qasem 2008).

Based on the analysis of newspapers,[10] there are at least three types of issues encountered in Spain that have had effects beyond the local place where the events took place: racism, the management of cultural (and religious) diversity and the politicization of multiculturalism. The latter type refers to using cultural diversity challenges as objects of political discourse and electoral campaigns. This politicization is clearly related to Muslim claims and the difficulties related to managing citizen protests against them.

These social conflicts are, however, not a clear reflection of Spanish public opinion. Most polls suggest that public opinion is predominantly concerned with immigration related to border issues, rather than issues related to cultural diversity. It is this apparent ambivalence which the governance hypothesis tries to explain. Negative public opinion is much more related to the vision citizens have of the government and its capacity to manage borders. This argument is built further in the next section.

The characteristics of Spanish public opinion on immigration

Importantly, most works dealing with immigration and public opinion in Spain focus on the number of immigrants.[11] Thus, the relationship between the number of immigrants and public perception is seen to be very close. We know, however, that this relationship is not so intuitive. Whether the number of immigrants plays a conditioning role is correlated with other variables, but it is not significant in itself in order to understand a negative attitude. For instance, supranational studies based on the results of the Eurobarometer suggest that there is no link between the number of immigrants in a country and negative perception. What is significant, however, is the speed of migratory flows. An increase in negative attitude is linked to the increase of immigration by over 35 per cent from 2000 to 2005.[12] The perception of the amount of immigrants must, therefore, be considered in relation to the frequency/speed of flows. This is a distinctive feature in Spain compared with other European countries.

Another widespread assumption lies within the framework of effects. Importantly, attitudes form part of the effects of immigration. It is these effects that have been the focus of the first studies on public opinion and immigration in Spain. We also know that it was under the VIth (1996–2000) and VIIth (2000–2004) legislatures, when the right-wing Partido Popular was in Government, that negative public opinion was first strongly linked to migratory flows in Spain. Politically it was assumed that 'the more immigration, the higher the percentage of negative opinion'. Studies in Spain have therefore worked under this conceptual framework generated by government policy itself.

The main sources of information in Spain are the Barometers of the *Centro de Investigaciones Sociológicas* (CIS).[13] By looking at its questions, two different interpretations can be made. On a first level, the Barometers are indicators of the state of public opinion on relevant matters, the famous 'public opinion thermometer'. On a second level, the inclusion of certain set questions and some that vary indicate specific government concerns at any given time. The questions on immigration started to become regular from 2000.[14] Thus, in this year immigration entered the government's agenda.[15]

If we look for arguments that separate Spanish public opinion from that of other countries, in addition to highlighting its tolerant nature (see, for example, Cea D'Ancona 2004), Spanish public opinion differentiates between issues relating to migratory flows and borders, and issues related to immigrant inclusion and accommodation. Taking this distinction into account, we observe that negative opinion is basically concentrated on the level of entry and flow management.

In the following section, I shall first undertake a transversal analysis from March 1999 to October 2006 to show how the perception of immigration as a basic concern evolves, trying to identify the main peaks of negative opinion, and to interpret them contextually. We shall see that legislative changes and periods of political innovation are the most likely to bring about more negative attitudes. Then, in a second section, I shall develop the results of the fourth peak of negative opinion (November 2005), as it was the month that saw the introduction of immigration related questions into the Barometer.

The emergence of immigration as a public concern

Since 1991, several CIS (*Centro de Investigaciones Sociológicas*) studies have focused on Spanish attitudes towards the immigrant population.[16] Since February 2000, questions related to migration issues are included in the survey on a monthly basis (Zapata-Barrero 2008). In the question about what people consider to be the three most important problems affecting the country, immigration becomes a permanent category starting from September 2000. Figure 9.1 gives an overview of the increasing importance of immigration as a problem. The *ranking* of 'immigration' is defined in relation to the frequency it is chosen over other answers (all answers are defined in advance). This can be found between brackets on the x-axis.[17]

Focusing on public concern there are several remarks to be made. First, throughout the entire period, immigration is perceived as one of the most important problems in the country, along with unemployment, civil

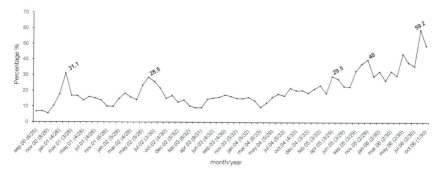

Figure 9.1 Trends in Spanish concerns about immigration. Answers to the question: According to you, what is the most important problem facing our country today? And second? And third? (max. 3 answers).

insecurity, terrorism, housing, economic, and political problems. Second, it is striking that since April 2005, immigration has been placed as the third most important problem, reflecting a growing and consolidated concern about immigration from 2004 onwards. Since October 2005, immigration has been ranked second, after unemployment and before terrorism. In September 2006 it reached the first position for the first time. Third, at least five peaks can be observed where concerns about immigration were high.[18] There are several concrete factors that influence the 'problematization' of immigration: illegal aliens, management of flows, specific conflicts related to exclusion, massive policies by decree, the reactive discourse of political parties, and so on (see Zapata-Barrero, 2009). All are ultimately linked to the legislative changes and the perception of a bad management of flows. I argue that it is not so much the media attention, but border management related factors and its subsequent policies that impact on negative attitudes.

It is at this level that the governance hypothesis takes meaning: as I will demonstrate in the remaining sections of this chapter, the negative attitude is not so much directed at immigration but at the government (and politics) and its (in)capacity to govern issues related to immigration and to respond to citizens' expectations. Now let us focus on the peaks identified in Table 9.1.

The first peak in February 2001 can be attributed to several factors. There were important legislative changes, a new immigration law came into force in January 2001 (*Ley de extranjeria 8/2000*), repelling the recent liberal Law (4/2000) (Aja 2006). The law was mainly aimed at fighting illegal immigration, but it also stripped immigrant workers of the rights of association, protest, and strike. The law was accompanied by a Royal Decree establishing the requirements for the regularization of foreigners able to prove that they were residing in Spain before 1 January 2001. The consequences of this legislative change affected negative perceptions. For example, there were several hunger strikes in Barcelona and sit-ins by illegal immigrants in various regions of the country in order to obtain legal status before the change in law came into

Table 9.1

February 2001 **(31.1%)**	Legislative change, aimed at fighting illegal immigration.
	Consequences: hunger strikes/sit-ins to obtain regularization; coach accident in Lorca, which killed 12 undocumented immigrant labourers and highlighted their precarious and illegal employment situation.
June 2002 **(28.5%)**	Control of (illegal) immigration topic on political agenda.
	Key event in the fight against illegal immigration: EU Seville Summit.
	Conflicts related to Muslims, racist protests against the building of mosques and conflicts over imams.
April 2005 **(29.5%)**	Two-month regularization process ('Normalization process') to end illegal employment of migrants and to control the black market.
	Protests and hunger strikes by immigrants.
	Growing numbers of undocumented Sub-Saharan Africans arriving at the Canary Islands, Ceuta and Melilla.
November 2005 **(40%)**	The escalation of the situation in Ceuta and Melilla.
	Political debate on measures to control the situation in Ceuta and Melilla, resulting in the building of another border fence in Melilla.
	Illegal immigration priority issue at Euro Mediterranean Partnership Conference.
	Riots caused by immigrant populations in large cities in France.
September 2006 **(59.2%)**	Arrival of undocumented immigrants to the Canary Islands breaks all records.

effect. Furthermore, a coach accident in Lorca, where 12 undocumented immigrants died, highlighted the precarious and illegal employment situation of many immigrants without residence and work permits. Finally, public figures adopted an alarmist tone on issues of immigration, which might have raised concerns (Zapata-Barrero 2008).

The second peak took place in June 2002. In this period the control of (irregular) immigration was a hot topic on the political agenda in Spain as well as in the rest of Europe. First of all, illegal immigration was one of the priorities of the Aznar government; this became evident in the more restrictive 8/2000 law, but also in the signing of new bilateral agreements with Colombia, the Dominican Republic, and Romania to return illegal immigrants. Between May and June there was a massive expulsion of Nigerian immigrants as a consequence of such bilateral agreements (SOS Racismo 2002: 116). A key event in the fight against illegal immigration was the EU Seville Summit under the Spanish Presidency on 21 and 22 June 2002. The basic summit agreement was to draft restrictive immigration policies to the point of sanctioning the sending countries if they did not demonstrate a will to control their population. The peak of June 2002 could be understood as growing public concern about immigration, in order to put pressure on the Spanish government to place it on the European agenda.

In the specific case of Catalonia, immigration similarly became a contested topic in its political agenda, where immigrants were increasingly seen as a threat to the Catalan society and identity. First, the growing number of Moroccan immigrants settling in Catalonia was interpreted as a national government policy initiative to weaken the autonomy of the Catalan community. Second, there were conflicts related to Muslims, manifested in racist protests against the building of mosques and conflicts over imams. These led the President of the *Generalitat* to claim a right to construct a Catalan immigration policy (Anguera 2002; Pérez 2002).

The third peak is in April 2005, coinciding with a two-month regularization process adopted by the Spanish Government (this time called the 'normalization process') to end illegal employment of migrants and to control the black market. Importantly it was not only the normalization policies themselves which led to negative public opinion, but also the political debate that followed and the reactions it raised in the European Union. Many protests and hunger strikes took place in Barcelona by immigrants that could not meet the conditions necessary to benefit from the regularization rounds and claimed to be driven into the hands of exploiting employers (*La Vanguardia*, 1 May 2005; Safont 2005). The media also reported on the growing numbers of undocumented Sub-Saharan Africans arriving at the Canary Islands, Ceuta, and Melilla. As reception centres could not take care of all arriving immigrants, flights had to be arranged to transport them to other parts of Spain (Morcillo 2005: 19).

The escalation of events in Ceuta and Melilla coincided with the highest peak observed in November 2005 (when immigration accounted for 40 per cent of the responses). As a consequence of the drama at the border, the issue of illegal immigration became a major topic in Spain's social and political agenda. It was also a priority issue discussed at the Euro Mediterranean Partnership Conference in Barcelona, in November 2005, and at the European Council Summit in Brussels in December 2005. The latter event resulted in the EU financing the extension of the *Sistema de Vigilancia Exterior (SIVE)* to cover the entire Mediterranean region, including the Canary Islands (Missé 2005). Another reason for this peak stems from the riots involving immigrant populations in large cities in France (see Simon and Sala Pala, this volume), which received a great deal of attention in the Spanish press, as well as the controversial cartoons of Mohammed in September 2005 in the Danish newspaper *Jyllands-Posten* (see Hedetoft, this volume).

Finally, the fifth peak took place in September 2006. It was caused by the dramatic arrival of undocumented immigrants to the Canary Islands in 2006, which made immigration one of the main preoccupations of the Spanish public and placed immigration at the forefront of Spanish and European political agendas. Between January and August, the Islands witnessed a large influx of African immigrants. The arrival of 4,772 immigrants to the Canary Islands in August 2006 broke all previous records. While the majority of immigrants, both regular and irregular, enter Spain by airplane or highway, the images of *cayucos* (people travelling by small boats) arriving at Spanish Islands and overcrowded reception centers made immigration the most important problem perceived by the Spanish public in September 2006 (corresponding to 59.2 per cent). In order to respond to the large influx of African immigration and to influence public opinion, the Spanish Socialist government under Prime Minister Rodríguez Zapatero attempted to arrange Return Agreements with sending countries while at the same time pressing the European Union for help to fight illegal immigration. The Spanish governance of EU borders poses normative questions (Zapata-Barrero and de Witte 2007). Here border management, lack of control, governance, and public opinion are directly linked.

The arguments related to public opinion concern are summarized in the analysis of the five basic peaks. The key focus here is that it is not so much the media attention, but factors related to governance that impact on negative attitudes. (See Table 9.1 for a summary.).

Differentiated attitudes towards immigration and equal rights

The fourth peak coincides with one of the last special surveys available.[19] Here, immigration is considered to be the second concern (40 per cent), below unemployment (54 per cent) and far above ETA terrorism (25.2 per cent) (question 5). 59.6 per cent consider that there are too many immigrants, and the vast majority supports a restrictive policy (84.7 per cent are of the opinion that the most suitable policy is that which allows entry only to those with a work contract).

When asked the question of who should enter, most respondents preferred an immigrant with a work qualification needed in Spain, a good level of education, and the ability to speak Spanish (or the official language of one of the Autonomous Communities). About a third consider being of Christian faith to be a significant criterion but less than a fifth think that immigrants should be white. This demonstration of tolerance (non-racism) is not just seen in all of the questions related to identity and emotional matters, but also in those related with inclusion policies (equal rights). For example, 78.9 per cent express that they 'greatly agree' or 'agree' that immigrants should have the same rights as everybody else, that things such as access to education (92.5 per cent) and health care (81.3 per cent) should be simplified for newcomers, that they should practise their religion if they so wish (81.2 per cent), and that they should have the right to vote on the local level (60.8 per cent) and in the general elections (53.4 per cent). With regard to acceptance in different spheres of their day-to-day lives (children's education, work, etc.) responses are also positive, with 71.7 per cent who agree that immigrants should maintain their language and culture, against 22.4 per cent who are of the opposite opinion.

We can therefore see that tolerance is expressed at different levels (school, work, etc.) but always relating to inclusion and not relating to issues of frontiers and the management of flows. However, this data should be treated with caution, given that some studies have demonstrated that this apparent positive tolerance changes in real situations of competition. For example, the study by Gimeno (2001) concentrates on citizens' perception of competition for access to, and the distribution of, scarce resources. Gimeno shows that if the population had to choose between egalitarian practices towards immigration or access to scarce resources before immigrants, they choose the latter.

An initial conclusion is that despite having a negative attitude towards *how many* enter (subject of frontiers and migratory flows), they display a pragmatic attitude to *who* enters (personal characteristics of the immigrant, not mentioning their nationality and provenance) and a tolerant attitude with regard to equal rights. However, all of these opinions are also related to perceptions of the number of immigrants.

In fact, according to Table 9.2, 52.4 per cent of the population has an exaggerated image of the number of immigrants that live in Spain, with 6.6 per cent of the population believing that over 50 per cent of the population are immigrants – half of the inhabitants of Spain. On average the responses indicate that the 'perceived amount' is 20.4 per cent whereas according to Ministerial data in 2005 the 'real number' was 6.2 per cent or 8.5 per cent (INE 2006).[20]

Table 9.2 Population's image of number of immigrants that live in spain

	%
Less than 10 people	15.9
10-19	20.5
20-29	13.1
30-39	8.0
40-49	4.2
50 or more people	6.6
Don't know	31.0
No reply	0.6
TOTAL	100.0

If we focus on the significant correlations regarding issues related to migratory flows (those that express the negative attitude), we may observe that the trends are similar to the results that have been highlighted in other studies. However, Spain also presents some relevant distinctions which I will attempt to underline.

With regard to the question relating to the percentage of immigrants believed to live in Spain, in almost all variables there is a lack of proportion between the 'real amount' and the 'perceived amount'. The disproportion between the real percentage of immigrants and the perceived percentage is to be found among a range of social categories. On average, unskilled workers perceive that over 23 per cent of the total population comprises immigrants, a similar percentage as women (saying 23.65 per cent), young people between 18 and 24 years of age (saying 25.35 per cent), the unemployed (saying 22.56 per cent), students (saying 20.14 per cent on average) and people working at home unpaid (saying 22.16 per cent). Those coming closest to the real percentage are right-wingers (saying 14.81 per cent), the upper and upper-middle classes (saying 15.97 per cent), people with higher education (saying 15.35 per cent), and managers and professionals (saying 16.61 per cent).

The correlation between the perception of number ('there are too many') and the defence of more restrictive policies (only allowing entry to those with a work permit), as pointed out by Alvira Martín and García López (2003: 191): is evident again in the November 2005 Barometer, though less intensely, 84.7 per cent of polled Spaniards are of the opinion that one should 'only allow entry to those who have a contract of employment' while at the same time 59.6 per cent say 'there are too many'. An ambivalence of public opinion is therefore evident.

Conclusion: towards a new democratic transition related to the management of diversities?

Immigration is a subject that gives rise to controversial debate, generates administrative ambivalence, fragments and polarizes society, and constantly places the capacity of governance in doubt. What makes the Spanish case so distinctive is that it highlights that the *backlash against multiculturalism in Europe* is more a matter of interpretation than of fact.

There are two issues that expose how, within the context of Europe, Spain is a laboratory for the management of diversities, where old questions (religious diversity and national diversity) are confronted by new challenges (immigration). The first issue is the question of how immigration is a factor that affects existent diversities and urges us to give political responses to related issues through the management of identities that were left unresolved in the past. The second issue is the question of how the important link to explore is not so much a political issue as an issue of societal opinion and its difficulties in interpreting the dynamics of diversity. These arguments lead us to defend the following: In Spain, we are witnessing a process of social, political, and cultural transformation without precedent. Due to the new dynamic created by immigration and the questions of multiculturalism it poses to Spanish identity and tradition, there is a revival of debates surrounding religious and multinational diversity that stimulate calls for a second democratic transition in Spain, taking the management of diversity as its main focal point.

The Spanish case also exemplifies apparent ambivalences of public opinion, illustrated by polls that indicate a widespread negative attitude in relation to levels of flows and frontier-related matters, and a positive, tolerant opinion on matters related to inclusion and equal rights. Specific factors can be seen to influence the 'problematization' of immigration, including: changes in legislation and the perception of poor management of immigration flows, specific conflicts that demand social and political positioning beyond the scope of the local administration where they occur, sweeping immigration decisions (especially regularization/normalization policies), and the reactive discourse of political parties (Zapata-Barrero 2009).

The governance hypothesis helps makes sense of the Spanish situation. Here, negative attitudes are not so much directed at the phenomenon of immigration itself, but at the Government and its policies which are deemed as incapable to govern issues related to immigration and to respond to citizens' expectations. Within this interpretative framework, three relevant arguments exist. First, it is not so much the actual volume of migratory flows itself that fosters negative attitudes, but rather its growth rate. A high rate is interpreted as evidence of governance problems and is reflected in negative public opinion. Second, socio-economic variables in Spain are highly significant in explaining negative attitudes. Third, the tolerant attitude shown with regard to immigrant inclusion raises questions as to how citizens' opinion is shaped. A set of questions subsequently arises: if policies would begin to focus more on immigrant-Spaniard coexistence, equal rights and inclusion, would the focus of public opinion divert away from borders issues? Might new negative attitudes arise around these governance measures? At present, one wonders whether the apparent 'tolerant attitude' of Spaniards evident in most studies actually reflects a rather baseless expression of public opinion since there are no political management reference points on these inclusion issues around which actually to base opinions. In other words, since the government does not have explicit policies of inclusion (or at least does not reveal them to citizens), whereas it does have them for border management, public opinion has no empirical reference point on which to shape its attitudes. Therefore, we stress that in Spain, attitudes towards immigration should not only be interpreted in a framework in which the immigration phenomenon is assessed, but also taking into consideration the implementation of policies and the government's capacity to respond to citizens' uncertainties.

What makes the Spanish case so interesting is not only that it highlights ambivalences in public opinions, but it shows ways in which 'what the government does' and 'what the citizens perceive' are linked. More broadly and in keeping with other chapters in this volume, then, such a situation is reflected in the fact that the backlash against multiculturalism in Europe is more a matter of interpretation than of fact.

Notes

1 See Mouritsen and Jørgensen (2008).
2 There are two linguistic models at work in Spain. While most autonomous communities are unilingual, there are Autonomous Communities that are bilingual, although they have different approaches to managing linguistic pluralism. From the perspective of the central administration, Spanish is established as the official state language that all citizens must learn throughout the country, while official status is also given to regional languages in their respective territories.
3 Constitución Española, 1987 (http://www.congreso.es/funciones/constitucion/indice.htm).
4 These include the right to receive instruction in Islam in public and private schools, the right to celebrate Muslim holidays and the right to have Muslim marriages recognized under civil law.
5 On Islam and Spain, see the authoritative studies and interesting comments of López García (2002), Martin-Muñoz (2003) and López Garcia and Berriane (2004).
6 See http://www.gencat.cat/benestar/societat/convivencia/immigracio/pni/index.htm.
7 On the case of Flanders, see the works of Swyngedouw (1992, 1995), and De Witte and Klandermans (2000).
8 See http://www.gencat.cat/benestar/societat/convivencia/immigracio/acollida/index.htm.
9 While the number of foreigners in Spain that held a valid residence card or permit on 31 December 2005 is 2,738,932 (Informe Estadístico 31–12–2005, Ministerio de Trabajo y Asuntos Sociales), the number of foreigners registered at the local level on 1 January 2006 is 3,884,573 (pádron municipal, Instituto Nacional de Estadística, 2006). While all foreign residents (independent of their status) can inscribe themselves within the local register, the number of foreigners provided by the Minister of Labour and Social Affairs only refers to foreigners that hold a valid residency permit. The total population is provided by the Instituto Nacional de Estadística.
10 News articles on immigration have been collected since September 2006 from the newspapers El País, El Periódico, El Mundo, ABC and La Vanguardia.
11 See, among others, Valles *et al.* (1999), Pérez Díaz *et al.* (2002), Alvira Martín and García López (2003), Campo Ladero (2004), Colectivo IOE (2005), Díez Nicolas (2006).
12 According to data from the Annual statistics on Foreigners 1996–2004 and the Statistical Report dated 31 December 2005, by the Ministry of Labour and Social Affairs and the National Statistics Institute, Municipal Census 1995–2005, in 2000 the immigrant population was 895,720 and in 2005 it was 2,738,932. This is a 37 per cent increase in five years.
13 Centre for Social Research – www.cis.es.
14 The first surveys which exclusively deal with attitudes towards immigration date from 1990. In March of that year, by the CIRES (Centro de Estudios sobre la Realidad Social or Centre for Research on Social Reality) and in September by the Centro de Investigaciones Sociológicas (CIS). For a list of the surveys carried out in Spain, see Cea D'Ancona (2004).
15 See Zapata-Barrero (2003).
16 See http://www.cis.es.
17 Ranking is based on the predetermined answer categories provided by the CIS. In some cases immigration shared its relative place with other answer categories.
18 The relatively low numbers (below 10 per cent) in November/ December 2001 and March/ April 2003 are mainly a result of concerns about ETA terrorism and in March 2004 due to the terrorist attacks in Madrid.

19 See http://www.cis.es/cis/opencm/ES/1_encuestas/estudios/ver.jsp?estudio=5118
20 It should also be stressed that 31 per cent prefer not to comment, expressing a doubt as to the number of immigrants that exists.

References

Aja, E. (2006) 'La evolución de la normativa sobre inmigración en España', in E. Aja and J. Arango (eds) *Veinte años de inmigración en España, perspectivas jurídica y sociológica [1985–2004]* (17–44), Barcelona: Fundació CIDOB.

Alvira Martín, F. and García López, J. (2003) 'Opinión pública e inmigración', in *Papeles de economia española*, 98: 182–97.

Anguera, I. (2002) 'Los partidos catalanes rompen la breve tregua en torno a la inmigración', *ABC,* 31 May.

Bader, V. (2008) Secularism or Democracy? Associational Governance of Religious Diversity, Amsterdam University Press – IMISCOE Research.

Cachón-Rodríguez, L. (2005) *Bases sociales de los sucesos de Elche de septiembre de 2004*. Madrid: Ministerio de Trabajo y Asuntos Sociales (Secretaria de Estado de inmigración y emigración).

Campo Ladero, M J. (2004), *Opiniones y actitudes de los españoles ante el fenómeno de la inmigración*, Madrid: CIS. Colección Opiniones y Actitudes, 48.

Cea D'Ancona, M A. (2004), *La activación de la xenofobia en España. ?Qué miden las encuestas?* Madrid: CIS.

Colectivo IOE (2005) 'Ciudadanos o intrusos: la opinión pública española ante los inmigrantes', *Papeles de Economía Española*, 104: 194–209.

De Witte, H. and Klandermans, B. (2000) 'Political racism in Flanders and the Netherlands: explaining differences in the electoral successof extreme right-wing parties', *Journal of Ethnic and Migration Studies*, 26 (4); 699–717.

Díez Nicolas, J. (2006) *Las dos caras de la inmigración*, Madrid: Madrid: Ministerio de Trabajo y Asuntos Sociales (Observatorio Permanente, n 3).

Gagnon, A.; Guibernau, M. and Rocher, F. (eds.) (2003) T*he Conditions of Diversity in Multinational Democracies*, Quebec: The Institute for Research and Public Policy (IRPP).

Gagnon, A.G. and Tully, J. (eds). (2001) *Multinational Democracies*, Cambridge: Cambridge University Press.

García Morente, M. (1938) *Idea de Hispanidad*. Buenos Aires: Espasa Calpe.

Garreta Bochaca, J. (2003) La integracion sociocultural de las minorias, Barcelona: Anthropos.

Gimeno, L. (2001) *Actitudes hacia la inmigración*, Madrid: Centro de Investigaciones Sociológicas (n. 34)

González Antón, L. (1997) *Espana y las Españas*. Madrid: Alianza

La Vanguardia (2005) 'La huelga de hambre que siguen 170 inmigrantes se mantendrá hasta el sábado', 1 May

López García, B. (2002) 'El islam y la integración de la inmigración en España', *Cuadernos de trabajo social*, 15; 129–44.

López Garcia, B. and Berriane, M. (eds) (2004) *Atlas de la inmigración marroquí en España*, Madrid: Taller de Estudios Internationales Mediterráneos (TEIM), Universidad Autonóma de Madrid

Martín Corrales, E. (2002) La imagen del magrebi en Espana una perspectiva historica, siglos XVI–XX, Barcelona: Bellaterra

Martin-Muñoz, G. (2003) Marroquíes en España, Estudio sobre su integración, Madrid: Fundación Repsol.

Missé, A. (2005) 'La UE pagará un sistema de control migratorio en todo el Mediterráneo, Los 25 crearán un fondo para la integración de inmigrantes promovido por Zapatero', *El País,* 12 December: 2.

Morcillo, C. (2005) 'Los vuelos de sin papeles hacia la Península se extienden desde Ceuta y Melilla tras solicitarlo el PP al Gobierno', *ABC,* 1 April: 19

Mouritsen, P. and Jørgensen, K. E. (eds) (2008) *Constituting Communities: Political Solutions to Cultural Conflict,* Basingstoke: Palgrave Macmillan.

Pérez, M. (2002) 'La alcaldesa de Premià pide ayuda a los gobiernos ante los brotes de racismo por la futura mezquita Jordi Pujol reclama más competencias para hacer una política de inmigración diferenciada', *El País,* 21 May.

Safont, C. (2005) 'Protesta de 200 guineanos por el elevado coste del certificado de penales', *La Vanguardia,* 10 April: 48.

SOS Racismo (2002 and 2003) *Informe Annual sobre el Racismo en el Estado español,* Barcelona: Icaria.

Swyngedouw, M. (1992) "L'essor d'Agalev et du Vlaams Block", *Courier hebdomadaire du CRISP,* 1362.

——(1995) "Les nouveaux clivages dans la politique belgo-flamande", *Revue française de science politique,* 45 (5); 775–90.

Valles, M., Cea, M.A. and Izquierdo, A. (1999) *Las encuestas sobre inmigración en España y Europa,* Madrid: OPI IMSERSO.

Vertovec, S. (2007) 'Super-diversity and its implications', *Ethnic and Racial Studies,* 30 (6): 1024–54.

Zapata-Barrero, R. (2003) 'The "Discovery" of Immigration: The Politicization of Immigration in the Case of El Ejido", *Journal of International Migration and Integration,* 4 (4): 523–39.

——(2006) 'The Muslim Community and Spanish Tradition: Maurophobia as a Fact, and Impartiality as a Desiratum', in T. Modood, A. Triandafyllidou, and R. Zapata-Barrero (eds) *Multiculturalism, Muslims and Citizenship: A European Approach,* New York: Routledge (chap. 8, 143–161).

——(2009) *Fundamentos de los discursos políticos en torno a la inmigración,* Madrid: Trotta

—— (ed.) (2009) *Immigration and Self-government of Minority Nations,* Brussels: Peter Lang editor, Col. Di versitad.

——(2009) "Policies and Public Opinion Towards Immigrants: The Spanish Case", *Journal of Ethnic and Racial Studies,* 32 (7), 1101–1120.

Zapata-Barrero, R. and Qasem, I. (2008) 'The Politics of Discourse towards Islam and Muslim Communities in Europe', in P. Mouritsen and K. E. Jørgensen (eds) *Constituting Communities: Political Solutions to Cultural conflict,* Basingstoke: Palgrave Macmillan; 73–93.

Zapata-Barrero, R. and de Witte, N. (2007) 'The Spanish Governance of EU Borders: Normative Questions', *Mediterranean Politics,* 12 (1), March: 85–90.

Internet resources (surveys and reports)

CIS: Centro de Investigaciones Sociológicas: http://www.cis.es

European Monitoring Centre on Racism and Xenophobia (2006) *Muslims in the European Union – Discrimination and Islamophobia*:
http://eumc.europa.eu/eumc/material/pub/ muslim/Manifestations_EN.pdf

US Department of State, Spain (2006) "International Religions Freedom Report 2006", Released on September 15 by the Bureau of Democracy, Human Rights, and Labor (http://www.state.gov/g/drl/rls/irf/2006/71409.htm).

Ley 4/2000-Ley Organica sobre derechos y libertades de los extranjeros en España y su integración social.http://www.boe.es/boe/dias/2000/01/12/pdfs/A01139–50.pdf

Ley Orgánica de Libertad Religiosa (LO 7/1980, de 5 de julio): http://www.boe.es/g/es/bases_datos/doc.php?coleccion=iberlex&id=1980/15955.Jefatura de Estado (1992) 'Ley 26/1992, de 10 Noviembre, por la que se aprueba el acuerdo de cooperación del estado con la comisión islámica de España', BOE 272, 12 November (www.boe.es/g/es/bases_datos/doc.php?coleccion=iberlex&id = 1992/24855).US Department of State Spain (2006) 'International Religious Freedom Report 2006', Released on September 15 by the Bureau of Democracy, Human Rights, and Labor (http://www.state.gov/g/drl/rls/irf/2006/71409.htm).

INE – Instituto Nacional de Estadística (2006, January 17) *Explotación Estadística del Padrón municipal a 1 de enero de 2005. Datos definitivos.* Available at http://www.ine.es

10 Multiculturalism

A Canadian defence

David Ley

The wide-ranging chapters in this book have shown the complexity not only of immigrant reception policies in Western Europe, but also the diversity between national understandings of multiculturalism itself. Non-Europeans might have limited knowledge of the less familiar models of French republicanism (see Simon and Sala Pala's chapter in this volume) contrasted with the German tradition of ethno-specific citizenship (see Schönwälder's chapter in this volume), but when they come to the multiculturalism enunciated for some time by countries such as Britain, the Netherlands or Sweden, a Canadian or Australian, with their own multicultural history, might expect to find some common ground. But what is clear is that multiculturalism bends with local political cultures. The Dutch version is shaped by the separate spheres model of pillarization, the long-established convention of institutional and cultural separation between dominant religious groups and the secular state (see Prins and Saharso's chapter in this volume), while the British variation, influenced by its own church–state relationships, has permitted the development of separate religious schools and their institutional offspring (see Grillo's chapter in this volume). A first and necessary realization, then, is that multiculturalism means different things in different places, including of course nations like Switzerland that are demographically multicultural but have no official multicultural policy (see D'Amato's chapter in this volume). The semantic breadth of the term has allowed, as I shall suggest later, its inflation to a size where is has become an easy target for critics lamenting the failure of settlement and integration policy.

Indeed, overriding national variations in the meaning and practice of multiculturalism in Europe is a unifying sense of unease, and periodic crisis, in assessing the failure of immigrant and refugee inclusion. Integration policy has become very unstable terrain, with significant policy turbulence accompanying the swings of public opinion, the oscillations of electoral behavior, and knee-jerk and sometimes opportunistic political responses. Former low-level anxieties accompanying the slow pace of cultural, economic, political and social integration are punctuated by unpredictable but increasingly common shocks creating national hypertension: the assassination of Theo van Gogh in the Netherlands, severe rioting in France and Britain, the cartoons crisis in Denmark, numbing terrorist attacks in Spain and Britain, and the existence of impulsive terrorist sleeper cells in Germany and elsewhere. The co-existence of the visible and publicized social exclusion of immigrant groups, the prospect of random violence and the rapidity of cultural change have, understandably, generated a fundamental sense of dislocation, casting long-established patterns of identity, affiliation and security into doubt. These are propitious conditions for backlash, with further polarization and deterioration of inter-group relations.

In this troubled context, a comparative perspective from the new world may be useful, not because the three largest immigrant-receiving countries of Australia, Canada and the United States are without integration challenges of their own – far from it – but because as settler societies they have had a longer experience with an intentional strategy of planning and managing cultural diversity, of nation-building within which immigration is a fundamental corner stone. The earlier inter-racial history of all three countries is in fact one of desperate, indeed atrocious failure, and includes aboriginal genocide and near genocide and entrenched racism solidified by institutionalized social exclusion, directed initially against those from outside north-western Europe, and later against non-Europeans. But the last third of the twentieth century has seen substantial cultural and institutional re-positioning, and in this more hopeful period, multiculturalism has played an important role, notably in Canada and Australia and to a much lesser degree in the United States. In light of the pessimism about multiculturalism in theory and practice in Europe, a Canadian perspective in particular may be helpful.

Multiculturalism as a Canadian institution

The origin of Canadian multiculturalism was to some extent unintended. In the 1960s, to address the growing challenge of the Quebec question during the 'quiet revolution' of growing self-expression in that province, the federal government set up a Royal Commission on Bilingualism and Biculturalism. As public hearings were held across the country representation was made by Ukrainian-Canadians and other groups of non-British and non-French ethnicity challenging the conventional national assimilation model of Anglo- and Franco-conformity. By 1961 citizens outside these two 'charter groups' accounted for 25 per cent of the national population, and immigration trends, notably after the 1967 reforms, suggested this share would grow steadily, as indeed it has. In an ambiguous positioning of this population, neither exclusionary but yet clearly partitioned and separate, the Royal Commission produced a fourth and final volume in 1969, entitled 'The Cultural Contribution of Other Ethnic Groups'. It was the political intuition of Prime Minister Pierre Trudeau, in a speech in the Canadian Parliament in October 1971, that reversed the bicultural (but not the bilingual) recommendations of the Royal Commission, ushering in multiculturalism as official government policy. The

Prime Minister's intent was that the 'Other Ethnic Groups' should become part of the mainstream.

Trudeau later oversaw the inscription of multiculturalism into the 1982 Constitution where article 27 of the Canadian Charter of Rights and Freedoms asserts a declaration of rights 'in a manner consistent with the multicultural heritage of Canadians'. I will want to return to that issue of rights later. Other legislative institutionalization was the 1988 Multiculturalism Act, followed by the 1995 Employment Equity Act, giving Canada the strongest legal and constitutional basis for multiculturalism in any country. In recent years the appointment by the Prime Minister of immigrant women of colour as Governor General of Canada, the Queen of Britain's official representative in Canada's constitutional monarchy, has provided symbolic and highly visible institutionalization of cultural diversity as a national norm. Reflecting large Caribbean- and Chinese-origin populations in Canada, Michaëlle Jean, the current Governor General, was born in Haiti, and her predecessor, Adrienne Clarkson, in Hong Kong. Interestingly, both women are married to white men, perhaps projecting a multicultural moral into the nuclear family itself. Following, and in some cases anticipating, this symbolic positioning of immigrants of colour, several provinces have also appointed members of visible minorities (to use the Canadian term) as Lieutenant Governor, filling the equivalent provincial constitutional role as the federal Governor General. Extending the modelling of inclusion to aboriginal populations, the past Lieutenant Governor of Ontario, James Bartleman, a diplomat and philanthropist, is a member of the Mnjikaning First Nation. His mandate included three key priorities: 'to eliminate the stigma of mental illness, to fight racism and discrimination, and to encourage aboriginal young people' (Government of Ontario 2007).

The federal Department of Canadian Heritage is official protector of cultural pluralism. Its website announces the official face of multiculturalism:

> Canadian multiculturalism is fundamental to our belief that all citizens are equal. Multiculturalism ensures that all citizens can keep their identities, can take pride in their ancestry and have a sense of belonging. Acceptance gives Canadians a feeling of security and self-confidence, making them more open to, and accepting of, diverse cultures. The Canadian experience has shown that multiculturalism encourages racial and ethnic harmony and cross-cultural understanding, and discourages ghettoization, hatred, discrimination and violence.
>
> (Government of Canada 2007)

Allowing for a certain level of public relations decorum, this summary statement still makes important claims. Multiculturalism is associated with equality, a sense of identity, acceptance of diversity, ethnic understanding and harmony, while discouraging social and spatial exclusion, bias and hatred. These are strong claims, and the Department sought to substantiate them in four pamphlets, 'The Evidence Series: Facts about Multiculturalism', that summarize academic research indicating that multiculturalism encourages attachment to Canada and that it promotes immigrant integration and citizenship. However, the pamphlets also document continuing bias in the labour market and the existence of hate crimes, suggesting that much remains to be done. But, above all, this dossier underscores that multiculturalism is part of the immigrant integration project, and stands opposed to parochial separation. Such an ideology was inherent in Trudeau's cosmopolitan view of Canada in the world and his persistent opposition to Quebec separatism that he regarded as divisive and small-minded. Multiculturalism continues to be seen in senior policy circles as a bridge-building tool between immigrants and the long-settled to achieve integration (Duncan 2005). That is why citizenship requires a short test of knowledge of Canadian institutions and the citizenship ceremony itself is a celebratory event before a judge and an officer of the Royal Canadian Mounted Police in iconic uniform. There is a rite of passage here, as immigrants and refugees are welcomed into citizenship as equal partners.

For equality to exist it must be monitored and this is the rationale for the extraordinarily detailed census record on indicators of cultural pluralism. From the Census of Canada, population data are available every five years on place of birth, citizenship, immigrant status, ethnic self-designation, racial self-designation, religious affiliation, mother tongue use and facility in English and French.[1] Many of these questions, accounting for almost a quarter of the census inventory, are nominated and paid for by the Department of Canadian Heritage. A principal objective is to monitor performance against standards required by compliance audits in such legislation as the 1988 Multiculturalism Act and the 1995 Employment Equity Act.

Outside government, multiculturalism is deeply embedded in school curricula, socializing children into the advantages of an open society. It has been promoted by public intellectuals, notably the political philosophers Charles Taylor (1992) and Will Kymlicka (1995, 1998). As a result, multiculturalism is often seen to be a defining characteristic of Canadian identity (Li 2003). Moreover, it continues to receive strong popular endorsement as a positive contribution to integration. A stratified random sample of 1500 Canadians in September 2006 showed that in Canada at least the demise of multiculturalism in public sentiment has been exaggerated (Jedwab 2006).[2] Among respondents, 76 per cent agreed that multiculturalism aids immigrant integration, 76 per cent that it aids equal participation in society, 74 per cent that it assists a sense of national belonging, 69 per cent that it assists national identity and citizenship, 69 per cent that it enhances the identification of shared values and 64 per cent that it aids social cohesion. These data seem to bear out the official pronouncement on the Canadian Heritage web site. The survey revealed that professional and university-educated respondents were more positive in their assessment, while low-income and retired Canadians were less supportive (but not negative). There was a slight but consistent tendency for respondents whose mother tongue was neither English nor

French, almost all of whom would be immigrants, to endorse multi-culturalism even more enthusiastically along these dimensions than the rest of the population.

There are frequently congruent attitudes between multiculturalism and immigration in national surveys, and it is notable that opinion polls typically find that, though cyclic, Canadian attitudes toward immigration are invari-ably affirmative. International surveys in 2002 and 2004 showed that Canadians were by far the most accommodating to immigration; in the 2002 poll, three out of four endorsed immigration, while in no other country was this position supported by a majority (Hiebert 2006). No political party opposes immigration and there has been no variation in annual entry targets in the transitions between Conservative and Liberal federal governments over the past 15 years – indeed there has been a slow but steady upward trajectory in target numbers.

Counter-flow: multiculturalism under attack

To a European reader this account must seem hopelessly utopian, perhaps even an unattractive form of national grandstanding. And so it should, for despite significant achievements, it would be disingenuous to present either immigration or multicultural policy as unflawed, and such a position would generate incredulity in Canada where academic and popular criticisms are unrelenting on such issues as immigrant and refugee selection, refugee adju-dication, discriminatory responses to racial diversity, harmonizing border policy with the United States, the adequacy of settlement services, the failure to recognize overseas professional credentials, the delayed economic, social and political integration of immigrants with Canadian society and the fundamental position of multiculturalism as a governance umbrella.

Multiculturalism has never been given an easy ride in Canada. Rather, there has been a spirited and sometimes cantankerous debate with dissenters representing a broad range of political positions (Ley 2008). I want first to review some of the older, typically, intellectual challenges before moving on to the current populist and sometimes more visceral attacks, where some con-vergence with, and inspiration from, European criticism has occurred.

From the political right has come the anxiety that multiculturalism is an exercise in post-modern identity politics that fragments the nation-building project. The charges of national separation with 'the proliferation of prob-lematic diversity' are widespread (Day 2000). This was also the *cri de coeur* of Pauline Hanson's One-Nation Party in Australia in the 1990s (Ang and Stratton 2001), and lies behind Samuel Huntington's (2004) recent interven-tions in the USA. Though no comparable political movement to Hanson's developed in Canada, nonetheless there were, and are (Gregg 2006), concerns that multicultural fracturing, superimposed onto periodically acute relations with Quebec and the growing mobilization of the aboriginal first nations, might over-extend the steering capacity of the state.

More troublesome for the federal advocates of multiculturalism was the response of certain representatives of the immigrant communities themselves. In general, as Jedwab's 2006 poll suggests, immigrants (and their organizations) are keen supporters of multiculturalism, seeing it as an endorsement of tolerance and respect toward their own cultural heritage and (more importantly) their citizenship rights. But that support is not shared by everyone, and particularly not by some articulate figures who, like the conservatives, also challenge the seeming partition of the nation into multicultural fragments, but unlike them do so from an immigrant perspective. They disagree with the cultural essentialism of multiculturalism, seeing not only the benign project of cultural recognition, but also a more troubling (if unintended) consequence that reproduces cultural difference, thereby prescribing the appropriate cultural repertoire for any hyphenated Canadian. This argument was raised most persuasively by Neil Bissoondath (1994) in *Selling Illusions: The Cult of Multiculturalism*, where he argued that his Trindadian past should have no bearing on his Canadian present. Rather he wanted to be a simple Canadian, unencumbered by ethnic expectations. Rebutting state mantras, he charged that multiculturalism contributed to the containment, marginalization and ghettoization of essentialized immigrant identities. Soon after, Canadian Heritage issued its Evidence Series of pamphlets defending multiculturalism by using academic research against such charges.

Bissoondath's challenge is a more measured version of Ghassan Hage's (1998) vigorous attack on Australian multiculturalism, where he objects to what he calls the ethnic caging of immigrant identities. This project of classification and containment by an older Anglo-Celtic elite is intended, writes Hage, to maintain their own power base as guardians and controllers of the national society, a charge he directs not only against transparent racists but also against the more subtle privileges of the middle-class 'cosmo-multiculturalist'. In a strategy of divide and conquer, he argues, new immigrants are sorted into groups predicated on cultural difference, an essentialization of identity that harks back to older and more pernicious models of ethno-racial classification (Anderson 1991). The tendency of categorization to homogenize and thereby limit the range of identities was brought home to me powerfully at a community meeting where, as part of a presentation, I showed a map plotting Vancouver residents of South Asian background. A voice from the audience took objection to this map. 'Am I on it? I object. I have almost nothing in common with all the other dots on the map. Don't limit our individuality.' This objection raised the relevant question of how far mapping, or any other use of ethnic classification as a form of academic representation, is itself a version of essentialization and containment.

These criticisms by no means exhaust the range of challenges to multiculturalism in Canada. It is not surprising that in a neo-liberal age a further charge against multiculturalism is that its founding purposes have been co-opted and that it has become commodified (Abu-Laban and Gabriel 2002). Katharyne Mitchell (1993) cites a speech of Prime Minister Mulroney from the 1980s, where he makes much of the capacity of multiculturalism to contribute to international trade and capital flows. Multiculturalism also enables elites to play the ethnic card as a sign of a worldly cosmopolitanism, and growth boosters have certainly taken advantage of the cultural diversity of large gateway cities in their place promotion activities. An ethnic advantage was fully claimed in Sydney's successful bid for the 2000 Summer Olympic Games and Vancouver's for the 2010 Winter Games.

A final critical challenge to multiculturalism is the claim, usually from the political left, that it is an exercise in false consciousness. Lisa Lowe (1996), an American scholar, has advanced an argument often heard in Canada that the gaiety of multicultural festival, the welcome diversity of immigrant cuisine, induce a soporific sense of cultural equality, concealing a more insidious reality of immigrant marginalization in economic and political integration to national life. Indeed and here her argument returns to some of Hage's themes, multiculturalism is supported because it adds variety, spice even, to the dull life of the middle-class native-born. But sustaining such bourgeois pleasures are legions of low-paid service workers, whose exotic self-presentation and smiling faces conceal an everyday life of poverty and social exclusion.

Defending multiculturalism in difficult times

There are responses to each of these challenges – for example an answer that has been given to the concern about national fragmentation is the statement that multiculturalism is a core Canadian value and thus a source of unity, not fragmentation, as Jedwab's survey indicates – but instead of working through each of these responses in turn, I want to address a broader issue about the understanding of multiculturalism upon which many of the challenges are assembled. For it is frequently the case that criticisms are derived from an imputed meaning of multiculturalism which is now largely obsolete in practice. The complaints about the fragmentation of a national culture, the commercial hijacking of ethnic culture, the essentializing of immigrant culture or the chimera of cultural equality all miss the point that in Canada today multicultural policy is only indirectly concerned with the maintenance of old-world cultures. The criticisms have not kept up with the evolution of a mutating practice.

Audrey Kobayashi (1993) has written cogently on the three stages of multiculturalism in Canada. The first stage is simply demographic multiculturalism, the recognition that a national society's charter group, in Canada the two English and French charter groups, are no longer the only teams in town. This acknowledgment occurred in Canada with the lobbying of other Canadians to the Bilingualism and Biculturalism Commission and the inclusion of their call for cultural pluralism in Volume IV of the Commission's Report. Trudeau's declaration of official multiculturalism in 1971 gave rise to a second stage of symbolic multiculturalism, a somewhat unfocussed support and celebration of heritage cultures through usually small grants for events, programmes and cultural centres. As Minister of State for Multiculturalism Joseph-Philippe Guay declared in 1977: 'If we accept our cultural pluralism then we assure our Canadian unity. It is as simple and as complicated as that ... assimilation is not an option we Canadians want or choose' (Kobayashi 1993: 216). This was the era of modest state support for elements of immigrant culture including music, literature, dance and pioneer histories, and respect for their worthy and equal status. Cultural difference was preserved, even promoted, and it is this emphasis on the accentuation of cultural difference that continues to be commonly understood as comprising multiculturalism today.

But in fact multiculturalism has moved on. According to the 2004–5 Annual Report on the Multiculturalism Act, 'As society has evolved and needs have changed so too have the priorities of the Multiculturalism Programme' (Government of Canada 2006: 9). The four programme areas in the report emphasize active citizenship, not heritage cultures. They comprise: 1) fostering cross-cultural understanding; 2) combating racism and discrimination; 3) promoting civic participation; and 4) making Canadian institutions more reflective of Canadian diversity. Similarly, the British Columbia multiculturalism programme is merged with anti-racism, and 'its primary goal ... is the elimination of racism and other forms of hate activity' (Government of British Columbia 2006). There are no longer grants to sustain heritage cultures, but there are grants for official-language programmes offered by NGOs to enhance integration.

Since the passing of the Multiculturalism Act, then, the emphasis has moved to a third stage of structural multiculturalism, the advancement of human rights as constitutionally protected in the Canadian Charter of Rights and Freedoms. Anti-racism, employment equity, equal treatment before the law in policing, education and immigration policy, and redress for group discrimination in the past are all agenda items of presently existing multiculturalism. The intent is integration and social inclusion through equality of opportunity and treatment. In June 2006 an official apology, with a small cash settlement, was granted by the Government of Canada to Chinese-Canadians and their descendants who were obligated to pay an invidious head tax, intended to block their immigration, from 1885 until 1923, when all Chinese entry was barred by the Chinese Immigration Act until it was annulled in 1947. Surviving head tax payers, family members and descendants successfully pressed their human rights for fair and respectful treatment, including redress for past injustices. Chinese redress follows the earlier Japanese redress settlement in 1988 when an apology and cash settlement was made to acknowledge and nominally compensate Japanese-Canadians for the suspension of their human rights when they were moved to internment camps during the Second World War, and their property was confiscated. The purpose of these redress settlements is not only to remove the stigma of past social exclusion but to testify to such exclusion as an historic error, thereby underscoring the contemporary commitment to an open inclusive society.

Like Canadian multiculturalism more generally the intent is the social integration of ethnic diversity.

Multiculturalism and the present crisis

But all of this may appear to be superseded and seemingly arcane in the face of urgent, populist challenges that have in part been agitated by media flows from Europe. Despite its human rights remit, it is multiculturalism that has borne the brunt of a renewed round of challenges this decade, more significant because they are now populist, politicized and widely publicized reactions to traumatic events. Troubling emergencies elsewhere that were generally viewed through the media from a safe distance came home with 18 arrests in 2006 in Greater Toronto of an alleged terrorist ring sympathetic to Al-Qaeda, whose bizarre plans are said to have included bombings, an invasion of Parliament and the beheading of the Prime Minister. Subsequent debate showed that Canada was not immune from the same anxious, sometimes shrill, reflections as Europeans.

Indeed much contemporary popular writing is inspired by the cross-national transmission of media text and images that selectively highlight points of crisis, presenting them as normative, eliding significant differences in national conditions and sliding across thin ice in prescribing causality. In this spontaneous and often uncritical transmission of tarnished ethnoscapes from elsewhere, multiculturalism has been projected as the abiding context, the grab bag for all manner of policy failures.

The spectre of spatial segregation

A seminal example is a widely read article in *The Walrus*, a magazine of art, politics and commentary, prior to the Toronto arrests but hard on the heels of the London bombings, *banlieue* riots and the Cronulla beach violence in Sydney. In March 2006, its lead article, written by Allan Gregg, a respected pollster and political commentator, was entitled 'Identity Crisis', with the revealing sub-title 'Multiculturalism: A twentieth century dream becomes a twenty-first century conundrum' (Gregg 2006). The article's first three paragraphs elaborated in turn the London, French and Sydney incidents, rolling them together in a common and alarmist semantic field. The fourth paragraph turns to Canadian multiculturalism, and raises fears of violence in Canada. Citing a poll, Gregg declares that the Canadian public want multiculturalism to be aimed at integration not separation. But that has always been its objective, and more explicitly in the third phase of structural multiculturalism than ever before. The perceived dysfunction of separation then leads in Gregg's argument to the familiar lament that 'ethnic groups are self-segregating'. The *bête noir* of spatial segregation is reminiscent of Trevor Phillips's anxiety in the United Kingdom of a society 'sleepwalking toward segregation'. It is undoubtedly the case that the huge immigration to Toronto and Vancouver in the past 25 years has led to higher levels of residential segregation, though these concentrations fall far short of any definition of ghetto (Walks and Bourne 2006), and many immigrants live in a district with pronounced ethnic mixing.

The anxieties associated with social isolation and residential segregation are ubiquitous in the popular media, as well as in charges directed by policy-makers and influential figures like Phillips or Gregg; compare, for example, the current Swedish policy imperative 'to break up segregation' (Andersson 2006). While multiculturalism is invariably blamed, such charges are far from the mark. In the United Kingdom, Deborah Phillips (2006) has discounted such accusations. She makes the pertinent observation that a comparable pattern of segregation of white Britons is not regarded as problematic: 'The white suburb and school thus become normalized, centralized spaces in the popular imagination, against which other spaces and lives are judged to be deviant or marginal' (2006: 29). The anxieties associated with 'parallel lives' and Muslim 'self-segregation', she points out, also overlook the effects of inner city disinvestment by more powerful groups as well as informal and institutional racism in shaping the residential choices of visible minorities. In England's northern cities, for example, British Muslims avoid residential areas where they fear harassment. The issue then is not simply one of self-segregation, but of societal intolerance. Moreover, segregation can serve positive ends. In Ceri Peach's oft-cited distinction there can be good segregation, encouraging mutual aid and shared problem-solving, as well as negative segregation (Peach 1996). Whenever appeals are made to the 'Muslim community' to 'police itself' against disruptive elements, policy-makers are themselves confirming that 'its' social cohesion does create a capacity for positive ends to be achieved.

But an even more important issue is that residential segregation is scarcely influenced by multiculturalism. The obvious example is the tenacious immigrant segregation in the *banlieues* around major French cities, existing despite the national policy of aggressive republicanism that rejects multiculturalism in favour of assimilation (Simon and Sala Pala, this volume). The same point has been made in a comparison of levels of residential segregation between cities in Canada and the United States, for aside from the much higher Black segregation in American cities, differences are minor and do not 'reveal any major distinction between a Canadian Mosaic and a US Melting Pot' (Peach 2005: 22). No relationship is evident between segregation and multiculturalism.

We need to challenge the false assumption that social and spatial separation have much if anything to do with multiculturalism.[3] Historically, one can easily find examples of cultural difference surviving in unexpected contexts that are free of multicultural influence. It was in the period of vigorous assimilation from 1910–60 that the Chicago School of urban sociology diffused the widespread study and measurement of ethnic segregation in American cities. They also pioneered the detailed study of the social worlds of the inner city, where social closure led to the creation of distinctive urban sub-cultures, distinctiveness sharp enough that social distance between groups became an operational and measurable concept (Bogardus 1925; Ley 1983). Consider the following familiar lament, which though it resonates with current complaints, occurred in the 1920s during the unchallenged period of the melting pot and assimilation in American cities. Moreover it was directed at European immigrants. The immigrant, complained an urban newspaper, 'has been all the time working for himself; he has kept to his own circles in the most clannish manner possible, he has learned too little English, familiarized himself all too little with our local laws and public movements and remained a [Dutchman], whereas he should have become more an American' (*Kalamazoo Telegraph*, 1922, cited in Jakle and Wheeler 1969: 447). The targets of this contemporary-sounding criticism against clannishness during the assimilationist era of the 1920s were the Dutch who were draining and farming the glacial muck lands of southwest Michigan. They needed no multicultural umbrella to assemble an institutionally complete and separate community, a community which a generation later had dispersed and Americanized (Jakle and Wheeler 1969).

The spectre of hostile difference

But in recent commentary the stakes have been raised, for it is not just separation and difference that are now the popular cause of concern, but rather hostile difference, introverted communities where social separation and economic marginality aid a receptiveness to ideologies and projects that challenge, in a few instances violently challenge, national values and civic order. It is multiculturalism we learn that has encouraged cultural difference, social isolation, the perpetuation and even the perversion of homeland beliefs, and disloyalty to the new state (see Hedetoft's chapter in this volume). The example of the Netherlands is produced repeatedly by critics as the object lesson of the failure of multiculturalism.

So Gregg (2006) like many others moves from the anxiety of segregation to the greater anxiety of segregation-bred violence among economically disenfranchised groups. A few months after his article was published, the arrest of the Toronto 18 revealed the apparent prescience of his argument, and his measured prose was replaced by the circulation in the media of more sensational and speculative opinion. More sober than many was the column by veteran journalist Robert Fulford (2006) in the right-wing *National Post*, two weeks after the Toronto arrests. His title, 'How we became a land of ghettos' is replete with sensational exaggeration of separateness (cf. Walks and Bourne 2006) that he attributes to multiculturalism. This is not his only example of false causal reasoning. His fullest example is a study revealing the apparent lack of cultural integration of Turkish-born women in Germany, leading to the conclusion that 'we need substantial criticism of multiculturalism and a redefinition of what it means'. Yet as Karen Schönwälder observes in her chapter in this volume, multicultural policy scarcely exists in Germany: 'No present or past federal or regional government has subscribed to an explicitly multicultural agenda'. Once again multiculturalism is inflated to a size where it becomes the only target that is visible.

A similar non sequitur was evident in the response of the British government to the London bombings in 2005. Prime Minister Blair announced in the wake of the bombings the creation of a Commission on Integration and Cohesion, a re-visioning that implied that previous British multicultural policy had not pursued such objectives. Launching the Commission in August 2006, two weeks after another terrorist plot to blow up planes leaving Heathrow had been foiled, Minister Ruth Kelly declared that Britain had moved away from a 'uniform consensus on the value of multiculturalism to one where we can encourage the debate by questioning whether it is encouraging separateness' (Woodward 2006). The coincidental timing between the announcement of the Commission following immediately upon a terrorist event and its launch right after a second event had been thwarted makes the imputed connection between multiculturalism and the formation of terrorist cells transparent. Multiculturalism is the permissive environment in which the state is 'sleepwalking toward segregation', sustaining a milieu of isolation and encouraging an exotic version of homeland culture to take root.

Yet the pattern in the current round of arrests in Canada and England makes that case hard to sustain. Suspects were invariably quite integrated: English-speaking, often native-born, sometimes middle-class and well-educated. Arrests in 2006 occurred in such places as Mississauga in middle-class suburban Toronto and Crawley, an equivalent middle-class town south of London. Why would my son give up his BMW convertible and corner office in a high-rise tower, protested one Canadian father of an arrested suspect. Some of the suspects and their families are converts to Islam: the wife of the alleged ring-leader in the Toronto cell was born Cheryl MacAulay in a Scots-Irish region of Atlantic Canada. British arrests have also included converts who did not grow up in an ethno-specific ideological hot-house.

It is not confinement within a warped cultural setting sustained by multiculturalism that is at issue here. More important is the identification of particular individuals with a larger national or pan-national political cause and their search for an extremist sub-culture, or their indoctrination into such a sub-culture by persuasive, even charismatic leaders. That cause is typically the war on terror, more specifically the war in Iraq, widely seen as a war on Muslims. But this cause, which is identified constantly in polls on Muslim opinion and is repeated by suspects themselves, is categorically and ideologically ruled out by the British government (Ash 2006; Bunting 2006). Multiculturalism is a much less embarrassing target than unpopular foreign policy and friendly fire is re-directed toward it.

Terrorist cells are not new in North America or Europe and they extend well outside the immigrant population. Are Timothy McVeigh, the Oklahoma City bomber, and the anti-government white militias in the US the fault of multiculturalism? Or what about the FLQ, Quebec separatists who undertook 200 acts of political terrorism in the 1960s culminating in the political assassination of the Deputy Premier of Quebec during the October Crisis of 1970, when tanks were called to the streets of Montreal? Should we blame multiculturalism that they did not learn core Canadian values? What these extremists, like jihadists, held in common was a political vision, however perverse, that had received and rejected both immigrant and homeland values in favour of a grand theory, an amoral meta-ideology. They repeat the familiar European twentieth-century story of ETA and the IRA, where the means justified the ends, whatever the collateral cost. From this perspective, 'immigrant integration and terrorism have nothing to do with each other' (Bunting 2006).

Conclusion

In December 2006, in its year-end review of the leading global migration issues, the Migration Policy Institute listed in first place the demise of multiculturalism. The brief review moved quickly through familiar episodes in Britain, the Netherlands and Denmark to make its case, ending by citing a Winnipeg-based journalist who suggested that not all was well in Canada. Surprisingly this Washington-based think tank made no reference to the United States, where 2006 had provided further evidence of its argument for the return of assimilation. After all, campaigning for his new immigration bill, President Bush had declared:

> One aspect of making sure we have an immigration system that works, that's orderly and fair, is to actively reach out and help people assimilate into our country ... That means learn the values and history and language of America ... When you hear people like me talking about assimilation, that's what we're talking about, helping people assimilate into America, helping us remain one nation under God.
>
> (Stolberg 2006)

In contrast, even under provocation, the Government of Canada has not followed this path. Two weeks after Mr Bush's statement, the Conservative Prime Minister of Canada had a somewhat different message at the opening of the World Urban Forum in Vancouver. The context of Stephen Harper's speech was the recent discovery of the terrorist plot in Toronto. But Mr Harper offered a defence of sustained immigration and multicultural policy: 'Canada's diversity, properly nurtured, is our greatest strength,' he observed (Mickleburgh 2006), asserting continued support for immigration and multiculturalism.

This chapter has similarly offered a defence of multiculturalism, policies that have evolved, and continue to evolve, in Canada over the past 35 years. A first premise is that the objective of multiculturalism is the integration of new immigrants into the Canadian mainstream – a definition that has not always been at the forefront of European applications (Entzinger 2008). An open society, not ethnic fiefdoms, was Trudeau's original objective, and the citizenship test and ceremony, only now being introduced in Europe, have been part of the status passage to inclusion in a national project since the 1970s. That inclusion is protected and enhanced by a battery of human rights legislation, monitored and audited by compliance requirements that are measurable through the census and other data bases. While providing individual rights, this legislation moves beyond assimilation by recognizing group rights nested within a larger commitment to Canada and its values. Anti-racism, employment equity, equal treatment before the law in such sectors as policing, education and immigration policy, and redress for group discrimination in the past, are all part of the multicultural agenda. The intent is integration and social inclusion through equality of opportunity and treatment. While funds for ethno-cultural projects are now minimal, public resources for settlement services, notably English- and French-language courses, are made available to NGOs that must represent a diversity of cultures and not a single ethnic origin. Like all nation-building, this is a work in progress, and evokes, as it should, criticism pointing to evident shortcomings and failures to reach mandated targets. But it is on the whole a system that has worked, granting Canada a reputation amongst immigrants and potential immigrants of being, albeit imperfectly, an open society (Bloemraad 2006).

Against these achievements and continued national support for the Canadian version of multiculturalism, criticisms commonly seem ill-directed. The repetitive argument that multiculturalism promotes segregation, separation socially and spatially, does not survive serious scrutiny. Segregation has always been a feature of sustained immigration and it always will be, and its extent has typically been exaggerated by critics. There was more segregation in the Chicago melting pot between 1880 and 1930 (Philpott 1978) than in multicultural Toronto or Vancouver in 2001 (Walks and Bourne 2006), and in both cases many more immigrants lived outside ethnic concentrations than within them. Chicago immigrant neighbourhoods were sometimes places of violence: in 1927, Frederic Thrasher wrote in great detail of the 1313 teenage gangs he had located in the Chicago slums (Thrasher 1927). Poverty and social exclusion were among their causes, the same conditions as have provided the setting for the 2005 French *banlieue* riots.

Terrorist cells are another matter. Many of the 2001 New York bombers were well educated, with pan-national connections; the core members met as students in Hamburg, Germany – a country not sympathetic to multicultural policy. They were motivated by American policy in the Middle East, articulated in the 1998 *fatwah* against the United States issued by Osama bin Laden. The prevalence of Western foreign policy in agitating young Muslims has been demonstrated repeatedly, most recently by the study *Living Apart Together*, for the conservative think-tank Policy Exchange (Mirza *et al.* 2007). Based on a survey of a thousand British Muslims, the study showed that British foreign policy mattered more to the respondents than economic issues, public services, or even ethno-specific Muslim issues such as discrimination.

'Foreign policy has become a major focus for Muslims in the West, as it concerns the persecution of fellow Muslims – the "imagined community" worldwide ... Muslim anger about foreign policy has been confirmed in numerous surveys over the past few years' (Mirza *et al.* 2007: 56). Yet, dutifully following the conservative impulse of 'sleepwalking toward segregation', the report overlooks its own findings and draws primary attention to the 'paradox of multiculturalism'.

Some of the most ardent challenges to multiculturalism in the recent past spring from a spurious causality. High levels of immigration, poverty and social exclusion have generated apartness, parallel lives, in the presence and the absence of multicultural policies. Hostile difference, currently the mobilization of small but militant Islamic cells in Western cities, derives its primary sustenance from an international movement that rejects Western foreign policy in the Middle East. These irritants of integration policy need fuller attention, in place of the fire drawn toward the inflated target of multiculturalism.

Notes

1 Census data are supplemented by several large databases assessing current and recent immigrant and ethnic attitudes, outcomes and conditions collected by government surveys, including the Longitudinal Survey of Immigrants to Canada (three waves, n = 12,000, 2001) the Ethnic Diversity Survey (n = 42,000, 2002), and continuing linked data bases such as the Landed Immigrant Data System (LIDS), developed from a landing card completed by all immigrants, and the longitudinal Immigrant Data Base (IMDB, 1980) linking landing cards with tax files of all immigrants landing in Canada since 1980 who submitted an income tax return.
2 The data were collected only a few months after Canada's worst terrorist incident, the arrest of 18 alleged terrorists in the Toronto region, reputedly affiliated with Al-Qaeda, who were apparently planning various attacks on public buildings and leaders in Ontario. We would expect the timing of the survey to have depressed the approval ratings of multiculturalism, but nonetheless they remain high. I am grateful to Jack Jedwab for access to these unpublished statistics.
3 Gregg (2006) seems to acknowledge this point in noting that Caribbean immigration in the United Kingdom under earlier 'generally assimilationist' policy was also associated with segregation, inequality and violence, but does not draw the obvious lesson concerning multiculturalism's alleged causal role.

References

Abu-Laban, Y. and Gabriel, C. (2002) *Selling Diversity: Immigration, Multiculturalism, Employment Equity and Globalization*, Peterborough, Ont: Broadview Press.

Anderson, K. (1991) *Vancouver's Chinatown: Racial Discourse in Canada, 1875–1980*, Montreal: McGill-Queen's University Press.

Andersson, R. (2006) ' "Breaking Segregation": rhetorical Construct or effective Policy?' *Urban Studies*, 43: 787–99.

Ang, I. and Stratton, J. (2001) 'Multiculturalism in Crisis: the New Politics of Race and national Identity in Australia', in I. Ang, *On Not Speaking Chinese: Living Between Asia and the West*, London: Routledge, pp. 95–111.

Ash, T. G. (2006) 'Divided Loyalties: why young British Muslims are angry', *The Globe and Mail*, 10 August.

Bissoondath, N. (1994) *Selling Illusions: The Cult of Multiculturalism in Canada*, Toronto: Penguin Books.

Bloemraad, I. (2006) *Becoming a Citizen: Incorporating Immigrants and Refugees in the United States and Canada*, Berkeley: University of California Press.

Bogardus, E. (1925) 'Measuring social Distance', *Journal of Applied Sociology*, 9: 299–308.

Bunting, M. (2006) 'Integration and Terrorism have nothing to do with each other', *Guardian*, 4 December.

Day, R. (2000) *Multiculturalism and the History of Canadian Diversity*, Toronto: University of Toronto Press.

Duncan, H. (2005) 'Multiculturalism: still a viable Concept for Integration?' *Canadian Diversity/Diversité Canadienne*, 4(1): 12–14.

Fulford, R. (2006) 'How we became a Land of Ghettoes', *National Post*, 12 June.

Government of British Columbia (2006) *Anti-racism and Multiculturalism Program*, Victoria, BC: Ministry of Attorney General, Settlement and Multiculturalism Division. Online. Available HTTP: http://www.ag.gov.bc.ca/sam/bcamp/index.htm (accessed 23 June 2006).

Government of Canada (2006) *Annual Report on the Operation of the Canadian Multiculturalism Act 2004–2005*, Ottawa: Department of Canadian Heritage, Catalogue Number CH31–1/2005.

——(2007) *What is Multiculturalism?* Ottawa: Department of Canadian Heritage. Online. Available HTTP: http://www.pch.gc.ca/progs/multi/what-multi_e.cfm (accessed 4 January 2007).

Government of Ontario (2007) The Hon. James K. Bartleman, O. Ont. 27th Lieutenant Governor of Ontario. Online. Available HTTP: http://www.lt.gov.on.ca/sections_english/welcome/hishonour_main.html (accessed 4 January 2007).

Gregg, A. (2006) 'Identity Crisis: A Twentieth-Century Dream becomes a Twenty-First Century Conundrum', *The Walrus,* March. Online. Available HTTP: http://www.walrusmagazine.com/archives/2006.03 (accessed 12 January 2007).

Hage, G. (1998) *White Nation: Fantasies of White Supremacy in a Multicultural Society*, Sydney: Pluto Press.

Hiebert, D. (2006) 'Winning, losing and still playing the Game: the political Economy of Immigration in Canada', *Tijdschrift voor Economischeen Sociale Geografie*, 97: 38–48.

Huntington, S. (2004) *Who Are We? The Challenges to America's National Identity*, New York: Simon and Schuster.

Jakle, J. and Wheeler, J. (1969) 'The changing residential Structure of the Dutch Population in Kalamazoo Michigan', *Annals of the Association of American Geographers*, 59: 441–60.

Jedwab, J. (2006) *Le Multiculturalisme au Canada*, Montreal: Association for Canadian Studies.

Kobayashi, A. (1993) 'Multiculturalism: representing a Canadian Institution', in Duncan, J. and Ley, D. (eds) *Place/Culture/Representation,* London: Routledge, pp. 205–31.

Kymlicka, W. (1995) *Multicultural Citizenship*, Oxford: Clarendon Press.

——(1998) *Finding our Way: Rethinking Ethnocultural Relations in Canada*, Toronto: Oxford University Press.

Ley, D. (1983) *A Social Geography of the City*, New York: Harper and Row.

——(2008) 'Post-Multiculturalism?', in Hanley, L., Ruble, B. and A. Garland (eds) *Immigration and Integration in Urban Communities*, Washington, DC: Woodrow Wilson International Center Press & Baltimore, MD: Johns Hopkins University Press, pp. 177–96.

Li, P. (2003) 'The Multiculturalism Debate', in Li, P. (ed.) *Race and Ethnic Relations in Canada*, Don Mills, Ont: Oxford University Press, pp. 148–77.

Lowe, L. (1996) 'Imagining Los Angeles in the Production of Multiculturalism', in L. Lowe, *Immigrant Acts*, Durham, NC: Duke University Press, pp. 84–96.

Mickleburgh, R. (2006) 'Harper defends Canadian Diversity', *The Globe and Mail*, 20 June.

Migration Policy Institute (2006) 'Top 10 Migration Issues of 2006: Issue #1 Goodbye Multiculturalism – Hello Assimilation?', *Migration Information Source*, December issue. Online. Available HTTP: http://www.migrationinformation.org/pdf/MISTop10MigrationIssues2006.pdf (accessed 12 January 2007).

Mirza, M., Senthilkumaran, A. and Zein, J. (2007) 'Living apart together: British Muslims and the Paradox of Multiculturalism', London: *Policy Exchange*. Online. HTTP: http://www.policyexchange.org.uk/images/libimages/246.pdf (accessed 30 January 2007).

Mitchell, K. (1993) 'Multiculturalism, or the united Colors of Benetton?', *Antipode*, 25: 263–94.

Peach, C. (1996) 'Good Segregation, bad Segregation', *Planning Perspectives,* 11: 379–98.

——(2005) 'The Mosaic versus the melting Pot: Canada and the USA', *Scottish Geographical Journal*, 121: 3–27.

Phillips, D. (2006) 'Parallel Lives? Challenging Discourses of British Muslim Self-Segregation', *Environment and Planning D: Society and Space*, 24: 25–40.

Philpott, T. (1978) *The Slum and the Ghetto: Neighborhood Deterioration and Middle-Class Reform, Chicago, 1880–1930*, New York: Oxford University Press.

Schönwälder, K. (2008) Chapter in this volume.

Stolberg, S. (2006) 'Bush suggests Immigrants learn English', *New York Times*, 8 June.

Taylor, C. (1992) *Multiculturalism and 'The Politics of Recognition': an Essay*, Princeton, NJ: Princeton University Press.

Thrasher, F. (1927) *The Gang: A Study of 1313 Gangs in Chicago*, Chicago: University of Chicago Press.

Walks, R. A. and Bourne, L. (2006) 'Ghettos in Canada's Cities?', *Canadian Geographer*, 50: 273–97.

Woodward, W. (2006) 'Kelly vows that new Debate on Immigration will engage critically with Multiculturalism', *Guardian*, 25 August.

Index

.